Democracy Promotion and the Challenges of Illiberal Regional Powers

This book examines Western efforts at democracy promotion, reactions by illiberal challengers and regional powers, and political and societal conditions in target states. It is argued that Western powers are not unequivocally committed to the promotion of democracy and human rights, while non-democratic regional powers cannot simply be described as 'autocracy supporters'. This volume examines in detail the challenges by three illiberal regional powers – China, Russia and Saudi Arabia – to Western (US and EU) efforts at democracy promotion. The contributions specifically analyse their actions in Ethiopia and Angola in the case of China, Georgia and Ukraine in the case of Russia, and Tunisia in the case of Saudi Arabia. Democratic powers such as the US or the EU usually prefer stability over human rights and democracy. If democratic movements threaten stability in a region, neither the US nor the EU supports them. As to illiberal powers, they are generally not that different from their democratic counterparts. They also prefer stability over turmoil. Neither Russia nor China nor Saudi Arabia explicitly promote autocracy. Instead, they seek to suppress democratic movements in their periphery the minute these groups threaten their security interests or are perceived to endanger their regime survival.

This book was previously published as a special issue of *Democratization*.

Nelli Babayan is a Fellow at the Transatlantic Academy in Washington, DC and Associate Fellow at the Center for Transnational Studies, Foreign and Security Policy, Freie Universität Berlin. She is the author of *Democratic Transformation and Obstruction: EU, US and Russia in the South Caucasus* (Routledge, 2015).

Thomas Risse is Professor of International Relations at the Otto-Suhr Institute of Political Science, Freie Universität Berlin. His latest publications include *A Community of Europeans? Transnational Identities and Public Spheres* (Cornell University Press, 2010) and *European Public Spheres: Politics Is Back* (Cambridge University Press, 2014).

Democratization Special Issues

Series editors: *Jeffrey Haynes, London Metropolitan University, UK*
Aurel Croissant, University of Heidelberg, Germany

The journal, *Democratization,* emerged in 1994, during 'the third wave of democracy', a period which saw democratic transformation of dozens of regimes around the world. Over the last decade or so, the journal has published a number of special issues as books, each of which has focused upon cutting edge issues linked to democratization. Collectively, they underline the capacity of democratization to induce debate, uncertainty, and perhaps progress towards better forms of politics, focused on the achievement of the democratic aspirations of men and women everywhere.

Democracy Promotion and the Challenges of Illiberal Regional Powers
Edited by Nelli Babayan and Thomas Risse

Religiously Oriented Parties and Democratization
Edited by Luca Ozzano and Francesco Cavatorta

Religion and Political Change in the Modern World
Edited by Jeffrey Haynes

Comparing Autocracies in the Early Twenty-first Century
Two-volume set:
1. Unpacking Autocracies – Explaining Similarity and Difference
2. The Performance and Persistence of Autocracies

Edited by Aurel Croissant, Steffen Kailitz, Patrick Koellner and Stefan Wurster

Twenty Years of Studying Democratization
Three-volume set:
1. Democratic Transition and Consolidation
2. Democratization, Democracy and Authoritarian Continuity
3. Building Blocks of Democracy

Edited by Aurel Croissant and Jeffrey Haynes

Political Opposition in Sub-Saharan Africa
Edited by Elliott Green, Johanna Söderström and Emil Uddhammar

Conflicting Objectives in Democracy Promotion
Do All Good Things Go Together?
Edited by Julia Leininger, Sonja Grimm and Tina Freyburg

PREVIOUSLY PUBLISHED BOOKS FROM DEMOCRATIZATION

Coloured Revolutions and Authoritarian Reactions
Edited by Evgeny Finkel and Yitzhak M. Brudny

Ethnic Party Bans in Africa
Edited by Matthijs Bogaards, Matthias Basedau and Christof Hartmann

Democracy Promotion in the EU's Neighbourhood
From Leverage to Governance?
Edited by Sandra Lavenex and Frank Schimmelfennig

Democratization in Africa: Challenges and Prospects
Edited by Gordon Crawford and Gabrielle Lynch

Democracy Promotion and the 'Colour Revolutions'
Edited by Susan Stewart

Promoting Party Politics in Emerging Democracies
Edited by Peter Burnell and Andre W. M. Gerrits

Democracy and Violence
Global Debates and Local Challenges
Edited by John Schwarzmantel and Hendrik Jan Kraetzschmar

Religion and Democratizations
Edited by Jeffrey Haynes

The European Union's Democratization Agenda in the Mediterranean
Edited by Michelle Pace and Peter Seeberg

War and Democratization
Legality, Legitimacy and Effectiveness
Edited by Wolfgang Merkel and Sonja Grimm

Democratization in the Muslim World
Changing Patterns of Authority and Power
Edited by Francesco Volpi and Francesco Cavatorta

Religion, Democracy and Democratization
Edited by John Anderson

On the State of Democracy
Edited by Julio Faundez

Democracy Promotion and the Challenges of Illiberal Regional Powers

Edited by
Nelli Babayan and Thomas Risse

LONDON AND NEW YORK

First published 2016 by Routledge

2 Park Square, Milton Park, Abingdon, Oxfordshire OX14 4RN
711 Third Avenue, New York, NY 10017

Routledge is an imprint of the Taylor & Francis Group, an informa business

First issued in paperback 2018

Chapters 1, 2, 4, 7 and 8 © 2016 Taylor & Francis
Chapters 3, 5 and 6 © the authors

All rights reserved. No part of this book may be reprinted or reproduced or utilised in any form or by any electronic, mechanical, or other means, now known or hereafter invented, including photocopying and recording, or in any information storage or retrieval system, without permission in writing from the publishers.

Notice:
Product or corporate names may be trademarks or registered trademarks, and are used only for identification and explanation without intent to infringe.

British Library Cataloguing in Publication Data
A catalogue record for this book is available from the British Library

ISBN 13: 978-1-138-65453-2 (hbk)
ISBN 13: 978-1-138-39174-1 (pbk)

Typeset in Times New Roman
by RefineCatch Limited, Bungay, Suffolk

Publisher's Note
The publisher accepts responsibility for any inconsistencies that may have arisen during the conversion of this book from journal articles to book chapters, namely the possible inclusion of journal terminology.

Disclaimer
Every effort has been made to contact copyright holders for their permission to reprint material in this book. The publishers would be grateful to hear from any copyright holder who is not here acknowledged and will undertake to rectify any errors or omissions in future editions of this book.

Contents

Citation Information ix

1. Democracy promotion and the challenges of illiberal regional powers 1
   Thomas Risse and Nelli Babayan

2. Democracy promotion and China: blocker or bystander? 20
   Dingding Chen and Katrin Kinzelbach

3. Not as bad as it seems: EU and US democracy promotion faces China in Africa 39
   Christine Hackenesch

4. The return of the empire? Russia's counteraction to transatlantic democracy promotion in its near abroad 58
   Nelli Babayan

5. Spoiler or facilitator of democratization?: Russia's role in Georgia and Ukraine 79
   Laure Delcour and Kataryna Wolczuk

6. Undermining the transatlantic democracy agenda? The Arab Spring and Saudi Arabia's counteracting democracy strategy 99
   Oz Hassan

7. Local actors in the driver's seat: Transatlantic democracy promotion under regime competition in the Arab world 116
   Tina Freyburg and Solveig Richter

8. The noble west and the dirty rest? Western democracy promoters and illiberal regional powers 139
   Tanja A. Börzel

Index 157

Citation Information

The chapters in this book were originally published in *Democratization*, volume 22, issue 3 (May 2015). When citing this material, please use the original page numbering for each article, as follows:

Chapter 1
Democracy promotion and the challenges of illiberal regional powers: introduction to the special issue
Thomas Risse and Nelli Babayan
Democratization, volume 22, issue 3 (May 2015) pp. 381–399

Chapter 2
Democracy promotion and China: blocker or bystander?
Dingding Chen and Katrin Kinzelbach
Democratization, volume 22, issue 3 (May 2015) pp. 400–418

Chapter 3
Not as bad as it seems: EU and US democracy promotion faces China in Africa
Christine Hackenesch
Democratization, volume 22, issue 3 (May 2015) pp. 419–437

Chapter 4
The return of the empire? Russia's counteraction to transatlantic democracy promotion in its near abroad
Nelli Babayan
Democratization, volume 22, issue 3 (May 2015) pp. 438–458

Chapter 5
Spoiler or facilitator of democratization?: Russia's role in Georgia and Ukraine
Laure Delcour and Kataryna Wolczuk
Democratization, volume 22, issue 3 (May 2015) pp 459–478

CITATION INFORMATION

Chapter 6
Undermining the transatlantic democracy agenda? The Arab Spring and Saudi Arabia's counteracting democracy strategy
Oz Hassan
Democratization, volume 22, issue 3 (May 2015) pp 479–495

Chapter 7
Local actors in the driver's seat: Transatlantic democracy promotion under regime competition in the Arab world
Tina Freyburg and Solveig Richter
Democratization, volume 22, issue 3 (May 2015) pp 496–518

Chapter 8
The noble west and the dirty rest? Western democracy promoters and illiberal regional powers
Tanja A. Börzel
Democratization, volume 22, issue 3 (May 2015) pp 519–535

For any permission-related enquiries please visit:
http://www.tandfonline.com/page/help/permissions

Democracy promotion and the challenges of illiberal regional powers

Thomas Risse and Nelli Babayan

Otto-Suhr Institute of Political Science, Department of Political and Social Sciences, Freie Universität Berlin, Germany

This special issue examines Western efforts at democracy promotion, reactions by illiberal challengers and regional powers, and political and societal conditions in target states. We argue that Western powers are not unequivocally committed to the promotion of democracy and human rights, while non-democratic regional powers cannot simply be described as "autocracy supporters". This article introduces the special issue. First, illiberal regional powers are likely to respond to Western efforts at democracy promotion in third countries if they perceive challenges to their geostrategic interests in the region or to the survival of their regime. Second, Western democracy promoters react to countervailing policies by illiberal regimes if they prioritize democracy and human rights goals over stability and security goals which depends in turn on their perception of the situation in the target countries and their overall relationships to the non-democratic regional powers. Third, the effects on the ground mostly depend on the domestic configuration of forces. Western democracy promoters are likely to empower liberal groups in the target countries, while countervailing efforts by non-democratic regional powers will empower illiberal groups. In some cases, though, countervailing efforts by illiberal regimes have the counterintuitive effect of fostering democracy by strengthening democratic elites and civil society.

Recent events in Ukraine have shown in a nutshell what this special issue is about. Abiding by strong pressures from Russia, the ousted Ukrainian President, Viktor Yanukovych, refused to sign the Association Agreement (AA) with the European Union (EU), which would have brought the country closer to the West. Mass demonstrations dubbed "Euromaidan" erupted against a corrupt and undemocratic regime. The resulting turmoil and violence led to various and initially rather uncoordinated mediation efforts by the United States (US) and the EU. When the Yanukovych government collapsed and an unelected transition government took over, Russian forces annexed the Crimean peninsula, instigating what some called the worst international crisis in Europe since the end of the Cold War. In Eastern Ukraine, Russian-supported rebel forces have engaged in a military conflict with the democratically-elected Ukrainian government, creating an area of limited statehood in the process in which the Ukrainian state is no longer able to enforce the law.[1]

Alternatively, take the events of the "Arabellions": for years, the US and Europe alike contributed to the stabilization of authoritarian regimes in North Africa for fear that sudden change would bring anti-Western and Islamist governments into power. At the same time, they cautiously supported civil society movements. Nevertheless, the Arab uprisings took Western powers by surprise and their reactions were slow and inconsistent.[2] They collaborated to prevent mass killings in Libya and intervened militarily with the UN Security Council, invoking the "responsibility to protect" (R2P). However, when Saudi Arabia and other Gulf states put down the uprising in Bahrain and when Russia (and China) blocked action against Syria in the United Nations Security Council (UNSC), the US and the EU ceased to respond more forcefully to what arguably have been mass atrocities and severe human rights violations.

The starting point of this special issue is the state of the art in the literature on transatlantic democracy promotion. This literature has shown that distinguishing the US as a "hard" power and the EU as a "soft" power is no longer valid.[3] Comparative studies of American and European democracy promotion programmes show that the two have converged with regard to goals, strategies, and instruments.[4] The literature has also looked into the substance of EU democracy promotion[5] and the EU's move from "leverage" to a "governance" model of promoting democracy.[6] Moreover, both the US and the EU rarely prioritize democracy and human rights in their foreign policies, but usually prefer stability over democracy[7] as has become obvious in their bewildered reactions to the "Arabellions". Various studies have also investigated conflicting objectives of initiating democracy promotion, but have so far focused only on the internal considerations of the US and Germany.[8] As to the effects of democracy promotion, scholars have focused predominantly on the domestic politics and societal conditions in target states as the main variables to explain democratization outcomes.[9] At the same time, there is also an emerging literature on "autocracy promotion".[10] It suggests that autocracy promotion may include deliberate diffusion of authoritarian values, borrowing of foreign models, assisting other regimes to suppress democratization, or condoning authoritarian tendencies.[11] The motivations for such actions have been explained by considerations of rent-extraction from target countries or by efforts to prevent democratization spillover,[12] while its effects have been explained by the balance of power between illiberal and liberal domestic elites.[13]

This special issue looks at the entire triangle: Western efforts at democracy promotion, reactions by illiberal challengers and regional powers, and political and

DEMOCRACY PROMOTION AND THE CHALLENGES

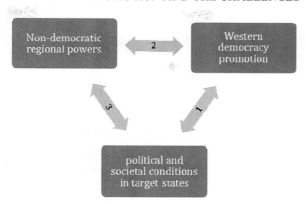

Figure 1. The focus of the special issue.

societal conditions in target states (Figure 1). We examine in detail the challenges of selected non-democratic or illiberal regional powers[14] – Russia, China, and Saudi Arabia – to Western (US and EU) efforts at democracy promotion. We argue that Western powers are neither unequivocally committed to the promotion of democracy and human rights nor can non-democratic regional powers simply be described as "autocracy supporters".

This special issue focuses on three sets of interrelated interactions:

- Interactions between Western efforts at democracy promotion and socio-political conditions in target states (arrow 1 in Figure 1);
- Interactions between illiberal regional powers and Western democracy promoters (arrow 2 in Figure 1);
- Interactions between illiberal regional powers and social and political actors in target states (arrow 3 in Figure 1).

This focus leads to three questions that this special issue tries to answer:

(1) How do non-democratic regional powers react to EU/US efforts at democracy promotion in target countries? In other words, which combination of Western democracy promotion and local conditions produces which reaction by illiberal regional powers?
(2) If non-democratic regional powers adopt countervailing policies, how do the US and the EU react to the policies of illiberal regional powers toward target states?[15]
(3) Which local effects do different combinations of Western policies and those of non-democratic regional powers produce? That is, how do the policies of non-democratic regional powers affect democracy promotion efforts by the US and the EU in target countries?

In response to the first question, we argue that illiberal regional powers are only likely to respond to Western efforts at democracy promotion in third countries if they perceive challenges to their geostrategic interests in the region or to the survival of their regime. We also suggest that non-democratic regional powers are unlikely to intentionally promote autocracy even though "autocracy strengthening" might be the consequence of their behaviour.[16] In some cases, illiberal regimes even promote democracy if it suits their geostrategic interests.[17]

In response to the second question, we claim that Western democracy promoters will only react to countervailing policies by illiberal regimes if and when they prioritize democracy and human rights goals over stability and security goals, which depends in turn on their perception of the situation in the target countries and their overall relationships to the non-democratic regional powers. As a result, the US and the EU might react differently to countervailing policies even though their strategies and instruments with regard to human rights and democracy promotion are similar.

With regard to the third question of the effects on the ground, this mostly depends on the domestic configuration of forces, both government and civil society.[18] Western democracy promoters are likely to empower liberal groups in the target countries, while countervailing efforts by non-democratic regional powers will empower illiberal groups. The differential empowerment of domestic forces depends in turn on the leverage of the EU and the US powers as compared to that of illiberal regional powers in terms of credibility of commitment, legitimacy, and resources. It also depends on economic and security linkages between the target state, on the one hand, and the Western powers as compared to the non-democratic regional powers, on the other.[19] As a result, Western democracy promotion and countervailing efforts by illiberal powers may sometimes have counterintuitive results: the US and the EU might actually foster illiberal outcomes, while autocratic regimes might promote democracy, albeit unintentionally.[20]

This introduction to the special issue elaborates on each of three questions raised above. We then proceed with a survey of US and EU strategies and instruments of democracy promotion, possible actions of non-democratic powers, followed by an overview of the contributions and how they fit into the special issue.

Research questions of this special issue

Illiberal regional powers reacting to democracy promotion: drivers and strategies

Within increasingly interdependent and globalized international affairs, US and EU democracy promotion programmes can no longer be regarded as the only game in town. A major contribution of this special issue to the literature consists of systematically investigating the role of illiberal regional powers that may counteract EU and US efforts at democracy promotion.

Counteracting democracy promotion is not a priority of non-democratic countries, but a means to achieving other objectives or a byproduct of other strategies. Despite their view of democracy promotion as meddling in internal affairs, little attention has been paid so far by the literature to actors such as Russia and China, who may counteract democracy promotion efforts for their own strategic interests.[21] Recent events concerning the EU's Eastern Partnership (EaP) policy in Armenia and Ukraine underline the significance of this question. Similar issues have been raised regarding China's role in sub-Saharan Africa and Saudi Arabia's role in the Middle East and North Africa (MENA).[22] We ask how and under which conditions non-democratic powers react to US and EU democracy promotion in countries in which they have particular interests. In this regard, we investigate the policies of three regional powers – China (article by Chen and Kinzelbach), Russia (article by Babayan), and Saudi Arabia (article by Hassan)[23] – and their interactions with the EU and the US. Three articles of this special issue then examine how these interactions between the US and the EU, on the one hand, and illiberal regional powers, on the other hand, play themselves out in particular target states – and what the effects are (Ukraine and Georgia, article by Delcour/Wolcuk; Ethiopia and Angola, article by Hackenesch; Tunisia, article by Freyburg/Richter).[24]

Successful democratization is possible if there is no major power in the region opposing democracy.[25] However, and partially in line with the emerging literature on "autocracy promotion",[26] we do not assume that counteracting democracy promotion necessarily implies fostering autocracy as an alternative regime type. The special issue rather identifies several possible actions by non-democratic regional powers in reaction to democracy promotion. "Non-democratic regional powers" are understood here as illiberal states (not necessarily autocratic ones, but also semi-authoritarian countries such as Russia) with the capability to counteract democracy promotion in their neighbourhood or in other parts of the world. The potential to influence stems from the military, economic, or cultural leverage of a non-democratic power over a democratizing country. In this special issue we only look at cases where this potential leverage is a given within a specific region (for example, Saudi Arabia and the Middle East; Russia and its "near abroad"; China in Asia and Africa).

In this context, we need to distinguish between intention and outcomes. We do not assume that Russia, China, or Saudi Arabia intentionally try to promote autocracy in the same way as Western powers try to foster human rights and democracy. Moreover, we do not assume that illiberal states perceive these Western efforts *per se* as a threat to their interests (see article by Hackenesch on China in Africa). Rather, we posit that US and EU efforts at democracy promotion only trigger a counter-reaction by illiberal regional powers when at least one of two conditions is present (hypothesis 1):

- The illiberal state perceives Western democracy promotion in a target state as a threat to its own regime survival.

- The illiberal state perceives Western democracy promotion in a target state as a threat to its geostrategic (political, economic, or military) interests.

The first condition is derived from liberal or domestic politics theories of international relations, while the second follows from realist thinking.

For example, higher resonance[27] of democracy in target countries among the elites and population may sway them away from the usual sphere of influence of non-democratic powers and trigger a counteraction, as has been the case in Ukraine (article by Delcour/Wolczuk). Popular protests in Bahrain directly affected the survival interests of the Saudi Kingdom (article by Hassan). In contrast, US/EU democracy promotion did not trigger a similar reaction by China in Africa, in spite of its considerable political and economic interests (article by Hackenesch).

Moreover, even if an illiberal state perceives its domestic or geostrategic interests at stake when faced with democracy promoters in a target state, the response might not be outright autocracy promotion. A non-democratic state may offer more appealing economic benefits or military partnerships to a target country without imposing democratic conditionality, thus becoming a less demanding partner for target countries. Counteracting may simply mean the presence of a powerful non-democratic actor offering alternative trade benefits and/or economic resources without an attempt to interfere with a country's choice of regime type (see China in sub-Saharan Africa, see article by Chen and Kinzelbach). In some cases, illiberal powers might actually promote democracy if it suits their interests.

Our arguments do not hinge on the strategies and instruments of human rights and democracy promotion used by the US or the EU. It does not particularly matter whether Western powers use persuasion, or positive (trade benefits) or negative incentives (conditionality or sanctions) in their efforts to promote democracy in a target country.[28] Rather, the reactions by illiberal powers are driven almost entirely by the effects of these democracy promotion efforts on the ground and by the sensitivity of the illiberal regime to these effects. For example, a non-democratic regime facing a domestic threat to its survival (such as Putin's Russia after the 2012 elections and faced with an economic crisis) is likely to be more sensitive to Western democracy promotion in its periphery (see articles by Babayan and Delcour/Wolczuk). However, and everything else being equal, we argue that it is the effectiveness of Western efforts at democracy promotion in a target country rather than the chosen strategies and instruments which is likely to trigger a response by illiberal regional powers.

To sum up, we only expect illiberal regional powers to react when they perceive Western efforts at democracy promotion as threatening their regime survival or particular geostrategic interests. The more regime survival of the illiberal power is threatened domestically, on the one hand, and the more effective Western efforts at democracy promotion are, the more likely is a reaction by the non-democratic state. We do not assume that the reaction will be "autocracy promotion" per se, but that it can be a whole variety of strategies and instruments in such a case of threatened interests. Under particular circumstances (see below), the effect of these counter-strategies may very well be "autocracy enhancing" or stagnation of democratization. But it would be misleading to discuss the reactions of illiberal regional powers to Western efforts under the heading "autocracy promotion", since this concept assumes intentionality.

This brings us to the second research question of this special issue, the Western reactions to countervailing efforts by illiberal regional powers.

Western reactions to countervailing strategies by illiberal regimes in target countries

We cannot assume that the US and the EU remain silent when faced with countervailing efforts by illiberal regional powers. Thus another question addressed, though briefly, in this special issue is: how are the US and the EU likely to react when faced with countervailing reactions of illiberal regional powers in target states? While not at the centre of this special issue, this question is addressed in some of the articles to underline the interactions between democracy promoters and illiberal regional powers (see for example, Hackenesch).

The Western responses are likely to depend on the particular combination of democracy and human rights-related foreign policy goals, on the one hand, and security and stability-related goals, on the other. In line with the extensive literature on democracy promotion,[29] we do not assume solely benign or even altruistic motives on the part of Western democracy promoters. Of course, democracy and human rights are constitutive parts of the foreign policy identity of both the US and the EU and, therefore, explicit promotion of these values forms part of their foreign policy strategies (in contrast to other states or organizations). In this sense, both the US and the EU are indeed "normative powers".[30] But the assumption that democracy and human rights (should) top the list of US and EU foreign policy goals is erroneous. Rather, efforts to promote democracy and human rights have to be balanced with other foreign policy goals, among them security, economic goals, and stability in one's own neighbourhood. These goals coincide in some cases, since, as the literature on the "democratic peace" reminds us,[31] democracy is the best long-term guarantee for security and stability. In other cases, these goals are at loggerheads with each other, as the US and EU reactions to the "Arabellions" show.[32]

However, the particular combination of human rights and democracy goals as compared to stability and security concerns is not a given, but we assume that it depends upon two conditions (hypothesis 2):

(1) Stability concerns regarding the target country;
(2) The strategic significance of the illiberal regional power.[33]

Regarding the first condition, the literature on democracy promotion suggests that both the US and the EU will compromise their support for human rights and democracy, if increased democratization and liberalization threaten the stability of the target country.[34] In such cases, neither the US nor the EU will forcefully react to countervailing policies by illiberal powers, but will align with them (see articles by Hassan and Freyburg/Richter).

As to the second condition, each of the illiberal states considered in this special issue has its own particular relationship with the US and the EU. As their reactions to Putin's land grabs in Crimea and eastern Ukraine demonstrate, neither of them was prepared to simply cut off all political and economic ties to Russia (see articles by Babayan and Delcour/Wolczuk). As to Saudi Arabia and the Middle East, the US was not prepared to support the Bahraini uprising against one of its most important allies in the Gulf region (see Hassan's article). Last but not least, both the US and the EU have significant economic and political interests with regard to China (see article by Chen/Kinzelbach). In addition, China and Russia are veto powers in the UN Security Council and confrontational Western policies may further increase tensions.

To sum up, we expect Western governments to decrease their efforts at democracy promotion in target countries when faced with countervailing reactions by illiberal powers, if they prioritize security and stability over human rights and democracy. This prioritization in turn depends on the stability of the target country and the overall significance of the non-democratic power with regard to Western foreign policies.

Yet, what are the effects of all these interactions on the ground, that is, in the target countries of democracy promotion? This is the third research question of this special issue to which we now turn.

Effects in target countries

Measuring the effects of external efforts at democracy promotion is a daunting task, which becomes even more difficult when we factor in the activities of illiberal regional powers. Simply looking at some quantifiable indicators for progress in human rights and democracy such as the "Polity IV" or "Freedom House" data sets will not do the trick. There are always too many alternative explanations to discard the notion that external actors played any role in moving a country toward democracy or toward autocracy.[35] The emerging consensus in the literature appears to be that the effects of external democracy promotion are rather modest under the best of circumstances, if not outright counterproductive in some cases. Moreover, scholars have converged on the proposition that such external efforts are doomed to fail unless there are considerable liberal domestic forces driving the fight for democracy and human rights.[36]

This special issue does not attempt to settle these concerns once and for all. Doing so would require detailed process-tracing of individual country cases, including historical comparisons. What we attempt to do – particularly in the country case studies – is to look at the effects of US/EU democracy promotion when those clash with non-democratic regional powers. With regard to non-democratic powers, we aim to determine what difference these attempts at counteracting democracy promotion make – whether intended or not. This special issue then contributes to answering the question whether the widely recognized failure of US/EU efforts to promote democracy is causally linked to the presence of other external actors, or whether it is "home-made", so to speak.

Possible effects

A clash of Western democracy promotion efforts with countervailing policies by illiberal powers might, first, have no impact at all. This is not an unlikely outcome given the limited effectiveness of external actors to promote regime change as documented in the literature (see Hackenesch's article). If Western democracy promoters are not effective, why should we assume that illiberal regional powers perform better in hindering democratization?

Second, the target country may improve its level of democracy irrespective of the activities of the illiberal regional power *and* at least some causal effect can be demonstrated with regard to the activities of the US and the EU. There is also the counterintuitive possibility that the polity further democratizes *because of* and in direct opposition to the interference of illiberal powers (see article on Ukraine and Georgia by Delcour/Wolczuk), in which case the latter's policies had unintended consequences (see conclusions by Börzel). This is actually one of the major findings of this special issue: Explicit efforts by illiberal powers to block democratization in target countries often strengthen rather than weaken domestic liberal forces and civil society in an effort to fight off "foreign intrusion". Russia's recent imperialism in its periphery might, thus, lead to democratization, as both Georgia and Ukraine seem to show.

Last not least, the illiberal power may "win" the battle and the country moves further away from democracy and toward autocracy. Note that this outcome must not necessarily result from a deliberate attempt by the illiberal power to promote autocracy (see above). Rather, it might simply derive from the non-democratic regime's attempt to move the country closer into its own sphere of influence by offering stronger economic or security ties.

Explaining outcomes

The main causal mechanism between our two "independent variables" – Western democracy promotion and countervailing reactions by illiberal regional powers – and its possible effects on the ground works through the (dis-)empowerment of liberal as well as illiberal forces in the target countries (including the possibility that undecided citizens or elites sway one way or the other). This proposition is well-established in the literature[37] and we extend it here to the possible effects of efforts by illiberal regional powers. In other words, the decisive struggle is being fought in the target country between pro-democratic and anti-democratic forces – and external actors cannot do much more than try to affect this domestic balance of power. The more local elites (and civil society actors) identify with democratic ideas, the more they should be, even if indirectly, empowered by external democracy promoters.[38] Thus, internalization of democratic rules promoted by the EU and the US is likely to proceed with fewer obstacles as compared to the cases where domestic actors do not identify with democracy and democracy promoters and promoted rules do not resonate domestically. However, this mechanism also works the other way round. The more local illiberal elites (and citizens) identify with the policies of non-democratic challengers or their promoted identity, the more this should sway the domestic balance of power toward them.

While this is the main causal mechanism in our view, there are a number of intervening factors that affect the ultimate outcome. First, economic and security conditions of the target country are likely to be significant. For example, economic interdependence[39] between the target country, on the one hand, and democracy promoters or non-democratic challengers, on the other hand, impact the effectiveness of democracy promotion. The security relationship between the target country and the external powers also matters including the existence or lack of so-called "protracted conflicts", as is also the case with the countries of the South Caucasus (for example, Armenia and Azerbaijan) or Moldova.[40] In a way, this is the "linkage" part in the linkage-leverage model as developed by Levitsky and Way.[41]

Second, the ability and willingness of the democracy promoting powers themselves to make credible commitments and to commit resources is another important intervening factor (see article by Freyburg/Richter). They need to match their democratic rhetoric with the respective deeds and "walk the walk". Lack of credibility is likely to damage the target's reliance on the promoter, making further similar actions ineffective. In a way, the answer to the second research question on the reactions of democracy promoters to countervailing efforts by illiberal regional powers becomes an intervening factor with regard to the final outcome on the ground. In the Levitsky and Way model, this is the "leverage" part.[42]

Third, non-democratic regional powers can employ their own leverage to affect the domestic balance of power between liberal and illiberal forces. For example, a non-democratic regional power can try to dominate local markets by *inter alia* providing an influx of capital, monopolizing energy resources, or purchasing national infrastructures.[43] Non-democratic powers can attain leverage over target countries by offering economic and financial benefits without conditionality, which is often attached to democracy and "good governance" promotion by Western states. Illiberal regional powers might also exploit ethnic cleavages and other internal political and security issues in target countries for their purposes.

In sum, we hypothesize that the outcome of Western efforts at democracy promotion faced with countervailing efforts by non-democratic regional powers depends upon the influence of these two types of actors on the domestic balance of power between liberal and illiberal elites and citizens. This influence is in turn conditioned by the economic and security linkages between and among the three actors (democracy promoters, non-democratic powers, target country) and by the leverage which the external actors – promoters and countervailing powers – have over the domestic forces, which in turn results in part from their credibility of commitment and their resources (see Figure 2).

Case selection and overview of the special issue

In this section we justify the case selection, including the focus on the EU and the US and provide an overview of the articles in this special issue. The EU and the US are among very few powers in the contemporary international system trying to export their own political regimes elsewhere. In addition, while individual states and international organizations such as the United Nations, Organization for Security and Cooperation in Europe, or the Council of Europe also engage in democracy promotion, none currently matches the breadth of EU and US policies or their potential economic and political leverage on target countries and the international arena.

In recent years, the US and the EU have increasingly converged in their democracy promotion policies.[44] This convergence is, first, observable with regard to goals. Democracy promotion policies of the EU and the US derive from similar rationales, which combine identity-derived normative interests as well as more traditional economic and security goals. As to identity, both the EU and the US are democratic powers and try to externalize these constitutive identities in their democracy promotion policies.

We also observe an increasing convergence with regard to instruments of democracy promotion. While until the late 2000s it was mainly the US paying more attention to the promotion of active civil society, this has changed with the creation of the European Endowment for Democracy (EED). The establishment of the EED indicates that the EU is ready to adjust its traditional democratic

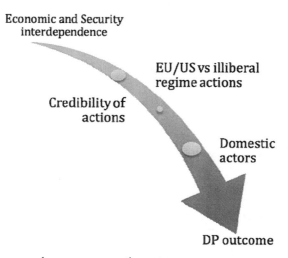

Figure 2. Influences on democracy promotion outcome.

script and to boost its leadership within democracy promotion. This convergence which pertains particularly to the new strategies and instruments of the EU, such as the establishment of the EED and the Civil Society Forum, has been more inadvertent rather than due to systematic coordination between the US and the EU.[45] There is no institutionalized coordination and cooperation between the US and the EU in general and on the ground in target countries, except in times of crisis, such as the one experienced in Ukraine.

The empirical analyses of this special issue start in 2011, since the unfolding of the "Arabellions". Even if the results are rather dubious in terms of democratization (except for Tunisia, see Freyburg/Richter, this special issue), their impact on general democracy promotion and the leadership of democracy promoters is undeniable. The timeframe also coincides with the second term of Obama's presidency and the establishment of the EED, allowing for a closer analysis of new policies and their outcomes.

As indicated above, the empirical article in this special issue focus on the policies of three illiberal regional powers in response to Western democracy promotion – Russia, China, and Saudi Arabia. As far as the three regional powers are concerned, we include two articles in each case, one adopting a "top-down" perspective (articles by Babayan, Chen/Kinzelbach, and Hassan) and the other taking a "bottom-up" view with regard to specific target countries (Angola and Ethiopia in the case of China, see article by Hackenesch; Ukraine and Georgia in the case of Russia, see article by Delcour/Wolczuk; and Tunisia with regard to Saudi Arabia, see article by Freyburg/Richter). A concluding article summarizes the findings and draws conclusions with regard to theory-building (article by Börzel).

Thus, following the abovementioned criteria, the issue starts with the chapter on China, where Chen and Kinzelbach show how, while determined to stop democracy promotion inside China, the Communist Party may not be as deterministic about democratization in other countries, depending on its own external objectives. Concentrating on the cases of Ethiopia and Angola in sub-Saharan Africa, the chapter by Hackenesch demonstrates how economic cooperation, which is not burdened by democratic conditionality, offered by China may render democracy promotion ineffective. In her chapter on Russia, Babayan argues that *inter alia* perceiving democracy promotion as a threat to its geostrategic interests, Russia has often counteracted democracy promotion, even if without explicitly promoting autocracy in its near-abroad. The following chapter by Delcour and Wolczuk correspondingly focuses on Ukraine and Georgia as Eastern European cases with Russia as the non-democratic power, and shows that counter-intuitively Russia's threats and counteraction have strengthened the influence of the EU and the US and bolstered pro-Western orientation of Georgia and Ukraine. The article by Hassan on Saudi Arabia demonstrates how any counteraction to democracy promotion is vested in inherent interest to protect the survival of the House of Saud, and that potential counteraction often goes in line with Western policies attempting to contain change in the volatile Middle East. Freyburg and Richter mainly focus on Tunisia and argue that in cases when democracy promoters demonstrate the credibility of their actions, persuading domestic actors by their actions, counteraction to democracy promotion, in this case Saudi Arabia, may remain without results. In her conclusions Börzel discusses the theoretical and policy implications of these findings. She argues that research on democracy promotion has to acknowledge the counterintuitive finding that while democracy promoters may inadvertently strengthen autocracy, illiberal regimes may unintentionally strengthen liberal reform coalitions.

Acknowledgements
A special thanks goes to two anonymous reviewers for their extremely helpful criticism and suggestions, as well as to the journal editors for their input.

Funding
This special issue originated in the framework of the TRANSWORLD project funded by the EU's 7th Framework Program for Socio-Economic Research (Grant agreement 290454). The Research College "Transformative Power of Europe", funded by the German Research Foundation DFG sponsored the authors' workshop on 23 May 2014. We thank the participants for their insights and their comments on the draft.

Notes
1. On limited statehood see Risse, *Governance Without a State*.
2. Dandashly, Börzel, and Risse, "Responses to the 'Arab Spring.'"
3. On these distinctions see Nye, *Soft Power*.
4. Risse, "Conclusions"; Babayan and Viviani, "Shocking Adjustments?"; Babayan, "Home-Made Adjustments?"; Cox, Ikenberry, and Inoguchi, *American Democracy Promotion*; Magen, Risse, and McFaul, *Promoting Democracy and the Rule of Law*.
5. Wetzel and Orbie, "Promoting Embedded Democracy?"; Schimmelfennig, "How Substantial Is Substance?"
6. Lavenex and Schimmelfennig, "EU Democracy Promotion in the Neighbourhood."
7. Börzel, Pamuk, and Stahn, "Democracy or Stability?"
8. Wolff, Spanger, and Puhle, *The Comparative International Politics of Democracy Promotion*; Poppe, Woitschach, and Wolff, "Freedom Fighter versus Civilian Power."
9. Higley and Burton, "The Elite Variable in Democratic Transitions and Breakdowns"; Cheibub et al., "What Makes Democracies Endure?"; Przeworski and Limongi, "Modernization"; Stradiotto and Guo, *Democratic Transitions*.
10. Burnell, "Is There a New Autocracy Promotion?"; Burnell and Schlumberger, "Promoting Democracy"; Vanderhill, *Promoting Authoritarianism Abroad*; Obydenkova and Libman, "Understanding the Foreign Policy of Autocratic Actors"; Horvath, "Putin's 'Preventive Counter-Revolution'"; Tolstrup, *Russia vs. the EU*; Obydenkova and Libman, *Autocratic and Democratic External Influences in Post-Soviet Eurasia*.
11. Burnell, "Is There a New Autocracy Promotion?"
12. Horvath, "Putin's 'Preventive Counter-Revolution'"; Obydenkova and Libman, "Understanding the Foreign Policy of Autocratic Actors."
13. Vanderhill, *Promoting Authoritarianism Abroad*.

14. Note that we do not use the term "autocracies" here. "Non-democratic" or "illiberal" states encompass a variety of regime types including what has been called "semi-autocracies" or "defective democracies" in the literature. Collier and Levitsky, "Democracy with Adjectives"; Levitsky and Way, "Linkage versus Leverage."
15. While not at the centre of this special issue, this question is addressed in some of the articles to underline the interactions between democracy promoters and illiberal regional powers.
16. This is also our understanding of the emerging literature on "autocracy promotion." Authors rarely assume that illiberal regimes are actively engaged in promoting their regime type, even though this might be the outcome.
17. Obydenkova and Libman, *Autocratic and Democratic External Influences in Post-Soviet Eurasia.*
18. This follows Schimmelfennig, Engert, and Knobel, *International Socialization in Europe*, but adds the potentially countervailing effects of the policies by illiberal powers.
19. On linkage and leverage see Levitsky and Way, "Linkage versus Leverage."
20. Börzel, "The Noble West and the Dirty Rest?"; Delcour and Wolczuk, "Spoiler or Facilitator of Democratization?"
21. Ambrosio, *Authoritarian Backlash*; Tolstrup, "Studying a Negative External Actor"; Vanderhill, *Promoting Authoritarianism Abroad*; Babayan, *Democratic Transformation and Obstruction.*
22. McGreal, "Chinese Aid to Africa May Do More Harm than Good, Warns Benn"; Brautigam, *The Dragon's Gift*; Vanderhill, *Promoting Authoritarianism Abroad*; Traub, "The Autocrat's Emergency Bailout Fund."
23. Chen and Kinzelbach, "Democracy Promotion and China"; Babayan, "The Return of the Empire?"; Hassan, "Undermining the Transatlantic Democracy Agenda?"
24. Delcour and Wolczuk, "Spoiler or Facilitator of Democratization?"; Hackenesch, "Not as Bad as It Seems"; Freyburg and Richter, "Local Actors in the Driver's Seat."
25. Whitehead, *The International Dimensions of Democratization.*
26. Burnell, "Is There a New Autocracy Promotion?"; Vanderhill, *Promoting Authoritarianism Abroad.*
27. Schimmelfennig, Engert, and Knobel, *International Socialization in Europe.*
28. Börzel and Risse, "Venus Approaching Mars?"
29. Carothers, *Aiding Democracy Abroad*; Carothers, *Critical Mission*; Zeeuw and Kumar, *Promoting Democracy in Postconflict Societies*; Burnell and Youngs, *New Challenges to Democratization*; Burnell, "Promoting Democracy"; Wolff, Spanger, and Puhle, *The Comparative International Politics of Democracy Promotion*; Babayan and Risse, "So Close but Yet So Far"; Babayan, *Democratic Transformation and Obstruction.*
30. On the EU see Manners, "Normative Power Europe."
31. Russett, *Grasping the Democratic Peace*; Oneal and Russett, *Triangulating Peace.*
32. Dandashly, Börzel, and Risse, "Responses to the 'Arab Spring.'"
33. A third condition pertains to the domestic support for value-based foreign policies inside the US and the EU. However, this special issue does not specifically look at public opinion in the US and the EU.
34. Dandashly, Börzel, and Risse, "Responses to the 'Arab Spring'"; Powel, "The Stability Syndrome"; Durac, "The Impact of External Actors on the Distribution of Power in the Middle East"; Darbouche and Zoubir, "The Algerian Crisis in European and US Foreign Policies."
35. Whitehead, "International Aspects of Democratization"; Schimmelfennig, Engert, and Knobel, "The Impact of EU Political Conditionality"; Schimmelfennig and Scholtz,

"EU Democracy Promotion in the European Neighbourhood"; Kelley, "D-Minus Elections."
36. For human rights see Risse, Ropp, and Sikkink, *The Power of Human Rights*; Risse, Ropp, and Sikkink, *The Persistent Power of Human Rights*; on democracy promotion see Schimmelfennig, Engert, and Knobel, "The Impact of EU Political Conditionality"; Börzel and Van Hüllen, "One Voice, One Message, but Conflicting Goals."
37. Welsh, "Political Transition Processes in Central and Eastern Europe"; Higley and Burton, "The Elite Variable in Democratic Transitions and Breakdowns"; Schimmelfennig, Engert, and Knobel, *International Socialization in Europe*; Vanderhill, *Promoting Authoritarianism Abroad*.
38. Bossuyt and Kubicek, "Advancing Democracy on Difficult Terrain."
39. Piggott, "Energy Security and Democracy Promotion"; Anyanwu and Erhijakpor, "Does Oil Wealth Affect Democracy in Africa?"
40. Nuriyev, "Azerbaijan and the European Union"; Simão, "The Problematic Role of EU Democracy Promotion"; Stewart, "The Interplay of Domestic Contexts and External Democracy Promotion"; Babayan, "Fear or Love Thy Neighbour?"
41. Levitsky and Way, "Linkage versus Leverage."
42. Ibid.
43. Babayan, *Democratic Transformation and Obstruction*.
44. Magen and McFaul, "Introduction"; Babayan and Risse, "So Close but Yet So Far."
45. Babayan and Risse, "So Close but Yet So Far."

Notes on contributors

Thomas Risse is Professor of International Relations at the Otto Suhr Institute of Political Science, Freie Universität Berlin. His latest publications include *A Community of Europeans? Transnational Identities and Public Spheres* (Cornell University Press, 2010), "External Actors, State-Building, and Service Provision in Areas of Limited Statehood" (co-edited with Stephen Krasner, special issue of "Governance", October 2014), and *European Public Spheres: Politics Is Back* (editor, Cambridge University Press, 2014).

Nelli Babayan is a senior researcher at the Center for Transnational Relations, Foreign and Security Policy at the Otto Suhr Institute of Political Science, Freie Universität Berlin. She is the author of *Democratic Transformation and Obstruction: EU, US and Russia in the South Caucasus* (Routledge, 2014).

References

Ambrosio, Thomas. *Authoritarian Backlash: Russian Resistance to Democratization in the Former Soviet Union*. Farnham: Ashgate, 2009.

Anyanwu, John C., and Andrew E. O. Erhijakpor. "Does Oil Wealth Affect Democracy in Africa?" *African Development Review* 26, no. 1 (March 1, 2014): 15–37. doi:10.1111/1467-8268.12061

Babayan, Nelli. "Fear or Love Thy Neighbour? EU Framework of Fostering Regional Cooperation in the South Caucasus." *Journal of Contemporary European Research* 8, no. 1 (2012): 40–56.

Babayan, Nelli. "Home-Made Adjustments? US Human Rights and Democracy Promotion." Transworld Working Papers, 2013. http://www.transworld-fp7.eu/?p=931

Babayan, Nelli. *Democratic Transformation and Obstruction: EU, US and Russia in the South Caucasus*. London: Routledge, 2015.

Babayan, Nelli. "The Return of the Empire? Russia's Counteraction to Transatlantic Democracy Promotion in Its Near Abroad." *Democratization* 22, no. 3 (2015): 438–458.

Babayan, Nelli, and Thomas Risse. So Close but Yet So Far: European and American Democracy Promotion. Transworld Working Paper, 2014.

Babayan, Nelli, and Alessandra Viviani. "Shocking Adjustments? EU Human Rights and Democracy Promotion." Transworld Working Papers, 2013. http://www.transworld-fp7.eu/?p=931

Börzel, Tanja. "The Noble West and the Dirty Rest? Western Democracy Promoters and Illiberal Regional Powers." *Democratization* 22, no. 3 (2015): 519–535.

Börzel, Tanja A., and Vera Van Hüllen. "One Voice, One Message, but Conflicting Goals. Cohesiveness and Consistency in the European Neighbourhood Policy." *Journal of European Public Policy* 21, no. 7 (2014): 1033–1049.

Börzel, Tanja, Yasemin Pamuk, and Andreas Stahn. "Democracy or Stability? EU and US Engagement in the Southern Caucasus." In *Promoting Democracy and the Rule of Law: American and European Strategies*, edited by Amichai Magen, Thomas Risse, and Michael McFaul, 150–184. Basingstoke, UK: Palgrave Macmillan, 2009.

Börzel, Tanja, and Thomas Risse. "Venus Approaching Mars? The European Union's Approaches to Democracy Promotion in Comparative Perspective." In *Promoting Democracy and the Rule of Law. American and European Strategies*, edited by Amichai Magen, Thomas Risse, and Michael McFaul, 34–60. Houndmills, UK: Palgrave Macmillan, 2009.

Bossuyt, Fabienne, and Paul Kubicek. "Advancing Democracy on Difficult Terrain: EU Democracy Promotion in Central Asia." *European Foreign Affairs Review* 16, no. 5 (2011): 639–658.

Brautigam, Deborah. *The Dragon's Gift: The Real Story of China in Africa*. Oxford; New York: Oxford University Press, 2010.

Burnell, Peter. "Is There a New Autocracy Promotion?" FRIDE Working Paper No. 96, 2010. http://www.fride.org/download/WP96_Autocracy_ENG_mar10.pdf

Burnell, Peter. "Promoting Democracy." *Government and Opposition* 48, no. 2 (October 31, 2013): 265–287. doi:10.1017/gov.2012.4

Burnell, Peter, and Oliver Schlumberger. "Promoting Democracy – Promoting Autocracy? International Politics and National Political Regimes." *Contemporary Politics* 16 (March 2010): 1–15. doi:10.1080/13569771003593805

Burnell, Peter, and Richard Youngs. *New Challenges to Democratization*. London: Routledge, 2009.

Carothers, Thomas. *Aiding Democracy Abroad: The Learning Curve*. Washington, DC: Carnegie Endowment for International Peace, 1999.

Carothers, Thomas. *Critical Mission: Essays on Democracy Promotion*. Washington, DC: Carnegie Endowment for International Peace, 2004.

Cheibub, Jose Antonio, Adam Przeworski, Fernando Papaterra Limongi Neto, and Michael M. Alvarez. "What Makes Democracies Endure?" *Journal of Democracy* 7, no. 1 (1996): 39–55. doi:10.1353/jod.1996.0016

Chen, Dingding, and Katrin Kinzelbach. "Democracy Promotion and China: Blocker or Bystander?" *Democratization* 22, no. 3 (2015): 400–418.

Collier, David, and Steven Levitsky. "Democracy with Adjectives: Conceptual Innovation in Comparative Research." *World Politics* 49, no. 3 (April 1997): 430–451.

Cox, Michael, G. John Ikenberry, and Takashi Inoguchi. *American Democracy Promotion: Impulses, Strategies, and Impacts*. Oxford: Oxford University Press, 2000.

Dandashly, Assem, Tanja A. Börzel, and Thomas Risse, eds. "Responses to the 'Arab Spring' – The EU in Comparative Perspective." *Journal of European Integration*, forthcoming.

Darbouche, Hakim, and Yahia H. Zoubir. "The Algerian Crisis in European and US Foreign Policies: A Hindsight Analysis." *The Journal of North African Studies* 14, no. 1 (2009): 33–55. doi:10.1080/13629380802383554

Delcour, Laure, and Kataryna Wolczuk. "Spoiler or Facilitator of Democratization? Russia's Role in Georgia and Ukraine." *Democratization* 22, no. 3 (2015): 459–478.

Durac, Vincent. "The Impact of External Actors on the Distribution of Power in the Middle East: The Case of Egypt." *The Journal of North African Studies* 14, no. 1 (2009): 75–90. doi:10.1080/13629380802383588

Freyburg, Tina, and Solveig Richter. "Local Actors in the Driver's Seat: Transatlantic Democracy Promotion under Regime Competition in the Arab World." *Democratization* 22, no. 3 (2015): 496–518.

Hackenesch, Christine. "Not as Bad as It Seems: EU and U.S. Democracy Promotion Face China in Africa." *Democratization* 22, no. 3 (2015): 419–437.

Hassan, Oz. "Undermining the Transatlantic Democracy Agenda? The Arab Spring and Saudi Arabia's Counteracting Democracy Strategy." *Democratization* 22, no. 3 (2015): 479–495.

Higley, John, and Michael G. Burton. "The Elite Variable in Democratic Transitions and Breakdowns." *American Sociological Review* 54, no. 1 (February 1, 1989): 17–32. doi:10.2307/2095659

Horvath, Robert. "Putin's 'Preventive Counter-Revolution': Post-Soviet Authoritarianism and the Spectre of Velvet Revolution." *Europe-Asia Studies* 63, no. 1 (January 1, 2011): 1–25. doi:10.1080/09668136.2011.534299

Kelley, Judith. "D-Minus Elections: The Politics and Norms of International Election Observation." *International Organization* 63, no. 4 (2009): 765–787.

Lavenex, Sandra, and Frank Schimmelfennig. "EU Democracy Promotion in the Neighbourhood: From Leverage to Governance?" *Democratization* 18, no. 4 (2011): 885–909. doi:10.1080/13510347.2011.584730

Levitsky, Steven, and Lucan A. Way. "Linkage versus Leverage. Rethinking the International Dimension of Regime Change." *Comparative Politics* 38, no. 4 (July 1, 2006): 379–400. doi:10.2307/20434008

Magen, Amichai, and Michael McFaul. "Introduction: American and European Strategies to Promote Democracy." In *Promoting Democracy and the Rule of Law: American and European Strategies*, edited by Amichai Magen, Thomas Risse, and Michael McFaul, 1–32. Basingstoke, UK: Palgrave Macmillan, 2009.

Magen, Amichai, Thomas Risse, and Michael McFaul. *Promoting Democracy and the Rule of Law: American and European Strategies*. London: Palgrave Macmillan, 2009.

Manners, Ian. "Normative Power Europe: A Contradiction in Terms?" *JCMS: Journal of Common Market Studies* 40, no. 2 (2002): 235–258. doi:10.1111/1468-5965.00353

McGreal, Chris. "Chinese Aid to Africa May Do More Harm than Good, Warns Benn." *The Guardian*, February 8, 2007, sec. World news. http://www.theguardian.com/world/2007/feb/08/development.topstories3

Nuriyev, Elkhan. "Azerbaijan and the European Union: New Landmarks of Strategic Partnership in the South Caucasus–Caspian Basin." *Southeast European and Black Sea Studies* 8, no. 2 (2008): 155–167. doi:10.1080/14683850802117773

Nye, Joseph S. Jr. *Soft Power. The Means to Succeed in World Politics*. New York: Public Affairs Press, 2004.

Obydenkova, Anastassia, and Alexander Libman, eds. "Understanding the Foreign Policy of Autocratic Actors: Ideology or Pragmatism? Russia and the Tymoshenko Trial as a Case Study." *Contemporary Politics* 20, no. 3 (May 14, 2014): 347–64. doi:10.1080/13569775.2014.911500

Obydenkova, Anastassia, and Alexander Libman, eds. *Autocratic and Democratic External Influences in Post-Soviet Eurasia*. London: Ashgate, 2015o. http://www.ashgate.com/isbn/9781472441249

Oneal, John R., and Bruce Russett. *Triangulating Peace: Democracy, Interdependence, and International Organizations*. New York: W. W. Norton & Company, 2000.

Piggott, Leanne. "Energy Security and Democracy Promotion in the Middle East: A Bush-Obama Continuum." In *American Democracy Promotion in the Changing Middle East: From Bush to Obama*, edited by Shahram Akbarzadeh, James Piscatori, and Benjamin Macqueen, 82–100. Routledge Chapman & Hall, 2013.

Poppe, Annika E., Bentje Woitschach, and Jonas Wolff. "Freedom Fighter versus Civilian Power: An Ideal-Type Comparison of US and German Conceptions of Democracy Promotion." In *The Comparative International Politics of Democracy Promotion*, edited by Jonas Wolff, Hans-Joachim Spanger, and Hans-Jürgen Puhle, 38–60. Abingdon, Oxon; New York: Routledge, 2013.

Powel, Brieg Tomos. "The Stability Syndrome: US and EU Democracy Promotion in Tunisia." *The Journal of North African Studies* 14, no. 1 (2009): 57–73. doi:10.1080/13629380802383562

Przeworski, Adam, and Fernando Limongi. "Modernization: Theories and Facts." *World Politics* 49, no. 2 (January 1, 1997): 155–183.

Risse, Thomas. "Conclusions: Towards Transatlantic Democracy Promotion?" In *Promoting Democracy and the Rule of Law: American and European Strategies*, edited by Amichai Magen, Thomas Risse, and Michael McFaul, Palgrave Macmillan, 2009.

Risse, Thomas. *Governance Without a State: Policies and Politics in Areas of Limited Statehood*. New York: Columbia University Press, 2011.

Risse, Thomas, Stephen C. Ropp, and Kathryn Sikkink. *The Power of Human Rights: International Norms and Domestic Change*. Cambridge: Cambridge University Press, 1999.

Risse, Thomas, Stephen C. Ropp, and Kathryn Sikkink. *The Persistent Power of Human Rights. From Commitment to Compliance*ct. Cambridge, UK: Cambridge University Press, 2013.

Russett, Bruce. *Grasping the Democratic Peace: Principles for a Post-Cold War World*. Princeton, NJ: Princeton University Press, 1994.

Schimmelfennig, Frank. "How Substantial Is Substance? Concluding Reflections on the Study of Substance in EU Democracy Promotion." *European Foreign Affairs Review* 16, no. 5 (2011): 727–734.

Schimmelfennig, Frank, Stefan Engert, and Heiko Knobel. "The Impact of EU Political Conditionality." In *The Europeanization of Central and Eastern Europe*, edited by Frank Schimmelfennig and Ulrich Sedelmeier, 29–51. Ithaca, NY: Cornell University Press, 2005.

Schimmelfennig, Frank, Stefan Engert, and Heiko Knobel. *International Socialization in Europe: European Organizations, Political Conditionality and Democratic Change*. London: Palgrave Macmillan, 2006.

Schimmelfennig, Frank, and Hanno Scholtz. "EU Democracy Promotion in the European Neighbourhood: Political Conditionality, Economic Development and Transnational Exchange." *European Union Politics* 9, no. 2 (June 1, 2008): 187–215. doi:10.1177/1465116508089085

Simão, Licínia. "The Problematic Role of EU Democracy Promotion in Armenia, Azerbaijan and Nagorno-Karabakh." *Communist and Post-Communist Studies* 45, no. 1–2 (2012): 193–200.

Stewart, Susan. "The Interplay of Domestic Contexts and External Democracy Promotion: Lessons from Eastern Europe and the South Caucasus." In *Democracy Promotion and the "Colour Revolutions"*, edited by Susan Stewart, 160–177. London: Routledge, 2012.

Stradiotto, Gary A., and Sujian Guo. *Democratic Transitions: Modes and Outcomes.* New York: Routledge Chapman & Hall, 2013.

Tolstrup, Jakob. "Studying a Negative External Actor: Russia's Management of Stability and Instability in the 'Near Abroad.'" *Democratization* 16 (October 2009): 922–944. doi:10.1080/13510340903162101

Tolstrup, Jakob. *Russia vs. the EU: The Competition for Influence in Post-Soviet States.* Boulder, CO: Lynne Rienner Publishers, 2013.

Traub, James. "The Autocrat's Emergency Bailout Fund." *Foreign Policy*, Accessed December 20, 2013. http://www.foreignpolicy.com/articles/2013/12/20/the_autocrats_emergency_bailout_fund

Vanderhill, Rachel. *Promoting Authoritarianism Abroad.* Boulder, CO: Lynne Rienner Pub, 2012.

Welsh, Helga A. "Political Transition Processes in Central and Eastern Europe." *Comparative Politics* 26, no. 4 (July 1994): 379–394. doi:10.2307/422022

Wetzel, Anne, and Jan Orbie. "Promoting Embedded Democracy? Researching the Substance of EU Democracy Promotion." *European Foreign Affairs Review* 16, no. 5 (2011): 565–588.

Whitehead, Laurence. "International Aspects of Democratization." In *Transitions from Authoritarian Rule. Prospects for Democracy*, edited by Guillermo O'Donnell, Philippe C. Schmitter, and Laurence Whitehead, 3–46. Baltimore, MD: Johns Hopkins University Press, 1986.

Whitehead, Laurence. *The International Dimensions of Democratization: Europe and the Americas.* 2nd ed. Oxford: OUP, 2001.

Wolff, Jonas, Hans-Joachim Spanger, and Hans-Jürgen Puhle. *The Comparative International Politics of Democracy Promotion.* Abingdon, Oxon; New York: Routledge, 2013.

Wolff, Jonas, Hans-Joachim Spanger, and Hans-Jürgen Puhle. *The Comparative International Politics of Democracy Promotion (Hardback) – Routledge.* London: Routledge, 2013. http://www.routledge.com/books/details/9780415826945/

Zeeuw, Jeroen De, and Krishna Kumar. *Promoting Democracy in Postconflict Societies.* Boulder, CO: Lynne Rienner Pub, 2006.

Democracy promotion and China: blocker or bystander?

Dingding Chen[a] and Katrin Kinzelbach[b,c]

[a]Department of Government and Public Administration, University of Macau, China; [b]Global Public Policy Institute, Berlin, Germany; [c]School of Public Policy, Central European University, Budapest, Hungary

The increasingly prosperous, mighty, and assertive China is arguably the most powerful country blocking democracy today. In addition to withholding democratic rights of one-fifth of the world's population, authoritarian China represents an alternative development model that has gained significant traction. China thus constitutes a challenge to democracy promoters. But does Beijing also countervail democracy promotion by the European Union and the United States? After a summary of the party-state's response to democracy promotion at home, we test the hypothesis that geostrategic interests or a perceived risk of regime survival will lead the People's Republic to countervail democracy promotion outside its own borders. We do so by focusing on the most likely cases in China's near-abroad: Myanmar and Hong Kong. Our analysis of Myanmar suggests that Beijing remains focused on securing economic and security interests irrespective of regime type when regime survival at home is not at risk. The case of Hong Kong, on the other hand, allows us to identify the tactics used by Beijing when there is a significant risk of democratic spillover. This case also demonstrates that the People's Republic of China is able to stifle United States and European Union democracy support when it wishes to do so.

Introduction

In April 2013, the Chinese Communist Party (CCP) reportedly distributed a confidential *Communiqué on the Current State of the Ideological Sphere*. The content of this document, referred to in short-hand as Document No. 9, was leaked to journalists and is said to have been released by the General Office of the Party's Central Committee and approved by the central leadership.[1] According to these reports, the secret communiqué lists seven contemporary perils, with the first among them being the promotion of constitutional democracy. Building on the party-state's own analysis in Document No 9, we offer a summary of current domestic and external democratization pressures vis-à-vis China, and the CCP's response to them. We then ask whether or not the People's Republic is pursuing an equally determined strategy to halt democratization outside China's borders as well.[2]

According to the theoretical framework presented in the introduction to this special issue, we start from the premise that the People's Republic has the ability to employ military and economic leverage to hinder democratization in its immediate neighbourhood. Risse and Babayan (see introduction) theorize that non-democratic regional powers will seek to countervail United States (US) and European Union (EU) democracy support when geostrategic interests are at stake or when regime survival at home is at risk. In recent years, it has been suggested by academics and foreign policy observers alike that authoritarian China hinders democratization outside its own borders and even promotes autocracy abroad.[3] However, whether China does in fact take targeted action to countervail US and EU democracy assistance remains an open empirical question. There has been a notable shift toward more assertiveness since President Xi Jinping assumed office in 2013, yet there is still not enough evidence to draw a definitive conclusion on his foreign policy.

To understand whether or not Beijing responded with any countervailing actions to US and EU democracy promotion in China's near-abroad during the period covered by this special issue (2011–2014), we adopted a most likely case research design. We assess whether China countervails democracy support due to geostrategic interests by looking at Myanmar. Myanmar shares a border with China, holds significant natural resources, is important for geostrategic reasons, and has been a longstanding ally of the People's Republic. Myanmar launched political reforms in 2011, which led the US and the EU to lift sanctions first imposed in the 1990s, normalize diplomatic relations, resume development aid, offer democracy support, and foster trade relations. Should geostrategic interests lead China to countervail EU and US democracy promotion, we should be able to find empirical evidence in China's response to the fledgling liberalization process in Myanmar.

In addition to Myanmar, we discuss recent developments in Hong Kong, a former British colony over which China regained sovereignty in 1997. Before the handover, the United Kingdom (UK) and China negotiated a special status for Hong Kong and signed a bilateral declaration that was ratified in May 1985. According to this agreement, Beijing promised to uphold the principle of "one country, two systems", thereby allowing Hong Kong a high degree of autonomy and, indeed, self-governance for issues other than defence and foreign affairs. Furthermore, it was also agreed that Hong Kong would continue to report to the United Nations (UN) on its compliance with the International Covenant on Civil and Political Rights – an international treaty that the People's Republic has not ratified. Therefore, while Hong Kong belongs to China, it is commonly considered a separate entity from the so-called "mainland". We argue that the Chinese leadership in

Beijing perceived the 2014 democracy movement in Hong Kong as a threat. If a perceived threat to regime survival leads China to countervail US and EU democracy promotion, we should be able to observe this in Hong Kong. Indeed, the case of Hong Kong demonstrates that Beijing does seek to stifle US and EU democracy support when it has reason to worry about democratic spillover; notably, this is true even though post-1997 US and EU democracy support toward Hong Kong has been limited to regular monitoring, carefully worded public statements, and modest technical and financial support.

Based on our analysis we conclude that the Chinese Communist Party counteracts EU and US democracy promotion only in cases threatening its own regime survival, but not in pursuit of geostrategic interests. The US and Europe, in turn, by and large respect the red lines drawn by Chinese diplomats. Both the US and the EU are hesitant to burden their bilateral relations with the rising China in the name of democracy. The outcome of this is that activists who are perceived to be a threat by the CCP cannot count on resolute international support when seeking to shift the local balance of power toward democracy.

China's response to domestic and international democratization pressures

In the period covered by this special issue (2011–2014), pro-democracy activism in China has been small in scale overall and only loosely organized. At the same time, the resilience of authoritarian rule in China has been tested by economic development trends, changes in Chinese political culture, competition among Chinese leaders, and the effects of globalization.[4] Andrew Nathan observed in 2013 that consensus was "stronger than at any time since the 1989 Tiananmen crisis that the resilience of the authoritarian regime in the People's Republic of China (PRC) is approaching its limits".[5] Minxin Pei postulated in the same year that "a transition to democracy in China in the next 10 to 15 years is a high probability event".[6]

It is striking that Document No. 9, the CCP's April 2013 communiqué on the state of the ideological sphere, essentially provides the same analysis, but with a view to stalling democratization pressures. It warns that democracy promotion is an "attempt to undermine the current leadership and the socialism with Chinese characteristics system of governance".[7] In addition to ideological challenges, the CCP also grapples with an increase in larger-scale protests around bread and butter issues, such as grievances about working conditions and salary levels, but also land grabbing and environmental degradation. Demonstrations, some of which turn violent, are said to continue to grow in frequency, and while there is a lack of clarity on the exact figures, public security spending has been rising as a result.[8] A sophisticated system of so-called social stability management (*weiwen*) was set up to deal with these pressures and to undermine organizations that could compete with the authority of the party-state.[9] According to Xie Yue, a political science professor at Tongji University in Shanghai, *weiwen* seeks to reduce social and political instability by enhancing coercive capacity rather than by moving forward to the rule of law and democracy.[10]

In the CCP's orthodoxy, domestic challengers of one-party rule are not only "anti-Chinese", they also play into the hands of China's international rivals that seek to undermine China's rise, notably the US. That is, the CCP employs a nationalist counter-discourse and it suggests that external actors (or rather: global rivals) try to politically destabilize the People's Republic for strategic reasons. According to Document No. 9, "Western anti-China forces" and "all kinds of so-called citizens movements" echo each other and rely on each other's support "to squeeze the Party out of leadership".[11] Finally, it concludes: "In the face of these threats, we must not let down our guard or decrease our vigilance."[12] Document No. 9 most likely spurred a number of recent arrests, notably of individuals belonging to the "New Citizen Movement". For example, Xu Zhiyong, who gave the movement its name,[13] received a four-year prison term in early 2014.

Three years earlier, in March 2010, China's State Administration of Foreign Exchange had already issued stricter rules on the receipt of foreign donations by Chinese organizations, thereby increasing the party-state's control over the flow of foreign resources to Chinese non-governmental organizations (NGOs). Chinese organizations can now only receive foreign funds if they have a special foreign exchange account and after getting their grant agreements notarized. Due to this procedure, it has become very difficult if not impossible for the US and the EU to make financial transfers to organizations that engage in democracy promotion in China. Therefore, foreign support for domestic civil society actors is, more often than not, designed so as to dispel possible concerns, thereby restricting the flow of foreign resources to activities that are palatable to the Chinese authorities.

The US and the EU continue to support Chinese human rights activists through financial grants, quiet diplomacy, and public statements, but both actors have scaled down their ambitions in recent years. This is not only because financial regulations have changed. China's rapidly increasing international weight, which was further accelerated by the subprime mortgage crisis in the US and the sovereign debt crisis in Europe, changed the dynamics of international politics, and significantly decreased the party-state's vulnerability to international pressure. Accordingly, high-ranking leaders in Beijing now dismiss Western criticism of China's governance model rather confidently. For example, according to confidential accounts of EU officials, Wu Hailong (since 2014 China's Representative at the UN in Geneva) noted repeatedly in closed-door meetings that China was no longer willing to be lectured on human rights and democracy because "times have changed".[14]

As this brief summary shows, the Chinese party-state has sought to countervail external and domestic democracy promotion by using a wide range of tactics, ranging from domestic repression, counter-discourse at home and abroad, to sticks and carrots at the international level. To what extent this policy extends beyond the borders of mainland China will be discussed in the following two sections on Myanmar and Hong Kong.

China's reactions to political reforms in Myanmar

Myanmar was ruled by a military dictatorship from 1988 to 2010. In early 2011, the defence services initiated a political reform process. While the reforms are significant, active-duty and retired officers continue to run the government; also, parliament remains under the control of the army and its proxy, the Union Solidarity and Development Party.[15] Despite the existing obstacles to genuine democratization in Myanmar, the EU suspended all its sanctions except for an arms embargo in response to by-elections held in 2012. A year later, the suspended sanctions were formally lifted and Myanmar was reinstated as beneficiary of the "Everything But Arms" initiative under the EU's generalized system of preferences, which helps developing nations to compete on the EU market.[16]

The US, in turn, normalized political relations by sending a US ambassador to Myanmar in July 2012 and easing its sanctions in the same month. This move entailed specific conditions and prior negotiations on the release of political prisoners.[17] American President Barack Obama visited Rangoon in November 2012, where he stressed in a public speech that America would support further reform in Myanmar "by using our assistance to empower civil society; by engaging your military to promote professionalism and human rights; and by partnering with you as you connect your progress towards democracy with economic development".[18] But Obama also used the occasion to send a geopolitical signal about America's so-called pivot to Asia: "The United States of America is a Pacific nation, and we see our future as bound to those nations and peoples to our West."[19]

The 2012 by-elections were not necessarily a step toward democracy, but rather the biggest institutional shake-up in Myanmar's history since the army took office in 1962.[20] According to Thant Myint-U, the final outcome of this shake-up is unpredictable. He also stresses that recent developments in Myanmar must be read in their broader geopolitical context, as Myanmar's place in the region has dramatically changed. Though it was "once the back of beyond", Myanmar is "now at the doorstep of the world's emerging superpower, China [...]"[21] In addition to normative objectives, both the US and the EU also pursue economic and strategic interests when supporting Myanmar's reform process, thereby challenging China's influence in the country. Thus, the case of Myanmar backs the argument presented in the introduction to this special issue: Western powers should not be regarded as unequivocally committed to the promotion of democracy and human rights; their concrete actions are also determined by other foreign policy interests.

We argue that Myanmar represents a most likely case for Chinese efforts to countervail EU and US democracy support because of strategic reasons. Myanmar is a buffer zone to China's national security and has been a longstanding ally of China. A close economic relationship between the two countries enhances China's economic development in the Western region. Last but not least, a good relationship with Myanmar's leadership can defeat US efforts to build what Beijing perceives as an "anti-China" circle in Southeast Asia. Although political liberalization is still at an early stage in Myanmar, some Chinese scholars do note that it already poses new challenges to China's strategic interests.[22] First, Myanmar's strategic reliance on China has declined and, as such, Myanmar's foreign policy becomes more autonomous and less dependent on China. Second, civil society groups and citizens in Myanmar increasingly oppose China's projects, notably the construction of dams and oil pipelines. Third, following the lifting of US and EU sanctions, a large number of foreign firms are entering Myanmar, posing serious competition to Chinese firms. Fourth, civil society in Myanmar has embraced democracy and human rights as desirable, facilitating a negative view of the People's Republic due to China's human rights and democracy shortcomings at home.[23] Yet, rather than counteracting democracy support in Myanmar, the Chinese government launched a multi-pronged public diplomacy effort in late 2011 which seeks to counteract anti-China resentment in Myanmar.[24]

A different view is promulgated by the Chinese Academy of Social Sciences (CASS), a research institute that is affiliated with the State Council. In a book report published in 2013, CASS-affiliated experts argue that China is not very concerned about Myanmar's political transition for several reasons. First, foreign policy experts in Beijing believe that Myanmar's political reforms are irreversible; at the same time, the transition process is not expected to be very smooth, notably because of the ethnic and religious conflicts in Myanmar. Myanmar was unlikely to entirely side with the West and to seek confrontation with China. A more likely scenario was that Myanmar would try to balance itself among several big powers. Finally, the CASS report argues that China's influence over Myanmar could not be replaced by other countries because of geostrategic reasons, and because of the close economic ties between Myanmar and China. CASS therefore advised Chinese leaders not to be overly worried about liberalization in Myanmar, except for any instability caused by the reform process.[25]

Accordingly, China's President Xi Jinping told Myanmar's new President Thein Sein in 2013 that China "sincerely hopes Myanmar can maintain social stability, develop its economy and improve people's livelihood". Crucially, President Xi also stressed that "China supports Myanmar to take the direction that fits its own reality".[26] This statement, of course, is not an explicit endorsement of democratization. In the past, similar phrases have been used by Chinese diplomats to shield Myanmar against international criticism. For example, in 2006, a Chinese delegate to the UN Human Rights Council stated: "As a neighbouring country, China hoped for stability, economic development, ethnic harmony and domestic reconciliation in Myanmar, but it was for the people of Myanmar to secure their own future."[27] Nevertheless, we consider it noteworthy that China's most senior leaders do not publicly condemn Myanmar's reform trajectory, nor do there seem to be concerted efforts to hinder political liberalization in Myanmar.

As far as could be ascertained by analysing Chinese language publications on Myanmar's transition and by consulting intellectuals that advise the Chinese government on China-Myanmar relations,[28] Chinese authorities do not currently seek to countervail EU and US democracy promotion in Myanmar. We have also not found any evidence that China is making its economic investments or military cooperation conditional on the restriction of democratic rights, or that it is using political leverage to foster autocracy in Myanmar. Since 2011, when Myanmar initiated political reforms, China's declared strategy has instead focused on three areas: engaging civil society, increasing contacts with opposition parties (this includes official meetings with Aung San Suu Kyi and even small donations to organizations affiliated with the National League for Democracy, NLD), as well as mediating peace talks.[29] These steps have one common purpose, which is to maintain Myanmar's domestic stability at the same time as China's political influence in the country – they do not focus on upholding authoritarian rule.

It is not entirely clear why China does not seek to countervail democratization support in Myanmar more forcefully. According to scholars from Yunnan University's Center for Myanmar Studies, which was set up in 2011 to study the political changes in Myanmar and to engage in public diplomacy, possible explanations for China's cautious approach include that China has limited influence over the military elites, despite China's overall influence in Myanmar after 1990. Moreover, Myanmar's elites were already suspicious of Chinese influence in Myanmar and a direct intervention from China into Myanmar's domestic affairs would only push Myanmar even further toward the West. Finally, the Chinese foreign policy establishment did not feel a serious threat from Myanmar's political liberalization as long as China's geostrategic interests remained largely protected.[30]

It is of course debatable whether Beijing's efforts to maintain influence in Myanmar are effective. After all, it has rapidly declined since 2011, evidenced by the drop of China's foreign direct investment to Myanmar. According to one report, China's investment in the 2013 fiscal year was less than 10% of what it was in 2012, mainly because the government of Myanmar had frozen several of China's investment projects.[31] Furthermore, China's investments in Myanmar are being criticized for human rights violations and the lack of environmental protection. The delay of a dam project at Myitsone is a case in point.[32] In taking such decisions, the government of Myanmar is most likely responding to more than just domestic critics; it also has strategic reasons to reduce its heavy reliance on Chinese investments. Indeed, Myanmar's dependence on China should be considered as one likely explanation for the country's recent political reforms.

The extent of China's influence in Myanmar may have inadvertently facilitated rather than hindered liberalization. To counterbalance China's power and guarantee Myanmar's independence, the military regime in Myanmar may have chosen to broker a rapprochement with the West, notably to overcome the long-lasting American and European sanctions. To achieve this strategic goal, the military leadership had to accommodate some US and EU concerns regarding political repression and human rights abuse. Contrary to this view, Lee Jones points out that China's influence in Myanmar was "tolerated as the price of Beijing's massive arms transfers, foreign investment, and diplomatic backing. Despite arousing popular and elite concern, Chinese influence did not suddenly escalate to intolerable levels that could explain an abrupt liberalization."[33] While the risk linked to Myanmar's dependence on China may not have been a sufficient factor for political reform, it likely contributed to elite interest calculations, thereby facilitating rather than hindering the country's opening to the West. US diplomats observe similar dynamics in Vietnam, where the political leadership has reportedly become more amenable to making concessions on human rights in recent years because it seeks to improve relations with the US in response to China's growing influence in the region.[34]

Despite these geostrategic dynamics in Southeast Asia, China has so far not systematically countervailed US democracy promotion in the region. The key priority for Beijing appears to be an active and good relationship with whatever government is in place so that China's strategic and economic interests will not be negatively affected.[35] Andrew Nathan calls this a "regime-type-neutral approach".[36] Fan Hongwei explains it with a dilemma: Beijing seeks to protect Chinese strategic interests while also trying to preserve its traditional policy of non-interference.[37] We do not wish to suggest, however, that China's role as a long-standing ally of the military junta as well as its influence as a non-democratic regional power do not negatively affect the ongoing reform process in Myanmar. Bader and Kästner argue that China does stabilize autocracy in Myanmar even though it only relies on cooperative measures rather than a coercive approach.[38] The introduction to this special issue rightly notes that obstacles to democratization do not only result from deliberate attempts by non-democratic regional powers to promote autocracy, but they can also result simply from strong economic or security ties. However, given that China does not seem to have a deliberate policy to countervail political reform in Myanmar, it should be a relatively benign environment for the EU and the US to project democratic values.

A thorough discussion of China's impact on Myanmar's fledgling reforms would require detailed field research beyond the scope of this article. The same is true for the impact of ongoing Western democracy promotion efforts in Myanmar. Nevertheless, we consider it likely that China's actions may not even be a key factor affecting EU and US impact, as Hackenesch has also shown in her African case studies (see Hackenesch in this special issue). Rather, the crucial question is whether local democratic forces can prevail. Final outcome aside, there is thus far no convincing evidence to suggest that China objects to Myanmar's political reforms on ideological grounds,[39] or that it is using economic or military leverage to promote an authoritarian form of government in the country. The most plausible explanation for this appears to be that Chinese leaders do not worry about democratic spillover[40] and a risk to their own hold on power. Perhaps this is because Myanmar is an exceptionally poor country; the Chinese population is therefore not likely to look at Myanmar as a model for China.[41]

We conclude that Beijing's response ultimately depends on whether democratization in China's near-abroad presents a serious threat to the CCP and its grip on power at home. This very factor, that is, the perceived attractiveness of an alternative political model in China's immediate neighbourhood, and the resultant threat of democratic spillover to the People's Republic, plays out very differently in the case of Hong Kong, to which we now turn.

China's reactions to democratization pressure in Hong Kong

According to the "one country, two systems" doctrine, Hong Kong enjoys a very high degree of autonomy. Hong Kong can decide its own policies except for issues concerning foreign policy and national defence. Although there is no authoritative and representative survey data on the matter, we have ample anecdotal evidence of Hong Kong's power of attraction vis-à-vis citizens of the Chinese mainland. To reference just one example: despite rigorous border controls, close to 36,000 pregnant Chinese women crossed the border to give birth in Hong Kong in 2011, thereby obtaining residence rights for their offspring.[42] Compared to China's richest cities, Shanghai and Beijing, Hong Kong remains far advanced economically. In 2013, Hong Kong's gross domestic product per capita was US$38,124,[43] while Beijing's stood at US$15,422 and Shanghai's at US$14,845.[44] Furthermore, there is an independent judiciary, a free press, and a vibrant civil society.

In September 2014, a civil disobedience movement launched by democracy activists under the name of "Occupy Central" blocked off government offices and Hong Kong's financial district. Tens of thousands demonstrated peacefully in the heart of Hong Kong. When the police force used tear gas to dispel demonstrators, it had the opposite effect: the crowd grew and the protests soon became known as the "umbrella revolution" because demonstrators on the street sought to protect themselves with umbrellas against tear gas. Following the theoretical framework of this special issue, we argue that Hong Kong is a most likely case, allowing us to test whether concerns over regime survival at home lead Beijing to countervail US and EU democracy support in China's immediate neighbourhood.

Beijing views local politics in Hong Kong primarily as a competition between two camps: pro-democracy groups and pro-Beijing groups. While the former mostly consists of democratic legislators and some grass-roots groups, the latter includes the rich and powerful business community and some traditional pro-China groups like trade unions. Partly responding to external democracy promotion efforts,[45] Beijing has employed a double strategy that has included both repression and co-optation strategies. One study notes that "the most powerful weapon employed by the PRC to co-opt the people of Hong Kong, to silence the critics, to buy off opportunists [...] and to curb the demands for democracy is economic enticement".[46] According to another study, big firms in Hong Kong that have strong ties with the mainland have benefited greatly from these ties.[47] However, Beijing's co-optation strategy has its own limits. Hong Kong's service and real estate sectors have benefitted from a great number of Chinese tourists in recent years, but the middle class has not shared in the benefits. Indeed, since 2010 there have been a series of incidents between mainland tourists and Hong Kong citizens that have increased tensions between mainland China and Hong Kong.[48] The Chinese government has increasingly turned to a repressive strategy for dealing with Hong Kong's growing desires to democratize. This can be seen in

Beijing's recent efforts to curb press freedom in Hong Kong, as evidenced by online attacks on *Apple Daily* (a pro-democracy newspaper),[49] physical attacks on journalists and legal accusations launched against Jimmy Lai (owner of *Apple Daily*).[50] Despite the "one country, two systems" doctrine, Hong Kong's freedom of speech has been eroding under the leadership of a pro-Beijing Chief Executive.[51] Against this background, the election of Hong Kong's next Chief Executive in 2017 became a contentious issue, and both the US as well as the EU paid close attention to the developments.

Support for the democratization of Hong Kong has been an element of US foreign policy for more than two decades. As the Hong Kong Policy Act of 1992 states, "support for democratization is a fundamental principle of United States foreign policy. As such, it naturally applies to United States policy toward Hong Kong. This will remain equally true after 30 June, 1997."[52] Twenty years later, in 2012, US Consul General Stephen M. Young confirmed that "long-standing U.S. policy has supported the express desire of the people of Hong Kong to participate in free elections by universal suffrage at the earliest possible date".[53] Public statements of this kind can either be seen as lip service to democracy in Hong Kong, or as acts of political support in their own right. We argue that they are more than lip service because they keep Hong Kong's democratization on the international agenda, thereby echoing domestic democratization pressure. US support has not been limited to public statements, it has included modest financial and strategic assistance as well. For example, the National Endowment for Democracy (NED) has supported Hong Kong's struggle for freedom, human rights, and democracy, an activity that is not well received in Beijing.[54] In 2014, Chinese state media claimed the NED instigated the civil disobedience movement Occupy Central, an allegation that the NED denied.[55] *China Daily* also smeared Hong Kong Labour Party Chairman Lee Cheuk-yan for receiving donations from the NED. The money was reportedly channelled through the American Center for International Labor Solidarity.[56] Via another partner, the National Democratic Institute for International Affairs (NDI), the NED financed seminars and media training for democratic parties in Hong Kong.[57] Another NED activity to promote democracy in Hong Kong has been to provide grants for public opinion surveys and to public policy think tanks such as Civic Exchange.[58] The US has thus maintained a very delicate position between publicly promoting democracy in Hong Kong and acting quietly behind the scenes, all the while trying to avoid backlash.

In response to the dispute over universal suffrage in Hong Kong, the US Congressional Commission on China organized a roundtable discussion on prospects for democracy in Hong Kong.[59] Two former legislators and well-known democracy activists, Martin Lee and Anson Chan, travelled to the US in April 2014 where they were received not only by US Assistant Secretary of State for Democracy, Human Rights and Labor, Tom Malinowski,[60] but also by Vice President Joe Biden.[61] In response, Chinese officials stressed that Washington should not interfere in Hong Kong.[62] In June 2014, Beijing released a white paper detailing its position on Hong Kong's political reforms, quelling hopes for universal suffrage in 2017.[63] Despite the diplomatic warning issued by Beijing, US Consul-General to Hong Kong and Macau, Clifford Hart, said that the US would back Hong Kong in striving for "genuine" universal suffrage in his first public speech after his appointment.[64] In November 2014, a bipartisan group of influential US lawmakers introduced the "Hong Kong Human Rights and Democracy Act (HKHRDA) in both House and Senate to ensure continued US monitoring of political developments in Hong Kong.

The public statements by the EU have remained comparatively reserved. On an annual basis, the EU issues a report on Hong Kong's political developments through its Office to Hong Kong and Macau. This monitoring arrangement honours a commitment given to the European Parliament at the time of the handover in 1997. Apart from the annual report, however, the EU Office focuses primarily on bilateral trade and investment relations.[65] In July 2014, the spokesperson for the European External Action Service commented on the Chinese white paper in a public statement that privileged diplomatic code over clear wording: "The EU is following this process closely and is looking forward to the forging of an ambitious consensus among the parties involved, within the framework of 'one country, two systems.'"[66] In December 2014, the EU also raised the issue of universal suffrage in Hong Kong during its regular human rights dialogue with Beijing.

Within the EU, the UK as former colonial power of Hong Kong and signatory to the Joint Declaration has paid particularly close attention to political developments in Hong Kong. The last British governor, Chris Patten, instituted significant constitutional reforms to broaden the electoral base, intended as a step toward universal suffrage. Yet after the handover, the CCP replaced the 1995-elected legislature with a Provisional Legislative Council. Since then, the UK's Foreign and Commonwealth Office has reported biannually on the implementation of the Sino-British Joint Declaration to the British parliament. In July 2014, when the Chinese issued their white paper on Hong Kong, the British parliament's Foreign Affairs Committee launched an inquiry into the implementation of the Joint Declaration.[67] Beyond regular monitoring and political attention, the UK also granted small-scale democracy support. For example, from 2009 onwards, the Westminster Foundation for Democracy, an NGO funded by the British government, made a modest grant of approximately £10,000 over three years to support seminars for political parties in Hong Kong.[68]

Even though the police dismantled the last barricades in December 2014, what is clear, however, is that Beijing and pro-Beijing groups in Hong Kong tried to delegitimize Occupy Central by framing it as a movement controlled and manipulated by so-called "black hands" and "hostile foreign forces". In the eyes of Beijing, it is American strategy to use Hong Kong's debates over democracy as an opportunity to keep its own dominant position in Southeast Asia, and to contain China's power and influence.[69] While the EU is hardly mentioned in this context, Beijing conspicuously seeks to re-frame Hong Kong's debate about democracy into a debate over China's international rise and the hidden agendas of foreign actors – a rhetorical refrain also characteristic of Document No. 9.

The Chinese party-state is evidently more concerned about US and EU democracy support in Hong Kong than Myanmar. A key reason for Beijing's opposition to democratization in Hong Kong appears to be that the city is viewed by many Chinese citizens as an attractive model for mainland China's future. Moreover, the Chinese government has reason to worry that Hong Kong, once fully democratized, could become a base for local and foreign democratic forces that could challenge the CCP. It remains to be seen whether or not the Chinese central government can win the battle against public opinion in Hong Kong regarding universal suffrage. Without doubt, Beijing has already shown that it can successfully moderate external support for democracy in Hong Kong. For example, when Anson Chan and Martin Lee visited London in July 2014 to lobby for support, Prime Minister David Cameroon and other senior Tory cabinet ministers declined to meet them. Deputy Prime Minister Nick Clegg from the Liberal Democrats, on the other hand, welcomed the two and complained to the press that the British Conservative Party was "too deferential towards China as they seek to boost British trade links with the country projected to soon be the world's largest economy".[70] Here it should be remembered that David Cameroon had already learnt his lesson about the power of Beijing's sticks and carrots after meeting the Dalai Lama in 2012. The result was a deep freeze of Sino-British relations that lasted more than a year. Despite having to report to the British parliament on the implementation of the Joint Declaration, it appears that the prime minister was not willing to risk another diplomatic fallout with China.

Although the US has been a stronger supporter of Hong Kong's democratization, it too has remained rather quiet with regard to Occupy Central. The peak of the movement came at a time when the US was distracted by two major events in Europe and the Middle East: the Ukraine crisis and the surge of the so-called Islamic State of Iraq and the Levant (ISIS). China's support for the US military campaign against ISIS is an important element for US foreign policy, and this might partly explain the low-key approach toward Hong Kong. For example, when US national security advisor Susan Rice visited China in early September 2014, she remarked that Hong Kong's political reform was an internal affair.[71] At the end of September, the US Consulate stated in a press release: "We do not take sides in the discussion of Hong Kong's political development, nor do we support any particular individuals or groups involved in it."[72]

These statements are most likely an expression of a policy that seeks to balance normative commitments with other national interests. As the introduction to this special issue already suggested, such a balancing act frequently leads to a downplaying of democracy promotion. Alternatively, the above US statements could also be interpreted as an attempt to counter Beijing's narrative that demonstrators in Hong Kong were puppets of foreign powers. Whatever the intention behind the above formulations, they confirm that Beijing has drawn clear red lines, especially with regard to public statements that US officials and politicians make in

Hong Kong and in China. When Chinese representatives travel to the West, on the other hand, carefully worded US references to normative aspirations remain common. For example, when China's Foreign Minister Wang Yi travelled to the US in October 2014, US Secretary of State John Kerry stated publicly in Wang's presence: "As China knows, we support universal suffrage in Hong Kong."[73] Such statements to the press should not be misunderstood as a promise for dedicated support, however. Instead, they form part of a diplomatic routine which, at least in part, serves to satisfy Western voters and journalists.

The lack of resolute support from the US and the EU on the one hand, and China's strategy to discredit demonstrators as foreign agents on the other, put Hong Kong's democratic forces in a delicate position. According to German media, student leader Joshua Wong called on the German Chancellor Angela Merkel to voice support for universal suffrage in Hong Kong when she met the Chinese cabinet for high-level consultations in October 2014. Wong argued that the protests only had a chance to succeed if Germany, Europe, and the whole world expressed solidarity and pressured China.[74] Different from Wong, the more experienced Benny Tai (Associate Professor of Law at the University of Hong Kong and initiator of Occupy Central), stressed that he would not actively ask a foreign government to support the demonstrations because Occupy Central was "a purely local movement". Evidently Tai was keen to counter Beijing's defamation of the movement as controlled by the West. But he still passed his message on by stating that Germany had a certain influence and if the German government decided to express support for Occupy Central, it would be welcomed.[75]

The case of Hong Kong confirms that the People's Republic of China countervails democratization where there is a risk of spillover, and that it does consider EU and US support significant enough to warrant diplomatic attention at the highest level. The US and the EU provide modest assistance, but by and large respect Beijing's red lines, while local pro-democracy activists walk a delicate line between soliciting external support for their cause and maintaining local legitimacy.

Conclusion: blocker or bystander?

The People's Republic of China is both a decisive blocker as well as an indifferent bystander of democratization. In this article, we looked at whether and how China countervails EU and US democracy promotion at home and in its immediate neighbourhood. In terms of domestic politics, the CCP is clearly determined to withstand, repress, outperform, and outsmart home-grown as well as external pressures for democratization. It is impossible to predict how long this approach will be sustainable.

With regard to China's foreign policy, we tested the hypothesis that geostrategic interests or a perceived risk of regime survival at home will lead the People's Republic to countervail democracy promotion outside its own borders as well. The case of Hong Kong confirms that a perceived risk of regime survival leads Beijing to countervail US and EU democracy support outside the Chinese mainland.

Although the scope of this article did not allow for additional case studies, we consider it likely that the CCP's focus on regime-survival at home does not only trump the "one country, two systems" doctrine, but ultimately also Beijing's declared non-interference principle in foreign policy. Yet, the fact that Beijing does not seem to use its significant leverage over Myanmar to hinder democracy support is an empirical challenge to the common proposition that authoritarian China is likely to export or protect autocracy, especially in its near-abroad. Given that we view Myanmar as the most likely case with respect to strategic interests, we suggest with considerable certainty that Beijing will only counteract democratization, including US and EU democracy support, where it perceives a challenge to the CCP's survival. Where this is not the case, Beijing is likely to focus on protecting its economic and strategic interests abroad, regardless of regime type.

While this finding might be taken to suggest that a focus on China's international influence should not be a priority for democracy supporters, we remain more cautious. China's economic performance has not only granted the CCP legitimacy domestically, it has also made China's development path – economic liberalization without political reform – appear desirable further afield. And the recent economic troubles in Europe and the US, in turn, have challenged the thus far common perception that democracy was required for prosperity. As democracy promoters, both the US and the EU should therefore ensure that the very real governance shortcomings in China, beyond as well as within the economic sphere, are publicly identified for what they are. Without such concerted efforts, it is likely that authoritarian China will continue to be looked at as an alternative development model, thereby challenging democracy's power of attraction.

Acknowledgements

We thank the participants of an authors' workshop for helpful comments on an earlier draft and three anonymous reviewers for constructive criticism. Andrew J. Nathan, Malin Oud, Minxin Pei, Christopher Walker, and others who asked that we withhold their names helped by sharing insights at the very beginning of our research. Allison West slightly edited the final text. Katrin Kinzelbach gratefully acknowledges a research grant from the Volkswagen Foundation.

Notes

1. *New York Times*, http://www.nytimes.com/2013/08/20/world/asia/chinas-new-leadership-takes-hard-line-in-secret-memo.html?pagewanted=all&_r=0, accessed 16 May 2014.
2. For China's approach to democracy promotion further afield, see the article by Christine Hackenesch in this volume.
3. See Walker, "Authoritarian Regimes Are Changing"; and Bader and Kästner, "Externe Autokratieförderung?"; also see Nathan "China's Challenge to Democracy."
4. Liu and Chen, "Why China Will Democratize."
5. Nathan, "China at the Tipping Point," 20.
6. Pei, "5 Ways China Could Become a Democracy."
7. ChinaFile, "Document 9."

8. Godement, "Control at the Grassroots," 3.
9. Ibid.
10. Xie, "Rising Central Spending," 104.
11. ChinaFile, "Document 9."
12. Ibid.
13. See http://xuzhiyong2012.blogspot.de/2012/11/blog-post_9281.html, accessed 16 May 2014.
14. Confidential interview with European official, conducted by Katrin Kinzelbach in January 2012.
15. See Callahan, "The Generals Loosen Their Grip"; and Myint-U, "White Elephants and Black Swans," for more details.
16. European Commission, "Press Release."
17. Martin, "Burma's Political Prisoners," 17–20.
18. The White House, http://www.whitehouse.gov/the-press-office/2012/11/19/remarks-president-obama-university-yangon, accessed 10 October 2014.
19. Ibid.
20. Myint-U, "White Elephants and Black Swans," 26.
21. Ibid., 30.
22. Sun, "China and the Changing Myanmar."
23. China Institute for International Studies, http://www.ciis.org.cn/chinese/2013-05/30/content_5992294.htm, accessed 24 July 2014.
24. Fan, "China Adapts to New Myanmar Realities."
25. Li, "Myanmar's National Situations."
26. Chinese Ministry for Foreign Affairs, http://www.fmprc.gov.cn/mfa_chn/zyxw_602251/t1028635.shtml, accessed 16 May 2014.
27. UN Human Rights Council, *Second Session*, § 106.
28. Personal interview with scholars at Myanmar Studies Center at Yunnan University by Dingding Chen on 16 September 2014.
29. Li, "China-Myanmar Relations," 17–33; also see Fan, "China Adapts to New Myanmar Realities," 6–7.
30. Personal interview with scholars at Myanmar Studies Center at Yunnan University by Dingding Chen on 16 September 2014.
31. *Nikkei Asian Review*, http://zh.cn.nikkei.com/politicsaeconomy/economic-policy/8635-20140328.html, accessed 16 May 2014.
32. Berger, "China's Troubled Myanmar Policy."
33. Lee, "Explaining Myanmar's Regime Transition," 2.
34. Confidential interview with US officials, conducted by Katrin Kinzelbach in October 2014.
35. See for example Cook, "Post-Myitsone Relations"; Li, "China-Myanmar Comprehensive Partnership"; Taylor, "Modern China-Myanmar Relations."
36. Nathan, "China's Challenge to Democracy."
37. Fan, "China Adapts to New Myanmar Realities," 8.
38. Bader and Kästner, "Externe Autokratieförderung?"
39. Sun, "China and Changing Myanmar," 51–77.
40. The only noteworthy spillover effect is that of the Kachin conflict into Yunnan province, where Beijing did not remain uninvolved but exercised "unprecedented pressure" according to Fan, "China Adapts to New Myanmar Realities," 9.
41. We thank Minxin Pei for advancing this explanation in a conversation about this article.
42. *New York Times*, http://www.nytimes.com/2012/02/23/world/asia/mainland-chinese-flock-to-hong-kong-to-have-babies.html?pagewanted=all&_r=0, accessed 27 June 2014.

43. The World Bank, http://data.worldbank.org/indicator/NY.GDP.PCAP.CD, accessed 27 June 2014.
44. Chinese Government, http://www.china.org.cn/top10/2014-03/13/content_31769827.htm, accessed 27 June 2014.
45. It should be kept in mind that Beijing's strategy to block democratization in Hong Kong does not necessarily reflect its concern about foreign actors. The democratization movement in Hong Kong is largely an internal movement, though it is supported by outside actors such as the US and the EU.
46. Lo, *Competing Chinese Political Visions*, 202.
47. Wong, "Authoritarian Co-optation," 205.
48. Lu, "Is Hong Kong Running Out of Room."
49. *South China Morning Post*, http://www.scmp.com/news/hong-kong/article/1535484/apple-daily-website-taken-offline-cyberattack-ahead-occupy-vote, accessed 21 September 2014.
50. *The Guardian*, http://www.theguardian.com/world/2014/aug/28/anti-corruption-raid-jimmy-lai-home-media-pro-democracy, accessed 21 September 2014.
51. Mak, "Opinion: Hong Kong Press Freedom Under Chinese Attack." *CNN*, 6 July 2012. http://edition.cnn.com/2012/07/05/opinion/hong-kong-press-freedom-eroded/, accessed 24 July 2014.
52. Martin, "Prospects for Democracy in Hong Kong," 1.
53. Consulate General of The United States, http://hongkong.usconsulate.gov/cg_sy2012050301.html, accessed 10 November 2014.
54. For more information, see http://www.ned.org/where-we-work/asia/china-hong-kong, accessed 10 November 2014.
55. National Endowment for Democracy, http://www.ned.org/for-reporters/the-national-endowment-for-democracy-and-support-for-democracy-in-hong-kong, accessed 10 November 2014.
56. *China Daily*, http://www.chinadaily.com.cn/hkedition/2014-10/17/content_18757549.htm, accessed 11 November 2014.
57. Brown, "Assessing Democracy Assistance," 11.
58. Kaldor, *Global Civil Society 2004/5*, 98.
59. Congressional-Executive Commission on China, http://www.cecc.gov/events/roundtables/prospects-for-democracy-and-press-freedom-in-hong-kong, accessed on 25 July 2014.
60. US Department of State, http://www.humanrights.gov/2014/04/04/assistant-secretary-malinowski-meets-with-hong-kong-democracy-leaders/, accessed 27 July 2014.
61. *South China Morning Post*, http://www.scmp.com/news/hong-kong/article/1465400/biden-backs-hong-kong-democracy-activist-meeting?page=all, accessed 25 July 2014.
62. *Reuters*, http://www.reuters.com/article/2014/04/07/us-hongkong-china-idUSBREA3608C20140407, accessed 10 November 2014.
63. Chinese Government, http://www.china.org.cn/chinese/2014-06/19/content_32637202.htm, accessed 16 July 2014.
64. *Wall Street Journal blog*, http://blogs.wsj.com/chinarealtime/2013/09/24/consul-u-s-will-continue-to-speak-out-for-democracy-in-hong-kong/, accessed 25 July 2014.
65. European Commission, *Joint Report to the European Parliament and the Council*.
66. European External Action Service, *Statement by the Spokesperson*, http://eeas.europa.eu/statements-eeas/2014/141209_04_en.htm, accessed 10 December 2014.
67. UK Parliament, http://www.parliament.uk/business/committees/committees-a-z/commons-select/foreign-affairs-committee/news/hong-kong-tor/, accessed 10 November 2014.

68. Brown, "Assessing Democracy Assistance," 11.
69. *Global Times*, http://opinion.huanqiu.com/special/Hong_Kong/, accessed 15 July 2014.
70. *The Guardian*, http://www.theguardian.com/world/2014/jul/15/nick-clegg-hong-kong-china-democracy, accessed 27 July 2014.
71. *South China Morning Post*, http://www.scmp.com/news/hong-kong/article/1591326/washington-pulls-back-beijing-clash-over-hong-kong-political-reform?page=all, accessed 20 September 2014.
72. US Consulate General to Hong Kong and Macau, http://hongkong.usconsulate.gov/pas_pr_2014092901.html, accessed 10 October 2014.
73. *The Guardian*, http://www.theguardian.com/world/2014/oct/02/hong-kong-protests-china-warns-us-not-to-meddle, accessed 12 October 2014.
74. *Süddeutsche Zeitung*, http://www.sueddeutsche.de/news/politik/demonstrationen-neue-proteste-in-hongkong-dpa.urn-newsml-dpa-com-20090101-141010-99-00692, accessed 12 October 2014.
75. *Der Spiegel online*, http://www.spiegel.de/politik/ausland/occupy-proteste-in-hongkong-interview-mit-wortfuehrer-benny-tai-a-996548.html, accessed 12 October 2014.

Notes on contributors

Dingding Chen is Assistant Professor of Government and Public Administration at the University of Macau as well as Non-Resident Fellow at the Global Public Policy Institute (GPPi) in Germany. He was a visiting instructor in the government department at Dartmouth College and was affiliated with the Olin Institute for Strategic Studies at Harvard University. Dingding was also a China and the World Program Fellow at Princeton University. Dingding holds a bachelor's in international economics from the Renmin University of China and a master's and PhD in political science from the University of Chicago.

Katrin Kinzelbach is Associate Director of the Global Public Policy Institute (GPPi) in Berlin and Visiting Professor at the Central European University in Budapest, School of Public Policy. Prior to joining GPPi, Katrin worked at the Ludwig Boltzmann Institute of Human Rights. From 2001–2007, she was a staff member of the United Nations Development Programme (UNDP). Katrin studied at the Universities of Bonn and Florence and at King's College London. Her PhD is from the University of Vienna and won the award "Deutscher Studienpreis" of the Körber Foundation, which honours outstanding research of particular value to society.

References

Bader, Julia, and Antje Kästner. "Externe Autokratieförderung? Das autokratiefördernde Potenzial russischer and chinesischer Außenpolitik." *Politische Vierteljahresschrift der Deutschen Vereinigung für Politische Wissenschaft*, no. 47 (2013): 564–586.
Berger, Bernt. "China's Troubled Myanmar Policy." *The Diplomat*, August 23, 2013. Accessed May 16, 2014. http://thediplomat.com/2013/08/chinas-troubled-myanmar-policy/.
Brown, Kerry. "Assessing Democracy Assistance: China." FRIDE Project Report, May 2010. Accessed May 16, 2014. http://fride.org/download/IP_WMD_China_ENG_jul10.pdf.
ChinaFile. "Document 9: A ChinaFile Translation: How Much Is a Hardline Party Directive Shaping China's Current Political Climate?" August 11, 2013. Accessed May 16, 2014. https://www.chinafile.com/document-9-chinafile-translation.

Cook, Alistair D.B. "Post-Myitsone Relations Between China and Myanmar – More Continuity than Change?" *East Asian Policy* 5, no. 4 (2013): 99–106.

European Commission. "Press Release: EU Re-opens its Market to Myanmar/Burma." doc. no. IP/13/695, Brussels July 18, 2013.

European Commission and High Representative of the European Union for Foreign Affairs and Security Policy. *Joint Report to the European Parliament and the Council. Hong Kong Special Administrative Region: Annual Report 2012*, doc. no. JOIN(2013) 13 final, Brussels, June 17, 2013.

European External Action Service. *Statement by the Spokesperson on the Introduction of Universal Suffrage for the Election of the Chief Executive in Hong Kong in 2017*, doc. no. 140718/01, Brussels, July 18, 2014.

Fan Hongping. "China Adapts to New Myanmar Realities." *ISEAS Perspectives*, no. 12 (2014). Accessed May 16, 2014. http://www.iseas.edu.sg/documents/publication/ISEAS_Perspective_2014_12-China_Adapts_to_New_Myanmar_Realities.pdf.

Godement, François. "Control at the Grassroots: China's New Toolbox." *China Analysis* no. 2 (2012). Accessed May 16, 2014. http://www.ecfr.eu/page/-/China_Analysis_Control_at_the_Grassroots_June2012.pdf.

Jones, Lee. "Explaining Myanmar's Regime Transition: The Periphery is Central." *Democratization* 21, no. 5 (2014): 780–802.

Kaldor, Mary. *Global Civil Society 2004/5*. London: Sage, 2005.

Li, Chenyang. "China-Myanmar Comprehensive Strategic Cooperative Partnership: A Regional Threat?" *Journal of Current Southeast Asian Affairs* 31, no. 1 (2012): 53–72.

Li, Chenyang. *A Report on Myanmar's National Situations, 2011–2012 [Miandian Guoqing Baogao, 2011–2012]*. Social Science Literature Publisher [Shehui Kexue Wenxian Chubanshe]. 2013.

Li, Chenyang. "China-Myanmar Relations since Political Transformation." *International Outlook* 33, no. 2 (2014): 17–33.

Liu, Yu, and Dingding Chen. "Why China Will Democratize." *The Washington Quarterly* 35, no. 1 (2012): 41–63.

Lo, Sonny Shiu-hing. *Competing Chinese Political Visions: Hong Kong versus Beijing on Democracy*. Santa Barbara, CA: Praeger, 2010.

Lu, Rachel. "Is Hong Kong Running Out of Room?" *Foreign Policy*, April 22, 2014. Accessed November 10, 2014. http://foreignpolicy.com/2014/04/22/is-hong-kong-running-out-of-room/.

Martin, Michael F. "Prospects for Democracy in Hong Kong: The 2012 Election Reforms." Congressional Research Service (2011). Accessed May 18, 2014. http://fas.org/sgp/crs/row/R40992.pdf.

Martin, Michael F. "Burma's Political Prisoners and U.S. Sanctions." Congressional Research Service (2013). Accessed April 24, 2014. http://fas.org/sgp/crs/row/R42363.pdf.

Myint-U, Thant. "White Elephants and Black Swans: Thoughts on Myanmar's Recent History and Possible Futures." In *Myanmar's Transition: Openings, Obstacles and Opportunities*, edited by Nick Cheesman, Monique Skidmore, and Trevor Wilson, 23–38. Singapore: ISEAS, 2012.

Nathan, Andrew J. "China at the Tipping Point, Foreseeing the Unforeseeable." *Journal of Democracy* 24, no. 1 (2013): 20–25.

Nathan, Andrew J. "China's Challenge to Democracy." *Journal of Democracy* 26, no.1 (2015): 156–170.

Pei, Minxin. "5 Ways China Could Become a Democracy." *The Diplomat*, February 23, 2013. Accessed November 10, 2014. http://thediplomat.com/2013/02/5-ways-china-could-become-a-democracy/.

Sun, Yun. "China and the Changing Myanmar." *Journal of Current Southeast Asian Affairs* 31, no. 4 (2013): 51–77.

Taylor, Robert H. "Modern China-Myanmar Relations: Dilemmas of Mutual Dependence." *Asian Affairs* 44, no. 1 (2013): 146–147.

UN Human Rights Council. *Second Session*: *Summary Record of the 16th Meeting*, UN doc. no. A/HRC/2/SR.16, Geneva, December 4, 2006.

Walker, Christopher. "Authoritarian Regimes are Changing How the World Defines Democracy," *The Washington Quarterly*, June 13, 2014. Accessed November 10, 2014. http://www.washingtonpost.com/opinions/christopher-walker-authoritarian-regimes-are-changing-how-the-world-defines-democracy/2014/06/12/d1328e3a-f0ee-11e3-bf76-447a5df6411f_story.html.

Wong, Stan Hok-wui. "Authoritarian Co-optation in the Age of Globalization: Evidence from Hong Kong." *Journal of Contemporary Asia* 42, no. 2 (2012): 182–209.

Xie, Yue. "Rising Central Spending on Public Security and the Dilemma Facing Grassroots Officials in China." *Journal of Current Chinese Affairs* 42, no. 2 (2013): 79–109.

Not as bad as it seems: EU and US democracy promotion faces China in Africa

Christine Hackenesch

Department of bi- and multilateral development cooperation, Deutsches Institut für Entwicklungspolitik / German Development Institute, Bonn, Germany

The rise of China in Africa is often described as a major challenge to the United States (US) and the European Union (EU) democracy promotion policies. China is accused of providing important volumes of loans, development aid, trade and investments without "political strings" attached, thereby undermining the US and the EU's possibilities to set material incentives for reforms. This article investigates Ethiopia and Angola as two cases where one would expect that the growing presence of China has made it more difficult for the EU and US to support reforms. Empirical findings presented in this article go against this argument. In both countries, the EU and the US face substantial difficulties to make the respective government address governance issues. However, the presence of China has not made it more difficult for the US and the EU to implement their strategies. Instead the empirical analysis suggests that domestic factors in Ethiopia and Angola, notably the level of challenge to regime survival both governments face, influence both governments' willingness to engage with the EU and US.

Introduction

The European Union (EU) and the United States (US) are among the most important actors that have the explicit objective to promote democratic reforms in Africa and other regions. However, as China has provided substantial volumes of aid, loans, trade and direct investments to African countries,[1] the context in which the EU and US seek to promote democratic reforms has been changing considerably. In the media, among policy-makers, and academia, the presence of China is widely assumed to make it more difficult for the US and EU to support democratic reforms in third countries, particularly in Africa. EU diplomats in Uganda, for

© 2015 The Author(s). Published by Taylor & Francis.
This is an Open Access article distributed under the terms of the Creative Commons Attribution-NonCommercial-NoDerivatives License (http://creativecommons.org/Licenses/by-nc-nd/4.0/), which permits non-commercial re-use, distribution, and reproduction in any medium, provided the original work is properly cited, and is not altered, transformed, or built upon in any way.

instance, openly complain that they are "rapidly losing influence".[2] The former United Kingdom Secretary for International Development, Hilary Benn, argued: "China's failure to match the conditions placed on aid by countries such as Britain – including evidence of good governance, respect for human rights and spending directed to alleviate poverty – could set back progress toward democratic administrations".[3]

The influence of China on EU and US democracy promotion policies has been rarely analysed in a systematic manner. Scholars interested in the implications of the rise of authoritarian powers for autocratic stability and for EU and US democracy promotion strategies have rarely investigated China's presence in Africa.[4] On the other hand, scholars interested in China-Africa relations have mostly focused on describing how China's relations with African countries have evolved during the past decade, who the main actors and what the main policy instruments are, and what factors explain the intensification of bilateral relations.[5]

How does China's presence affect the US and EU's democracy promotion strategies in sub-Saharan Africa? This article deals mainly with the third question outlined in the Introduction to this special issue. Hence, it is interested in whether the EU and US have faced more difficulties in implementing their strategies and in engaging with African governments on political reforms, given that China has become an alternative cooperation partner. Similar to the Introduction in this special issue, the article is not interested in the impact of the US and EU's democracy promotion strategies on the level of democracy or possible countervailing effects by China.

This article selects Ethiopia and Angola as two cases where China is most likely to negatively affect the US and EU's democracy promotion policies. Both are among those few African countries where China has indeed become a cooperation partner as important as the US and EU since the mid-2000s. Moreover, Ethiopia and Angola can both be classified as authoritarian regimes. Engaging with the EU and US on political reforms is therefore assumed to produce substantial costs for both governments. In this regard, one would expect both governments to become *less* willing to engage with the US and EU on political reforms in light of China's presence.

However, the findings from the case studies do not give any indication that China has made it more difficult for the EU and US to implement their democracy promotion strategies. Instead the analysis suggests that domestic factors in Ethiopia and Angola, notably the level of challenge to regime survival, influence both governments' willingness to engage with the US and EU.

The following sections first analyse the US and EU's democracy promotion strategies in Africa in light of China's influence. Afterwards, the analysis focuses on Angola and Ethiopia since the early 2000s. In both countries, China became an important cooperation partner in the mid-2000s, which allows for a "before/after" within-case analysis.[6] Counterfactual arguments and alternative explanations are explored to analyse the relative importance of China.

US and EU democracy promotion encounters China in Africa
The US and EU's democracy promotion strategies in Africa

Since the early 2000s, the EU and US have both invested considerably in developing their positive instruments to support democratic reforms in sub-Saharan Africa. Both mainly seek to promote democratic reforms through (political) *dialogue*, different forms of *democracy aid* and positive *incentives* rather than sanctions and other forms of negative conditionality. Both have established political dialogues with African governments; they have considerably increased their democracy aid volumes,[7] and have developed instruments to set positive incentives to support reforms, for example the Millennium Challenge Corporation in the case of the US or the governance incentive tranche in the case of the EU.[8] For both, the objective of promoting democratic reforms conflicts with other foreign policy, economic, security and development policy interests and objectives,[9] not too differently to their relations with other regions. Moreover, they ultimately prefer stability over democracy in their relations with Africa.[10] The EU and US democracy promotion strategies in Africa thereby confirm what has been argued for their strategies towards other regions: more similarities than differences exist regarding their objectives, strategies and instruments for promoting democratic reforms.[11]

Research on the effectiveness of democratic sanctions, on economic conditionality, democracy aid, political dialogue or the EU's support for political reforms in the neighbourhood, concur that the willingness of the government in the target country to engage with the EU and US is a pre-condition for these instruments to work.[12] This is particularly relevant for EU and US democracy promotion instruments in Africa since the early 2000s. Most of the US and EU's democracy promotion instruments require the active engagement of governments in African countries. Only if African governments accept the inclusion of debates on democratic reforms in political dialogues, directing at least some parts of overall development aid to support political reforms, or debating comprehensive governance action plans with the EU, can these instruments eventually contribute to political reforms. Even the US and EU's support to civil society organizations (CSO), opposition parties or other potential reform entrepreneurs require at least some consent of the respective government. Put differently, only if the EU and US manage to establish an active engagement with African governments on the implementation of their democracy promotion instruments can they eventually have an influence on political reforms.

How could China's engagement in Africa affect the US and EU's democracy promotion strategies?

While the EU and US have made support for democratic reforms a more prominent issue in engaging with African countries, China has rapidly become a more important cooperation partner for African governments. Particularly from 2006 onwards, activities including trade, investments, assistance and diplomatic events have reached previously unknown heights. At the same time, the Chinese government projects its engagement with Africa as an alternative to the US and EU and highlights that it rejects the conditioning of aid, trade and loans to economic or political reforms.[13]

In line with the Introduction to this special issue, this article assumes that China does not intentionally promote autocracy in a similar way to how the US and EU seek to promote democracy. However, under certain conditions China's economic support "with no strings attached" could still have negative effects for the US and EU's democracy promotion. Previous research has shown that China (not too different from the EU and US) mostly engages with the government and rarely with opposition forces.[14] If China provides attractive cooperation packages for African governments, this could change their calculations and their willingness to engage with the EU and US on political reforms.

One would expect that the effect of China's engagement is not the same for all countries. Research on external democracy promotion generally starts by assuming that democracy promotion produces substantial costs for governments in authoritarian regimes. The risk of losing power is identified as a key factor shaping the willingness of the target government to accept engaging on the implementation of democracy promotion instruments.[15] One would therefore expect that the EU and US face considerable difficulties to implement their democracy promotion instruments in authoritarian regimes. At the same time, engaging with the Chinese government which does not condition economic support to democratic reforms should be particularly attractive for governments in these regimes.

In addition to these domestic factors, research on sanctions, on the effectiveness of EU political conditionality towards the neighbourhood, as well as macro-quantitative studies on the influence of aid and democracy aid on political reforms all highlight the importance of a country's economic dependence on the EU or US to explain why authoritarian governments may still be willing to engage with the EU or the US on political reforms, even if this engagement produces costs.[16] Findings from these bodies of research thus give reason to expect that the EU and US would face even *more* difficulties in establishing an active cooperation with governments in African authoritarian regimes, if China offers loans, aid, trade and investments without political conditions attached. The more cooperation with China reduces African countries' economic dependence on the EU and US, the less willing governments in African authoritarian regimes should be to engage with the EU and US on political reforms.

Research on external democracy promotion in authoritarian regimes suggests that the growing presence of China is only one factor that may influence the willingness of African authoritarian governments to engage with the EU and US on political reforms. Focusing on the domestic factors of regime survival, research on authoritarian regimes has identified different ways in which authoritarian regimes' political survival can be challenged and how this affects external democracy promotion. Governments in authoritarian regimes may come under serious threat from mass movements and civil society protests, the military, or factions of the ruling party that may decide to defect.[17] One would expect that the more governments in African authoritarian regimes are under threat from domestic opposition, the less they are willing to engage with the US and EU on the implementation of democracy promotion instruments as this type of engagement may produce imminent threats to regime survival.

EU and US democracy promotion strategies face China in Angola and Ethiopia

Ethiopia and Angola constitute two cases, where one would expect that the EU and US are most likely to face *more* difficulties in establishing an active engagement with both governments in light of the rise of China. First, Angola and Ethiopia can both be classified as authoritarian dominant party systems.[18] Both have adopted formally democratic institutions and introduced multiparty elections. At the same time both allow for similarly low levels of political competition, when measured in terms of macro-level indices such as Freedom House.[19] In both countries, political life is dominated by a ruling party that has strongly entrenched itself in power. In Ethiopia, the EPRDF (Ethiopian Peoples' Revolutionary Democratic Front) has dominated Ethiopian politics, since it overthrew the militarist Marxist Derg regime in the early 1990s.[20] In Angola, since the end of the civil war in 2002, the ruling party MPLA (People's Movement for the Liberation of Angola) has used the reconstruction process to bolster its grip on power.[21] One would expect that in authoritarian regimes such as Angola and Ethiopia, engaging on governance reforms with the EU and US is costly for the government, making it difficult for the EU and US to implement their democracy promotion strategies. At the same time, one would expect that the presence of China, as an alternative cooperation partner who does not ask for democratic reforms, would be particularly attractive for the Ethiopian and Angolan governments and reduce their willingness to engage with the EU and US on political reforms *even further*.

Second, Angola and Ethiopia are among those few African countries where China has indeed become a cooperation partner as important as the EU and US since the mid-2000s.[22] At the same time, Angolan and Ethiopian dependence on the EU and US varies. Ethiopia is strongly aid dependent on the EU and US. During the past decade, aid has represented about 13% of gross national income. The EU and US are among Ethiopia's largest donors. Contrary to this, Angola is clearly not dependent on the EU or the US in terms of aid; aid only accounts for 1% of gross national income. However, the country has substantial oil deposits and the EU and particularly the US have traditionally been the largest market for Angola's oil exports and important sources of official flows. Due to these different levels of dependence, one would expect that Ethiopia is more forthcoming to engage than Angola. Moreover, one would expect that the *relative* decrease in both countries' dependence on the EU and US in light of the rise of China has made it even *more* difficult for the EU and US to implement their strategies since the mid-2000s.

Angola

Almost 30 years of civil war left the country devastated with basic infrastructure destroyed and millions of people displaced. After the end of the civil war in 2002, the Angolan government faced several interlinked challenges. It needed to transform the economy from a war to a peace economy and it had to show that it was not only able to bring peace but also an economic and social "peace dividend".

EU and US democracy promotion in Angola

In this context, the EU and US support for democratic reforms has largely diverged from the preferences of the Angolan government and both faced substantial difficulties in implementing their democracy promotion strategies. This section further elaborates on this claim.

After the end of the civil war in 2002, support for democratic reforms became more important in the US and EU's policies towards Angola. Both launched political dialogue and allocated democracy aid to support political reforms (Table 1). Moreover, the EU and US pressured the Angolan government to improve the transparency of oil revenues and to hold parliamentary and presidential elections soon after the end of the war. The EU and US conditioned the organization of an international donor conference to the holding of elections and improvements in the transparency of government revenues.[23]

Between 2000 and 2004, the Angolan government very reluctantly started to engage with the EU and US in the implementation of democracy aid and political dialogue. The government agreed to launch Article 8 political dialogue with the EU in 2003 and accepted to implement some of the US and EU's democracy aid.[24] However, at the same time, it refused to comply with the EU and US demands to introduce political reforms. The date for the elections was postponed several

Table 1. EU and US foreign aid and democracy assistance to Angola.

	Total aid (million US$)	Democracy aid total (million US$)	Democracy aid/total aid (%)	Support for democratic government/ democracy aid (%)	Support for effective government/ democracy aid (%)	Share democracy aid targeted to CSO
2000–2004						
US	497	17	4	59	41	–
EU	355	14	4	21	79	–
2005–2012						
US	515	48	9	30	70	56%
EU	286	49	17	20	80	12%

Source: OECD Development Assistance Committee (DAC), Creditor Reporting System; own calculation.[71]

times before they were finally held in 2008. Moreover, the government made limited attempts to improve the transparency of public finances.

Since 2005, both the EU and US have become more reluctant to use aid funds to exert pressure on the Angolan government. Instead, both relied mainly on political dialogue and democracy aid to support political reforms. The EU geared its efforts mainly towards promoting the effectiveness of government institutions rather than the democratic quality of decision-making processes. The US has put slightly more emphasis on also supporting the democratic quality of decision-making processes, with more support for elections and the media than the EU (Table 1).[25]

Moreover, the EU provided only a little assistance to civil society organizations, but instead engaged mainly with the Angolan government. Only 12% of the EU's democracy promotion aid was allocated to support CSO (Table 1). The EU has mostly funded capacity-building activities such as seminars and training, but has been reluctant to support non-government organizations (NGOs) that monitor Angola's human rights record.[26] The US has been slightly more active than the EU in working with civil society organizations and empowering civil society organizations to hold the government accountable. More than half of US democracy aid was directed to support CSO (Table 1).

Since 2005, the EU and US have both faced even more difficulties in implementing their democracy promotion instruments than in the early 2000s. The government has become even less willing to engage in political dialogue with the EU; since 2008, no dialogue has taken place.[27] It was also reluctant to engage in political dialogue with the US.[28] It has largely refused to engage in the implementation of the US and EU's democracy aid and has ignored positive incentives such as the EU's governance incentive tranche.[29] In sum, since the mid-2000s, the Angolan government has largely ignored the US and the EU's attempts to foster cooperation on political reforms.

China: alternative economic cooperation partner

According to the Angolan President dos Santos: "China needs natural resources and Angola wants development".[30] This short statement nicely captures Angola and China's interests in the bilateral relationship. Both sides are primarily interested in economic cooperation.

China strengthened its engagement with Angola in 2004, when the EU and US sought to pressure the Angolan government to hold elections and improve the transparency of oil revenues. In 2004, the China Export-Import (EXIM) Bank negotiated a US$2 billion loan contract with the Angolan government. As Soares de Oliveira[31] puts it: "one [cannot] underestimate the extent to which the Chinese credit mattered in 2004, or the symbolic role of the Chinese arrival in the broader transformation of Angolan external relations". The size of the loan outweighed support that Angola had expected from the EU and US. The loan had a catalytic effect, because it gave the government access to international commercial loans again.[32] The timing and the Chinese offer to extend not only a credit line but to also *deliver* much needed infrastructure projects closely matched the need of the Angolan government to launch infrastructure rehabilitation before the 2008 parliamentary elections.[33]

Since this first EXIM Bank loan, China has quickly emerged as a major economic cooperation partner for the Angolan government. In 2007, China overtook the US as the largest destination for Angolan oil exports. By 2012, the EXIM Bank and other Chinese Banks had extended credit lines totalling US$14.5 billion, making China the largest source of official flows (much larger than the EU or US).[34]

The presence of China: What effects for the US and EU's policies?

The previous section has shown that in the case of Angola, the EU and US both faced considerable difficulties in implementing their democracy promotion strategies. For both, it has become even more difficult to make the Angolan government address governance issues since the mid-2000s, in parallel to China's growing engagement. At first sight, the Angolan case thus seems to confirm the expectation that China's presence makes it more difficult for the EU and US to establish engagement with African governments on political reforms. However, when exploring alternative explanations and counterfactual arguments, it becomes clear that China's presence has had limited effects on the Angolan government's willingness to engage with the EU and US on governance reforms.

There is little evidence supporting claims that Angola might have been more cooperative should China not have emerged as an alternative partner. In parallel to China's growing presence, since the mid-2000s domestic opposition against the Angolan government has been mounting, making it more costly for the government to engage with the EU and US on political reforms. In the first few years after the end of the civil war, the Angolan government faced very few domestic challenges to regime survival. Societal opposition was weak as "Angolans were exhausted after four decades of conflict and keen on predictability in their lives".[35] Moreover, the opposition party UNITA (the National Union for the total Independence of Angola) was clearly not in a position to politically challenge the MPLA as it was disorganized internally after the death of UNITA leader Savimbi.[36] In light of a very low level of domestic opposition, engaging with the EU and US on political reforms did not produce a direct threat to regime survival for the Angolan government.

However, since the mid-2000s, opposition from outside and within the ruling elite has gradually become more pressing. Compared to the early 2000s, the Angolan government has hardly engaged with the EU and US on political reforms, since that would have incurred higher political costs. Dissatisfaction fermented within the MPLA itself. Several high level figures in the MPLA defected and joined the opposition.[37] At the same time, societal opposition has become much more important, as indicated most clearly in anti-government demonstrations in Luanda in 2011 and 2012. Even though demonstrations remained largely peaceful and did not escalate into a full-scale mass movement, they clearly showed the mounting dissatisfaction with the social and economic performance of the regime.[38] In this context, engaging with the EU or US on reforms to strengthen freedom of the media, political spaces for civil society organization or elections would have been more costly for the Angolan government compared to the early 2000s.

At the same time, the US and particularly the EU have few incentives to offer that could potentially outweigh the costs of engaging on political reforms. The EU and US offered Angola a strategic partnership in 2010. These strategic partnerships are intended to foster closer cooperation beyond a traditional "donor-recipient" relationship. The EU and US both seek to signal to the Angolan government that they consider Angola to be among their three most important partners in Africa – together with South Africa and Nigeria. Yet, the Angolan government's interest in a strategic partnership has been limited.[39]

In summary, in light of the substantial costs that cooperation with the EU and US would have produced and the limited economic incentives for Angola to engage, it seems unlikely that in the absence of China the government would have been more interested engaging with the EU or US.

How have the EU and US reacted to the rise of China in Angola? The rise of China as an alternative cooperation partner for Angola was very visible for the EU and US. The EXIM Bank loan in 2004, in the midst of negotiations between the Angolan government and Western donors, was widely reported in (international) media and the subject of controversy among donors.[40] Interviews with Western government officials and leaked diplomatic cables suggest that the relationship between China and Angola has been closely observed by European and US officials since then. Moreover, the US also made attempts to reach out to China and to establish joint cooperation projects (for instance in agriculture and health), albeit with limited success.[41] Nevertheless, beyond a general interest in China-Angola relations, little indication could be found that the EU or US has adapted its democracy promotion strategies in light of China's presence.

Ethiopia

After the end of the war with Eritrea in 2000, in light of Ethiopia's strategic importance in the war on terror since 2001, and due to the Ethiopian government's willingness to align with the priorities of the Millennium Development Goals, the EU and US quickly scaled up their aid to Ethiopia in the early 2000s.[42]

EU and US democracy promotion in Ethiopia

In Ethiopia, too, the EU and US support for democratic reforms has partly diverged from the preferences of the government. Both faced substantial difficulties to implement their democracy promotion strategies. Nevertheless, as the analysis shows, both were more successful than in Angola.

The EU and US both strengthened their engagement with Ethiopia in the early 2000s (Table 2). Support for democratic reforms became an important issue for the EU as well as the US. Both have launched political dialogue with the Ethiopian government that should also address issues related to political reforms. In the early 2000s both were reluctant to exert pressure on the Ethiopian government to strengthen political reforms.[43]

The Ethiopian government, in turn, reluctantly started to engage with the EU and US on political reforms. It was more forthcoming to engage than the Angolan government. Ethiopia agreed to establish regular political dialogue with the EU and US. It accepted to implement some democracy aid. Ahead of the 2005 elections it agreed to establish aid policy dialogues that would address political reforms; it moved ahead with the establishment of the Human Rights Commission and finally agreed to launch the EU's Civil Society Fund (CSF).[44]

However, during the 2005 election period, relations between the Ethiopian government, the EU and the US altered fundamentally. The EPRDF won the elections, but opposition parties gained about 30%. Shortly after the elections, protests broke out and were violently repressed. More than 200 people died.[45] In response to the crisis, the US and EU pressured the Ethiopian government to reconcile with the opposition and to release political prisoners.[46] In December 2005, the EU and other budget support donors decided to withhold direct budgetary aid.[47] The US had not provided budget support and did not make substantial modifications in its aid strategy.[48] Despite considerable pressure by the EU and other donors, the Ethiopian government showed little willingness to reconcile with the opposition and to comply with EU and US demands to modify its approach to the crisis.[49]

After the election crisis, the EU and US both made support for political reforms a more prominent issue in their relations with Ethiopia (Table 2). For instance, the EU contributed to the Democratic Institutions Programme (DIP) that is jointly

Table 2. EU and US foreign aid and democracy assistance to Ethiopia.

	Total aid (million US$)	Democracy total (million US$)	Democracy aid/total aid (%)	Support for democratic government/ democracy aid (%)	Support for effective government/ democracy aid (%)	Share democracy aid targeted to CSO
2000–2004						
US	1.501	15	1	28	72	–
EU	777	26	4	35	65	–
2005–2012						
US	5.864	47	1	48	52	41%
EU	1.877	73	4	49	51	15%

Source: OECD DAC, Creditor Reporting System; own calculation.[72]

managed by the United Nations Development Programme (UNDP) and the Ethiopian government. EU aid has also supported institutions in the justice sector.[50] The EU has continued to address problems in the human rights situation and democratic reforms in the context of its political dialogue with the Ethiopian government.[51] The US also broadened its strategy after the 2005 election crisis, using its political dialogue with the Ethiopian government to raise issues related to democratic reforms.[52] Similar to the EU, the US Agency for International Development (USAID) provided some support to the DIP. Moreover, USAID allotted some assistance to the media and justice sector.[53]

Since the 2005 election crisis, the EU and US both have faced more difficulties in implementing their democracy promotion strategy compared to the early 2000s. At the same time, both have been more successful than in Angola as will be shown in the following. The Ethiopian government has been relatively reluctant to engage in political dialogue with the EU and US.[54] Political dialogue has taken place relatively regularly (and more often than in Angola).[55] The EU and US both have faced considerable difficulties in engaging with the Ethiopian government in the implementation of democracy aid projects (but were more successful than in Angola). The US, for instance, had to abandon its support to civil society actors when a new civil society law entered into force in 2009.[56] The EU faced considerable difficulties during the 2010 parliamentary elections when the government did not allow the EU to present the final results from the election observation mission in Addis Ababa – something that has never happened before in the history of EU election observer missions.[57] However, in contrast to Angola, in the case of Ethiopia the EU and US could support democratic institutions such as the Human Rights Commission or the Parliament through the DIP.

China: alternative economic cooperation partner

Similar to Angola, in the case of Ethiopia, China has also become an economic cooperation partner as important as the EU and US since the mid-2000s. China's engagement has considerably reduced the Ethiopian government's vulnerability to pressure from the EU and US to engage in governance reforms.

Similar to Angola, in the case of Ethiopia the Chinese EXIM Bank has extended a first sizable loan during a period when the US and the EU tried to use their aid funds to pressure for political reforms. The Chinese government offered Ethiopia a US$500 million loan for various infrastructure programmes in early 2006,[58] a few weeks after the EU and other donors had decided to freeze budget support and before the Ethiopian government agreed with donors that budget aid should be rechanneled to other programmes. The volume of the loan equalled the volume of funds that the government would have been losing if the EU and other donors were to decide to cut their aid.[59]

Since 2006, China has successively become a more important economic cooperation partner. China has considerably increased its loans and grants; the Chinese EXIM bank supports large infrastructure projects in hydro power, transport or railways.[60] For the period 2006–2012, the total volume of Chinese loans and grants to Ethiopia has been estimated to amount to US$7 billion,[61] which would be similar to what the EU and US have provided as grants (Table 2). In 2008, China became Ethiopia's second largest export destination, after the EU and ahead of the US. Trade with China contributed to the diversification of Ethiopia's trade and thereby generated important windfall profits for the government.[62] As Ethiopia has no exploitable natural resources, China's growing economic engagement with Ethiopia seems surprising at first sight. However, Ethiopia's position within the Horn of Africa, the size of its (potential) market and its influence in African regional debates make the country an attractive partner for the Chinese government.[63]

The presence of China: What effects for the US and EU's policies?

As argued in the previous section, the EU and US faced considerable difficulties in implementing their democracy promotion strategies in Ethiopia, but they were more successful than in Angola. For both, it has become more difficult to engage with the Ethiopian government on political reforms since 2005, in parallel to China's growing presence. However, even though China started to strengthen its economic cooperation with Ethiopia at a point in time when the EU (and to a lesser extent the US) used aid funds to pressure the government to cease coercive measures, and even though China has since emerged as an economic cooperation partner as important as the EU and US, counterfactual arguments and alternative explanations suggest that China's presence has had limited influence on the Ethiopian government's willingness to engage with the EU and US in democratic reforms.

Whereas the Ethiopian government faced relatively little domestic opposition ahead of the 2005 election, the 2005 election crisis produced a fundamental threat to regime survival for the government.[64] The strong gains for the opposition took the ruling party by surprise. It showed that the EPRDF had considerably underestimated the perception within the population that economic achievements were poor, particularly in rural areas.[65] In response to the 2005 election crisis, the Ethiopian government gradually closed political spaces for the media, civil society and opposition parties.[66] In contrast to the early 2000s, in this context engaging on the implementation of the EU and US democracy promotion instruments could have directly threatened the survival of the regime.

Against this background it seems surprising that the Ethiopian government has continued to at least very reluctantly cooperate on governance reforms with the EU and US. Instead, one would have expected that Ethiopia completely refuses to engage if China becomes a cooperation partner as important as the EU and US. However, due to fundamental challenges to regime survival during the election crisis in 2005, output legitimacy through economic growth and provision of social services also became more important for the Ethiopian government to strengthening its grip on power.[67] As the EU and US continue to remain important donors to the Ethiopian government, engaging on political reforms thus still yields some benefits for the government. In sum, it seems unlikely that in the *absence* of China, the Ethiopian government would have been any more forthcoming to engage with the EU or the US on political reforms since 2005.

How have the EU and US responded to China's engagement with Ethiopia? In contrast to Angola, China's growing engagement with Ethiopia happened largely unnoticed by the EU and US. When China provided a loan to the Ethiopian government in 2006 at the height of tensions between the government and its traditional donors, this was hardly reported in the media. The presence of China became more visible for the EU and US only after 2009, when China started to provide loans for large scale infrastructure projects. Moreover, it is only since 2010 that the Ethiopian government has used the presence of China more explicitly as a bargaining chip in its negotiations with the EU and US.[68] On the other hand, the US and EU's reaction towards the growing presence of China have been minimal. Little indication can be found that the US or EU have adapted and modified their democracy promotion strategies or their overall strategy to engage with Ethiopia in response to the growing presence of China.[69] Two factors could explain why the US and the EU's response towards China's rise been even more limited in Ethiopia compared to Angola. In contrast to Angola, little economic competition exists between the EU, the US and China in Ethiopia. Moreover, the EU and US have questioned the developmental effects of China's support for infrastructure development in Ethiopia to a far lesser extent than in Angola.

Conclusion

The cases of Angola and Ethiopia show the limitations of the "China threat" argument. In contrast to widely held assumptions in academic and policy debates, the analysis in this article suggests that during the past decade the presence of China has had limited influence on the implementation of the US and the EU's democracy promotion strategies in Ethiopia and Angola. The article has selected Ethiopia and Angola as two most likely cases; if China has no influence there it is not likely that China has had an influence in the cases of other African countries.

The US and the EU faced considerable difficulties in engaging with the Angolan and Ethiopian government on political reforms; in both countries it has become even more difficult for the EU and US to implement their democracy promotion instruments since the mid-2000s. For Angola and Ethiopia, China has emerged as a cooperation partner as important as the EU and US and its importance increased at a point in time when the EU and US sought to exert pressure on the governments to induce political reforms. Yet, this article has argued that the presence of China has limited explanatory power to account for the US and EU's difficulties in implementing their strategies.

Instead, findings from this study resonate with an emerging debate that highlights the importance of domestic factors to explain differential effects of external democracy promotion in authoritarian regimes. This article has shown that the challenges to the survival of authoritarian regimes at a certain point in time considerably affect their willingness to engaging with the EU and US on political reforms. Whereas previous research has focused on the level of political liberalization or the type of authoritarian regime,[70] empirical findings in this article point to an additional variable that would need to be further explored in future research: the level of challenge to regime survival that governments in authoritarian regimes face.

Notes

1. African Development Bank et al., *African Economic Outlook.*
2. Süddeutsche Zeitung, "Wettlauf gegen die Zeit und gegen andere", 6.
3. The Guardian, "Chinese Aid to Africa May Do More Harm than Good."
4. Bader et al., "Autocracies Promote Autocracy?"; Chen and Kinzelbach, "Democracy Promotion and China."
5. Brautigam, *Dragon's Gift*; Alden, *China in Africa.*
6. The empirical analysis draws on research from area studies and an extensive review of EU and US policy documents. This information is triangulated with about 60 interviews conducted between 2009 and 2013 with representatives of the EU and member states, Ethiopian, Angolan and Chinese government officials and civil society actors.
7. Between 1995 and 2009 the volume of EU democracy aid increased from US$50 million to US$520 million and the volume of US democracy aid from US$60 million to about US$450 million, http://stats.oecd.org (accessed 5 July 2014).
8. Molenaers and Nijs, "From the Theory of Aid Effectiveness."
9. Wetzel and Orbie, "Promoting Embedded Democracy"; Crawford, "EU and Democracy Promotion Africa"; Del Biondo, "Democracy Promotion Meets Development Cooperation."
10. Olsen, "Europe and the Promotion of Democracy"; Brown, "Foreign Aid and Democracy Promotion."
11. Risse and Babayan, "Democracy Promotion and the Challenges"; Magen and Morlino; "Methods of Influence."
12. Portela, *European Union Sanctions*; Killick, "Principals, Agents and the Limitations of BWI Conditionality"; Wright, "How Foreign Aid can Foster Democratization"; Checkel, *Compliance and Conditionality*; Schimmelfennig and Sedelmeier, *The Europeanization of Central and Eastern Europe*; van Hüllen, "Europeanization through Cooperation?"
13. Brautigam, *Dragon's Gift*; Alden, *China in Africa*; Information Office of the State Council, "China's Foreign Aid."
14. Bader et al., "Autocracies Promote Autocracy?"
15. Wright, "How Foreign Aid can Foster Democratization"; Cornell, "Regime Type."
16. Portela, *European Union Sanctions*; Schimmelfennig and Sedelmeier, *The Europeanization of Central and Eastern Europe*; Vachudova, *Europe Undivided*; Börzel and Risse, "When Europeanization Meets Diffusion"; Wright, "How Foreign Aid can Foster Democratization"; Dietrich and Wright, *Foreign Aid and Democratic Development.*
17. Bratton and van de Walle, *Democratic Experiments*; Geddes, "Authoritarian Breakdown."
18. Hadenius and Teorell, "Pathways."
19. Angola has been classified as "not free" on the Freedom House index for the last 10 years. Ethiopia has been classified as "partly free" during most of the last decade but was labelled "not free" in 2012. This small difference between the two countries results from Ethiopia's better scores on political rights. The data was obtained from

DEMOCRACY PROMOTION AND THE CHALLENGES

http://www.freedomhouse.org/report-types/freedom-world#.U9UFPbGmrDd (accessed 5 May 2014).
20. Abbink, "Discomfiture of Democracy?"
21. Soares de Oliveira, "Illiberal Peacebuilding."
22. Grimm and Hackenesch, "European Engagement with Emerging Actors."
23. Soares de Oliveira, "Illiberal Peacebuilding"; Interviews with EU officials, Brussels, April 2010; Luanda, October 2009.
24. Ibid.; Angola and European Community, Country Strategy Paper; USAID, Angola's Democratic Transition Program.
25. USAID annual report 2009, 2010; Wikileaks 14/01/2009, "Advancing Political Competition and Consensus Building in Angola."
26. Foley et al., *Capitalisation Study of the EIDHR Programme Angola.*
27. Angola and European Community, *Country Strategy Paper*; Interviews with EU officials, Brussels, October 2012; Luanda, October 2009.
28. Wikileaks 11/02/2008, "Angola Optimistic that its Elections won't Mirror Kenya's"; Interviews with donor officials in Luanda in October 2009.
29. Interviews with EU officials, Brussels, April 2010; Luanda, October 2009; see also EU-Angola Joint Annual Reviews of EDF assistance, various years; US State Department, Freedom and Democracy Reports; US State Department, Freedom and Democracy Reports.
30. Campos and Vines, "Angola and China", 18.
31. Soares de Oliveira, "Illiberal Peacebuilding", 301.
32. Corkin, *Uncovering African Agency.*
33. Ibid., 154.
34. Ibid.; Campos and Vines, "Angola and China."
35. Soares de Oliveira, "Illiberal Peacebuilding", 293.
36. Ibid.
37. Croese, "Angola."
38. Ibid.
39. The EU labels this partnership Joint Way Forward (JWF). Interviews with EU officials, Brussels, April 2010 and October 2012; USAID, *Country Development Cooperation Strategy.*
40. The New York Times, *China's African Adventure*, 19 November, 2006, http://www.nytimes.com/2006/11/19/magazine/19china.html?pagewanted=all&_r=1&
41. Wikileaks 15/05/2009, "China's Africa aid aims to achieve political goals"; Interviews with EU officials, Brussels, April 2010; Luanda, October 2009.
42. Borchgrevink, "Limits to Donor Influence."
43. DAG, Annual Report 2004; Ethiopia and European Community, *Country Strategy Paper.*
44. Ibid.; Interviews with donor officials and Ethiopian government officials, Addis Ababa, October 2009, November 2010.
45. Abbink, "Discomfiture of Democracy?"
46. Council of the EU, "Statement on Ethiopia."
47. Interviews with EU officials, Brussels, October 2012; Addis Ababa, October 2009; Ethiopia and European Community, *Country Strategy Paper.*
48. A proposed bill to sanction Ethiopia for human rights violations was sidelined in Congress because of US security interests; Borchgrevink, "Limits to Donor Influence."
49. Abbink, "Discomfiture of Democracy?"
50. European Commission, *Commission Decision.*
51. Ethiopia and European Community, *Country Strategy Paper.*
52. Wikileaks 31/01/2010 "Undersecretary Otero meeting with Prime Minister Meles"; Wikileaks 08/06/2009 "Understanding Ethiopia's hardliner;" Interviews with US officials, Addis Ababa, October 2010.

53. USAID, *Ethiopia US Foreign Assistance*; US State Department, *Advancing Freedom and Democracy Reports, Ethiopia*.
54. Interviews with EU and US officials, Addis Ababa, October 2009, October 2010, June 2013.
55. Ibid.
56. The civil society law does not allow Ethiopian NGOs engaged in human rights, elections or other aspects related to democratic reforms to receive international funding and thus restricts possibilities for donors to support Ethiopian NGOs. Interviews with donor officials, Addis Ababa, October 2010.
57. European Union, Declaration by the High Representative Catherine Ashton on the publication of the Final Report of the EU Election Observation Mission to Ethiopia, 8 November 2010, http://europa.eu/rapid/press-release_PESC-10-295_en.htm (accessed 5 July 2014).
58. BBC. Ethiopian finance minister holds talks in China on economic cooperation. *BBC Asia Pacific*, 11 January 2006; Interviews with Ethiopian government officials and civil society actors, Addis Ababa, October 2009.
59. Furtado and Smith, "Ethiopia."
60. Interviews with Ethiopian officials, Addis Ababa, October 2009, October 2010.
61. Hackenesch, "Aid Donor."
62. Interviews with Chinese and Ethiopian government officials and businessmen, Addis Ababa, October 2010; Beijing, June 2010.
63. Ibid.
64. Abbink, "Discomfiture of Democracy?"
65. Ibid.
66. Vaughan, "Revolutionary."
67. This is exemplified by substantial increases in government spending on social services since 2005 (see World Development Indicators) and heated debates among donors and the government on whether Ethiopia's growth figures reflect the reality.
68. Interviews with EU and Ethiopian officials, Addis Ababa, October 2009, 2010.
69. Ibid.
70. Cornell, "Regime Type"; Vachudova, *Europe Undivided*; van Hüllen, "Europeanization through Cooperation?"
71. Data is based on aid activity data from the OECD Development Assistance Committee Credit Reporting System. "Democracy assistance" refers to data reported as "Government and Civil Society"; Support for "democratic government" refers to data reported as Legal and judicial development, democratic participation and civil society, elections, legislature and political parties, media and free flow of information, human rights, women's equality organizations and institutions as a share of total "governance aid"; Support for "effective government" refers to data reported as public sector and administrative management, public finance management, decentralization and anti-corruption as a share of total "governance aid". No data on civil society is available for the early 2000s, since DAC donors have only reported their aid to civil society since the mid-2000s, http://stats.oecd.org (accessed 5 July 2014).
72. Ibid.

Acknowledgements

I thank the participants of an author's workshop for helpful comments on an earlier draft. A special thanks goes to the two anonymous reviewers, Thomas Risse, Nelli Babayan, Kai Striebinger and Svea Koch for constructive criticism.

Notes on contributor

Christine Hackenesch is a researcher at the German Development Institute/Deutsches Institut für Entwicklungspolitik (DIE). Her research areas are China's engagement in Africa, EU–Africa relations, EU external relations with a specific focus on development policy and EU democracy promotion. She holds a Ph.D. in political sciences from the Free University of Berlin, a diploma in political sciences from same university and a master in comparative politics from Sciences Po in Paris.

References

Abbink, Jon. "Discomfiture of Democracy? The 2005 Election Crisis in Ethiopia and its Aftermath." *African Affairs* 105, no. 419 (2006): 173–199.
African Development Bank, Development Centre of the OECD, United Nations Development Programme and United Nations Economic Commission for Africa. *African Economic Outlook. Special Theme: Africa and its Emerging Partners*. Paris, 2011.
Alden, Chris. *China in Africa*. London: Zed Books, 2007.
Angola and European Community. *Country Strategy Paper and National Indicative Programme for the period 2008–2013*. Luanda: Angola and European Community, 2008.
Bader, Julia, Jörn Grävingholt, and Antje Kästner. "Would Autocracies Promote Autocracy? A Political Economy Perspective on Regime-Type Export in Regional Neighbourhoods." *Contemporary Politics* 16, no. 1 (2010): 81–100.
Borchgrevink, Axel. "Limits to Donor Influence: Ethiopia, Aid and Conditionality." *Forum for Development Studies* 35, no. 2 (2008): 195–220.
Börzel, Tanja A., and Thomas Risse. "When Europeanization Meets Diffusion. Exploring New Territory." *West European Politics* 35, no. 1 (2012): 192–207.
Bratton, Michael, and Nicholas van de Walle. *Democratic Experiments in Africa: Regime Transitions in Comparative Perspective*. New York: Cambridge University Press, 1997.
Brautigam, Deborah. *The Dragon's gift. The Real Story of China in Africa*. Oxford: Oxford University Press, 2009.
Brown, Stephen. "Foreign Aid and Democracy Promotion: Lessons from Africa." *The European Journal of Development Research* 17, no. 2 (2005): 179–198.
Campos, Indira, and Alex Vines. "Angola and China. A Pragmatic Partnership." Working Paper Presented at a CSIS Conference, "Prospects for Improving US-China-Africa Cooperation", London, December 2007.
Checkel, Jeffrey. *Compliance and Conditionality*. Oslo: ARENA Working Papers, 2000.
Chen, Dingding, and Katrin Kinzelbach. "Democracy Promotion and China: Blocker or Bystander?" *Democratization* 22, no. 3 (2015): 400–418.
Corkin, Lucy. *Uncovering African Agency: Angola's Management of China's Credit Lines*. Surrey: Ashgate, 2013.
Cornell, Agnes. "Does Regime Type Matter for the Impact of Democracy Aid on Democracy?." *Democratization* 20, no. 4 (2013): 642–667.
Council of the EU. "Joint Statement of the European Union and the United States on Ethiopia of July 13, 2005." Brussels, 2005.
Crawford, Gordon. "The EU and Democracy Promotion in Africa: High on Rhetoric, Low on Delivery?." In *EU Development Policy in a Changing World. Challenges for the 21st Century*, edited by Andrew Mold, 169–197. Amsterdam: Amsterdam University Press, 2007.
Croese, Sylvia. *Angola: Chronicle of an Unfulfilled Promise: A Hundred Days after the Elections*. Berlin: Friedrich Ebert Stiftung, 2013.
DAG. *Annual Report 2004*, Addis Ababa: Development Assistance Group Ethiopia, 2005. www.dagethiopia.org/index.php?option=com_docman&task=doc_download&gid=80&Itemid=120

Del Biondo, Karen. "Democracy Promotion Meets Development Cooperation: The EU as a Promoter of Democratic Governance in Sub-Saharan Africa." *European Foreign Affairs Review* 16, no. 5 (2011): 659–672.

Dietrich, Simone, and Joseph Wright. *Foreign aid and democratic development in Africa*. Helsinki: UNU World Institute for Development Economics Research, 2012.

Ethiopia and European Community. *Country Strategy Paper and National Indicative Programme for the period 2008–2013*. Lisbon: Ethiopia and European Community, 2008.

European Commission. *Commission Decision of 21 December 2009 on the Annual Action Programme 2009 in favour of Ethiopia to be financed from the 10th European Development Fund*. Brussels: European Commission, 2009.

Foley, Conor, Bert Fret, and Clément Lorvao. *Capitalisation Study of the EIDHR Programme in Angola*. Brussels: European Commission, 2010.

Furtado, Xavier, and Jim Smith. "Ethiopia: Retaining sovereignty in aid relations." In *The Politics of Aid. African Strategies for Dealing with Donors*, edited by Lindsay Whitfield, 74–107. Oxford: Oxford University Press, 2009.

Geddes, Barbara. "Authoritarian Breakdown", Unpublished manuscript, Department of Political Science, UCLA, 2004.

Grimm, Sven, and Christine Hackenesch. "European Engagement with Emerging Actors in Development: Forging new Partnerships?" In *The European Union and Global Development. An enlightened superpower in the making?*, edited by Stefan Gänzle, Sven Grimm, and Davina Makhan, 211–228. Houndmills: Palgrave McMillan, 2012.

Hackenesch, Christine. "Aid Donor Meets Strategic Partner? The European Union's and China's Relations with Ethiopia." *Journal of Current Chinese Affairs* 42, no. 1 (2013): 7–36.

Hadenius, Axel, and Jan Teorell. "Pathways from Authoritarianism." *Journal of Democracy* 18 (2007): 143–157.

Information Office of the State Council. "China's Foreign Aid (2014)," 2014. http://www.china.org.cn/government/whitepaper/node_7209074.htm

Killick, Tony. "Principals, Agents and the Limitations of BWI Conditionality." *The World Economy* 19, no. 2 (1996): 211–229.

Magen, Amichai, and Leonardo Morlino. "Methods of Influence, Layers of Impact, Cycles of Change. A Framework for Analysis." In *International Actors, Democratization and the Rule of Law. Anchoring Democracy?*, edited by Leonardo Morlino and Amichai Magen, 26–52. London: Routledge, 2009.

Molenaers, Nadia, and Leen Nijs. "From the Theory of Aid Effectiveness to the Practice: The European Commission's Governance Incentive Tranche." *Development Policy Review* 27, no. 5 (2009): 561–580.

Olsen, Grye R. "Europe and the Promotion of Democracy in Post Cold War Africa: How Serious is Europe and For What Reason?." *African Affairs* 97, no. 388 (1998): 343–367.

Portela, Clara. *European Union Sanctions and Foreign Policy: When and Why Do They Work?*. Abingdon: Routledge, 2010.

Risse, Thomas, and Nelli Babayan. "Democracy Promotion and the Challenges of Non-Democratic Regional Powers: Introduction to the Special Issue." *Democratization* 22, no. 3 (2015): 381–399.

Schimmelfennig, Frank, and Ulrich Sedelmeier, eds. *The Europeanization of Central and Eastern Europe*. Ithaka: Cornell University Press, 2005.

Soares de Oliveira, Ricardo. "Illiberal Peacebuilding in Angola." *The Journal of Modern African Studies* 49, no. 2 (2011): 287–314.

Süddeutsche Zeitung. "Wettlauf gegen die Zeit und gegen andere," 3 June, 2013: 6.

The Guardian. "Chinese aid to Africa may do more harm than good," 8 February, 2007.

U.S. State Department. *Advancing Freedom and Democracy Reports, Angola*. Washington, DC: U.S. State Department, 2010.

U.S. State Department. *Advancing Freedom and Democracy Reports, Angola*. Washington, DC: U.S. State Department, 2009.

U.S. State Department. *Advancing Freedom and Democracy Reports, Ethiopia*. Washington, DC: U.S. State Department, 2010.

USAID. *Country Development Cooperation Strategy*. Washington, DC: U.S. Agency for International Development, 2014.

USAID. *Ethiopia U.S. Foreign Assistance Performance Publication Fiscal Year 2009*. Washington, DC: U.S. Agency for International Development, 2009.

USAID. *Support to Angola's Democratic Transition Program. Final Evaluation Report*. Washington, DC: U.S. Agency for International Development, 2005.

Vachudova, Milada A. *Europe Undivided: Democracy, Leverage and Integration After Communism*. Oxford: Oxford University Press, 2005.

van Hüllen, Vera. "Europeanization through Cooperation? EU Democracy Promotion in Morocco and Tunisia." *West European Politics* 35, no. 1 (2012): 117–134.

Vaughan, Sarah. "Revolutionary Democratic State-Building: Party, State and People in the EPRDF's Ethiopia." *Journal of Eastern African Studies* 5, no. 4 (2011): 619–640.

Wetzel, Anna, and Jan Orbie. "Promoting Embedded Democracy? Researching the Substance of EU Democracy Promotion." *European Foreign Affairs Review* 16, no. 5 (2011): 565–588.

Wright, Joseph. "How Foreign Aid can Foster Democratization in Authoritarian Regimes." *American Journal of Political Science* 53, no. 3 (2009): 552–571.

The return of the empire? Russia's counteraction to transatlantic democracy promotion in its near abroad

Nelli Babayan

Otto-Suhr Institute of Political Science, Department of Political and Social Sciences, Freie Universität Berlin, Berlin, Germany

> Russia's recent actions in its neighbourhood have not only upset Western policies but have also reinvigorated arguments that Russia may be promoting autocracy to counteract democracy promotion by the European Union and the United States. They have also underlined a broader problem: that of how illiberal powers may react to democracy promotion, especially when their strategic interests are at stake. This article investigates these issues by studying Russia's interactions with the countries in its neighbourhood and democracy promoters. First, the article argues that even if Russia has contributed to the stagnation of democratization and ineffectiveness of democracy promotion in its neighbourhood, its actions do not constitute autocracy promotion and largely lack ideological underpinnings. Second, Russia's counteraction to democracy promotion stems from its ambitions of restoring its great power status, maintaining its regional influence, and perceiving Western policies as a threat to its interests. Third, when it considers its strategic interests undermined, Russia employs economic and military threats (sometimes incentives) against its neighbourhood countries to make the compliance with Western policies less preferable.

One of the overarching aims of this special issue has been to understand how illiberal regional powers react to the efforts by the European Union (EU) and the United States (US) at democracy promotion.[1] While addressing this question, the special issue studies the interactions between (1) Western democracy promoters and illiberal regional powers; and (2) illiberal regional powers and political actors in target states. Following the objectives of the special issue, this article focuses on these issues by investigating Russia's interactions with the EU and the US and countries that are targets of democracy promotion. Thus, the main focus of this article is on

Russia's actions on the backdrop of EU and US policies in the countries included in one of the EU's flagship democracy promotion initiatives, Eastern Partnership (EaP): Armenia, Azerbaijan, Belarus, Georgia, Moldova, and Ukraine. The issue of the effectiveness of EU and US democracy promotion from the perspective of Russia's near abroad (or the interactions between democracy promotion and socio-political conditions in target countries) is thoroughly discussed by Delcour and Wolczuk[2] in this special issue on the cases of Georgia and Ukraine and is beyond the scope of this article. Central Asian countries are also included in Russia's neighbourhood, yet due to comparatively limited democracy promotion by the EU and the US they do not provide ample evidence of interaction between democracy promoters and Russia.

The focus on Russia as a "countervailing illiberal regional power"[3] stems from its strengthened authoritarianism and heightened activities in its neighbourhood that some analysts even classify as autocracy promotion.[4] Encouraged by the West in the early 1990s, the initial promise of Russia's speedy democratization is long gone and its relations with the West have grown more complicated. Yet, it is not only Russia's democratic performance that deteriorates, but also that of its so-called *blizhnee zarubezhye* – near abroad. Democracy indices such as Freedom House or Polity IV show that democratization stagnated almost simultaneously both in Russia and within its neighbourhood. This stagnation may seem surprising, since it happened despite continued democracy promotion in Russia's near abroad by the EU and the US, which on its own has been supported by the rhetorical commitment of local societal and political actors to democratization. At the same time, through business acquisitions, security and trade agreements, and institutional structures[5] Russia has become more active in its near abroad compared to its role after the break-up of the Soviet Union. More often than not these actions have counteracted the ones by the EU and the US and blocked some of their initiatives, for example, the Nabucco pipeline or signing of EaP Association Agreements (AA).

Thus, while following the framework of the special issue and investigating the aforementioned problems, this article further narrows its focus to the following questions:

- Does Russia promote autocracy or any other regime in its neighbourhood?
- How does Russia (and why would it) counteract democracy promotion by the EU and the US in its neighbourhood?

Dealing with the overarching questions of this special issue, Risse and Babayan have hypothesized that illiberal regional powers may counteract democracy promotion only when their geostrategic interests or regime survival are challenged. Moreover, illiberal powers are unlikely to promote autocracy, even if their actions may inadvertently result in strengthening of authoritarianism in target countries. By analysing the case of Russia's actions in its near abroad, this article confirms these hypotheses. The article argues that even if Russia's potentially confrontational policies may have contributed to the stagnation of democratization in its near abroad, Russia does not seem interested in promoting a specific regime type in the manner of democracy promoters. However, Russia continues to perceive the countries of the former Soviet Union as its inalienable spheres of influence and Western policies, including democracy promotion, as a threat to that influence. Being interested in restoring its international and domestic image of importance through strengthening (though not promotion) of its own regime and through safeguarding of its geostrategic interests, Russia has developed a more decisive approach to the region, starting from the first election of Vladimir Putin.

These questions and arguments are further explained by first juxtaposing the arguments on the drivers and mechanisms of EU and US democracy promotion with Russia's actions. The article demonstrates that contrary to popularized opinions, Russia has not engaged in promoting autocracy or any other regime for that matter. Quite the contrary – it has abided by democratic rhetoric similar to that of the West. Capitalizing on democratic rhetoric, it has consistently styled itself as a democracy and rendered any democracy promotion within its own borders as redundant. Second, the article shows how bilateral relations of Russia with the EU and the US have been affected by rapid EU and NATO (North Atlantic Treaty Organization) enlargements, transforming not only democracy promotion but also any Western supported policy into a potential threat to Russia's geostrategic interests in its near abroad. On the cases of EaP countries the article shows how this threat perception along with Russia's power ambitions, rather than concerns over regime survival, are the main drivers behind Russia's actions countering democracy promotion and how they shape its strategies toward its neighbours. The democratization of EaP countries is perceived as a threat to Russia's influence in its near abroad and induces it to apply a spectrum of economy and security-related measures to steer them away from Western policies. Third, the article shows how Russia's counteraction to Western policies is especially aggressive when EU and US policies meet the approval of local political actors and increase the likelihood of their successful implementation. To prevent this, Russia has exploited the domestic conditions of the others, and often-unsure policies of the EU and the US, as happened in the case of Armenia and its unexpected preference for Russia's Customs Union over the EU's AA. Russia has created conditions that make compliance with its demands preferable to compliance with democracy promotion or Western policies' objectives. However, from the cases of Belarus and Azerbaijan, it is also evident that Russia applies its counteraction strategies even when Western policies (including democracy promotion) are unlikely to succeed, yet again demonstrating that instead of promoting autocracy Russia simply safeguards its interests. These actions on their own may have induced stagnation of the democratization process in Russia's near abroad since most Western policies come in bundles of interrelated policies and objectives.

Does Russia promote autocracy?

While Russia's own regime has become more autocratic, this article argues that judging from Russia's practices and ideological bases it has hardly been interested in promoting autocracy, or, for that matter, any regime abroad. However, given Russia's consolidated authoritarianism (in Freedom House parlance), and actions during the 2008 conflict in Georgia and 2014 conflict in Ukraine, it may not be surprising that some analysts have tended to qualify Russia's actions as autocracy promotion. In addition, there is no denying that Russia's regime – often dubbed as Putinism – and its methods have found followers in other countries.[6] Yet, this process can be attributed to passive learning or contagion[7] rather than active regime promotion. While addressing the possible issue of autocracy promotion, it seems Russia's actions have been previously explained by a reverse logic of democracy promotion. The literature on democracy promotion argues that democracies promote their regime types for the achievement of greater security and trade opportunities.[8] Thus, it has been expected that Russia may promote its own regime to simplify rent-extraction from neighbouring countries.[9] In addition, as Whitehead[10] has suggested, democratization of neighbouring countries might be "contagious" to nearby autocracies, thus Russia may promote its regime to prevent any spillover of democracy over its own borders.[11] These explanations clearly shed light on the drivers for possible autocracy promotion. They also corroborate the hypothesis posited in the introduction to this special issue that counteracting democracy promotion is likely to be driven by safeguarding geostrategic interests and the concerns over regime survival.

Yet, while these explanations do demonstrate why Russia may engage in autocracy promotion, they do not clearly show that it does so, since autocracy promotion would require active advancement of an autocratic regime, very much in the style of democracy promotion. Even if autocracy promotion may seem a feasible alternative to EU and US actions classified as democracy promotion, the literature on the issue has yet to provide a clear understanding of what autocracy promotion is. Scholars of the emerging autocracy promotion literature have suggested that it may include deliberate diffusion of authoritarian values, assisting other regimes to suppress democratization, or condoning authoritarian tendencies.[12] While these considerations point to possible activities of an autocracy promoter, some of them may equally be ascribed to democracy promoters: for years both the EU and the US condoned autocratic regimes of the allies in the Middle East and North Africa based on their geostrategic interests.[13]

Democracy promotion as a rule consists of transferring to democratizing countries the components of democracy, such as free and fair elections, viable political parties, and civil society. Hence, autocracy promotion may include advancing the abolition of elections (or at least competition), promotion of one-party (if any) rule, and curtailing of civil and political rights in target states. However, in some cases Russia has adopted the practices of democracy promoters. For instance, it dispatched election observation missions to the US and European countries, among others, and in the summer of 2014 published human rights reports such as the one on Ukraine. Whether the content of these reports corresponds to the reality is not important, since by the production of such reports autocratic states acknowledge the prevalence of human rights and democracy rhetoric. In addition, supporting whatever regime it deems profitable, Russia has also used democracy promotion rhetoric and to some extent "mimic[ed] Western countries".[14] It has also shrewdly adopted much-celebrated concepts such as the "responsibility to protect" when launching military operations in Georgian breakaway regions in 2008 and sending troops to Ukraine in 2014 Thus, instead of actively promoting certain, perhaps, autocratic rules as the EU and the US do in the case of democracy promotion, Russia has simply adapted to democracy's prevalence and bended its concepts according to its interests.

During the Cold War there was a clear ideological divide between the democratic West and the communist Soviet Union. Yet, the ideological underpinnings of the current Russian regime are derivatives of democracy. Moreover, they are often based on the consideration of increasing Russians' patriotism[15] rather than propagating regimes that are alternative to democracy. Even much-publicized terms such as managed democracy and *suverennaya demokratia* (sovereign democracy)[16] do not mean that Russia has coined another regime type or even an alternative understanding of democracy. The intended message being that Russia was democratic and its democracy could not be doubted by anyone.[17] This is not to say that Russia's regime is inherently democratic, but to underline that the Russian political elite has also agreed to the dominance and popular appeal of the democratic script. Possible arguments that Russia equates the political and economic relations of its neighbours with the EU to yielding to homosexual culture and surrendering traditional values[18] cannot serve as evidence of autocracy or regime promotion either, since similar debates persist also in Western democracies.[19] Undoubtedly, the law criminalizing "gay propaganda" has diminished certain human rights in Russia. However, Putin's move has largely been guided by considerations of ensuring "[Russian] public acquiescence",[20] sense of patriotism, and national values in the wake of possible political isolation without clear evidence yet that similar laws have been promoted abroad.

Russia's disinterest in promoting its "consolidated authoritarianism" with a strengthened presidency, dominant ruling political party, and tolerated elections can also be noticed, for example, in its disregard of possible constitutional changes in Armenia announced in 2014. If implemented, Armenia would transform into a parliamentary regime[21] with a ceremonial president: a regime that the scholarship considers more conducive to democratization.[22] Such disinterest in promoting its regime may seem surprising, especially given that Russia's illiberal practices have found followers even in the EU member Hungary.[23] Yet, the realization of Russia's obvious economic and military advantages over its near abroad countries makes active promotion of a regime, which may be resisted by local actors, a cumbersome and inefficient strategy in comparison to sanctions or threats.

Why would Russia counteract democracy promotion?

Russia's problem with the democratization of its near abroad has not been in the establishment of democracy, it has rather been in the possible westernization of these countries as a result of democratization and their possible turn from their forced allegiance to Russia, as happened in the case of the Baltic States. Russia realizes that the congestion of competing international actors in the post-Soviet space and often attractive incentives – for example, free trade with the EU, visa-liberalization, or additional financial aid from the US – may further loosen its grip on its near abroad. Even if, unlike the Baltic States, the EaP countries largely lack pre-Soviet democratic legacies, they have often listed closer economic, political, and security cooperation with the EU and the US among their top priorities. The US, and especially the EU, have also launched a multitude of policies, including democracy promotion, targeting the countries in Russia's near abroad. In most of the cases these policies aimed for closer integration into European political and economic structures, often at the expense of Russia's interests. Thus, the perceived threat to Russian leverage in the post-Soviet space is far from illusory and has been largely shaped by the activities of the EU and the US in these countries, their negligence of Russia's geostrategic interests, and Russia's reinvigorated strive to restore its great power status. The combination of these factors has induced Russia to perceive democracy promotion and possible westernization as a threat to its power and its objective of restoring that great power status. The overview of Russia's relations with the EU and the US and its approach to democracy promotion support these arguments.

The collapse of the Soviet Union delivered a major blow to Russia but boosted the US's position in international affairs. Russian political elites lamented "Moscow's lost empire"[24] and perceived its decline as the negative side of liberalization, exacerbated by rapid expansions of the EU and NATO to the east. Russia's nostalgia for its great power past became more outspoken after NATO's bombing of Serbia in 1999 despite strong Russian opposition.[25] The appointment of the then unknown former KGB officer as prime minister surprised many in and outside of Russia. However, Putin's confirmation speech already indicated the direction of his foreign policy toward the restoration of Russia's great power status:

> Russia has been a great power for centuries and remains so. It has always had and still has legitimate zones of interest abroad in both the former Soviet lands and elsewhere. We should not drop our guard in this respect, neither should we allow our opinion to be ignored.[26]

Thus, the restoration of its great power status and the preservation of its traditional sphere of influence have become the primary tasks of Putin's Russia, as it has moved to build foreign policy "projecting Russian strength".[27] Putin's approach toward foreign affairs reflected his vision that "national might ... [is] the main engine that drives global politics",[28] while maintaining its influence over post-Soviet countries is one of the keys to restoring Russia's might. Russia's foreign policy has been shaped from within Russian politics by the centralization of power in the Kremlin, prolonging presidential terms, personification of power in Putin,[29] and by re-imagining democratic principles, although, as shown above, not rejecting them.

Broadening the assumption of this special issue, the article suggests that Russia's counteractions are also fuelled by its concerns over regime strengthening rather than regime survival, as may be the case with Saudi Arabia (on Saudi Arabia see Hassan in this special issue). As also argued in this special issue and demonstrated by a series of recent revolts, regime survival can first of all be threatened from within. The 2011–2012 protests in Russia generated arguments that Putin's regime may be under threat. However, not only have protests subsided, which of course can be the result of the government's actions, but the approval rankings of Russia's policies and of Putin himself have increased. Surveys conducted in April 2014 by the Levada Center, an independent polling institution often itself a target of the Kremlin's disapproval,[30] showed that 88% of Russian respondents believed that Crimea's annexation was a free act of self-determination, which according to 75% of the respondents demonstrated the return of the "traditional great power status".[31] The same pollster showed that Putin's approval ranking increased from 64% in September 2013 to 86% in September 2014, while 62% in September 2014 thought that "things go in the right direction in Russia" as opposed to 42% in September 2013.[32]

The centralization of power in the Kremlin and the evolution of a stronger foreign policy have proceeded on the background of rather lackadaisical democracy promotion in Russia by both the EU and the US. Similarly to the policies toward China and Saudi Arabia (see also Chen and Kinzelbach and Hassan in this special issue),[33] US administrations have preferred to engage in trade and "implicit"[34] rather than active democracy promotion in Russia. EU democracy promotion in Russia has not been as systematic as in the rest of Eastern Europe or EaP countries. The dynamics of US-Russia relations have been characterized by an on-off rivalry,[35] and EU-Russia relations by tenacious clash of interests amidst the background of a porous strategic partnership.[36] Russia interpreted EU and US support for the wave of "colour revolutions" and its engagement with civil society as a direct threat[37] and to prevent a possible spillover restricted the activities of politically involved or foreign-funded non-governmental organizations (NGOs) in Russia.[38] The much-discussed "reset" of US-Russia relations of 2009[39] also did not last long. By expelling[40] the main US democracy promoting institution – the United States Agency for International Development (USAID) – Russia demonstrated that US activities, especially in democracy promotion, are not welcome. USAID's expulsion may not come as a surprise since President Putin has repeatedly characterized democracy promotion as a "waste of money" and such democracy promotion-related activities as election observation as attempts to influence elections.[41] The EU's plans to diversify its energy source by building gas pipelines that bypass Russia have further antagonized the latter, since any alternative pipeline was viewed as direct competition with Russia's plans.[42] The 2014 events in Ukraine have further emphasized the divisions between Russia and the West: each repeatedly blamed the other for instigating the conflict and imposed mutual sanctions.[43]

This article has suggested that embedded in its historical past as a great power, Russia's counteraction to democracy promotion can be explained as a result of policies aiming to restore its international position and maintain its sphere of influence. With these aims Russia has been acting on the opportunities presented by the actions of the EU, the US, and post-Soviet countries. These objectives have been pursued internationally by attempts to project a more decisive foreign policy position than in the 1990s; regionally by shaping the actions of neighbours to Russia's interests; and domestically by strengthening the state's authority and image. Playing on the still-remaining sentiments from the Cold War period, Putin's rhetoric and policies have presented the West at large as the antagonist of Russia's efforts to restore its position or improve its economy. As a result, Russia's actions have clashed with the policies of the EU and the US, especially when the latter have concerned the countries of Russia's near abroad. Hence, the association with the EU was depicted as a betrayal of historical ties and national interests. The next section explores these arguments and focuses on the counteraction to the EU's policies, which have also been repeatedly supported by the US.[44]

How does Russia counteract democracy promotion?

This special issue has suggested that from the perspective of target countries, the resonance of promoted democratic rules among domestic elites and the population, the economic and military importance, and to some extent cultural/historical proximity to an illiberal power are likely drivers for counteraction of democracy promotion. This section considers these assumptions by overviewing Russia's actions in EaP countries and proceeds to more detailed discussion of Russia's strategies in counteracting democracy promotion using the example of Armenia's withdrawal from initialling the EU's AA. While not a frontrunner in democratization, Armenia has endeavoured to develop closer relations with both Russia and the EU, being particularly enthusiastic about new targeted policies. Precisely this endeavour to integrate into European structures rather than to democratize induces Russia to counteract Western policies. To reinforce the argument that counteraction to democracy promotion is a byproduct of Russia protecting its strategic interests, the article briefly refers to Russia's relations with Azerbaijan and Belarus. Due to their already consolidated authoritarian regimes and disregard of European "shared values", Azerbaijan and Belarus are least likely to be pressured by Russia because of their possible democratic aspirations. However, their interactions with Russia show that the latter used the same instruments toward these countries whenever the latter ignored its interests.

Realizing that the previously forced allegiance of Eastern Europe had moved to the EU, president Putin prioritized the post-Soviet countries in Russia's foreign policy.[45] Along with its historical ties, Russia has vested economic and security interests in all EaP countries. Thus in terms of the drivers for possible counteraction to democracy promotion (see the introduction to this issue by Risse and Babayan) all three apply to Russia's near abroad, though to different extents depending on the country. While geographic proximity and shared history apply to all six EaP partners, resonance of democracy among local political actors is most pronounced in the cases of Georgia and Ukraine (see Delcour and Wolczuk in this special issue). Economic and military interests and leverage are emphasized in the cases of Armenia – a host to the only Russian military base in an EaP country – and Azerbaijan – a potential though smaller rival in energy exports to Europe. While both Armenia and Azerbaijan are democratic laggards, the rhetorical resonance of democracy and the willingness to participate in EU policies is more pronounced among Armenian political elites and the population.[46] Apart from democracy indices such as Freedom House, frequent and tolerated criticism of the authorities in the media, and the visibility of opposition parties'[47] support this observation. These factors and the argued attractiveness of the EU's incentives have induced Russia to realize that democratization of these countries may result in their closer partnership with the EU and the US at the expense of Russia's own regional interests. Thus, democracy promotion policies have been viewed by Russia as contradicting its own interests in the region.

By pressuring its neighbouring countries through military power and economic investments or sanctions, Russia has, perhaps, inadvertently countered democracy promotion and stabilized authoritarian regimes in the post-Soviet space. To extend its influence and to counter the policies of the EU and the US even before the launch of the EaP in 2009, Russia had forgiven debts in exchange for military-industrial enterprises and purchased large shares in telecommunications, energy, electricity networks, and banking industries.[48] Thus, it *inter alia* engaged in specific business development based on its own strategic interests, however, framing those as serving the development of its neighbours. This strategy has underlined the employment of non-military instruments in reinforcing Russia's policies and obtaining a dominant status in the economies of its former satellites. It has also presented the post-Soviet countries with potentially less cumbersome opportunities for economic gains: unlike EU and US policies, Russia's cooperation has not been tied to domestically costly political reforms or lengthy harmonization processes.

Russia considered its growing regional dominance to be challenged when in 2010 the European Commission started negotiations on Deep and Comprehensive Free Trade Agreements (DCFTA) with EaP countries. Despite the reassurances from the former EU foreign policy chief Javier Solana that the EaP had not been designed against Russia, foreign minister Sergey Lavrov interpreted the choice given to EaP partners as either being with Russia, or with the European Union. Russia *inter alia* reacted by urging EaP countries to join its Customs Union with Belarus and Kazakhstan – a precursor to Putin's envisaged Eurasian Union. The EU has repeatedly stated that signing any customs agreements with Russia would endanger the AA, since the prerequisites of Russia's aspiring Eurasian Union contradicted the EU-offered DCFTA. Russian Prime Minister Dmitry Medvedev also underlined the incompatibility of the two structures.[49] However, the Customs Union has been viewed not only as another alternative agreement but also as possible leverage over the EU's neighbours, since, as expected, Russia did apply pressure, including:

- misuse of energy pricing;
- artificial trade obstacles such as import bans of dubious World Trade Organization (WTO) compatibility and cumbersome customs procedures;
- military cooperation and security guarantees; and
- the instrumentalization of protracted conflicts.[50]

To "minimize the impact of ... new ties with the EU",[51] Russia took more substantial measures when it engaged in trade wars with the countries which were most enthusiastic about their European aspirations. While Moldova repeatedly stated that signing of the AA would not damage its export prospects and economic relations with Russia, the latter banned the import of Moldovan wine.[52] Largely viewed as retaliation against a pro-EU Ukrainian businessman – later Ukrainian President Petro Poroshenko – Russia banned imports of a Ukrainian chocolate brand in July 2013 and dairy products in April 2014.[53] The coordinated action by the EU and the US guided Georgia and Ukraine to the signing of the AA in June 2014; however, the determination of Russia to prevent shifts in its regional dominance persisted. Under admitted Russian pressure and threats of "asymmetric measures" in response to Western sanctions, in September 2014 the EU suspended the enforcement of DCFTA with Ukraine and postponed it from November 2014 to December 2015.[54] In this special issue Delcour and Wolczuk discuss interactions between Russia, Georgia, Ukraine, and democracy promoters in more detail.

Yet, not only EU-enthusiasts may be targeted by trade sanctions, showing that these instruments do not aim to restrict democratization *per se* but to punish incompliance with the Kremlin's interests. Russia has employed similar strategies against long-time partners, who do not even welcome democracy promotion. Trade wars between Belarus and Russia and Russia's mass purchase of Azerbaijani energy are cases in point. Given the resistance of the Belarusian regime to democratization and the string of EU and US sanctions,[55] trade and cooperation with Russia are vital for Belarus. Nevertheless, on several occasions President Alexander Lukashenko denounced Russia's dominance in their relations. In response, Russia imposed various sanctions at the end of the 2000s and early 2010s, including banning import of Belarusian food products and flights of the Belarusian national carrier. Similarly, Azerbaijani authorities display no willingness to democratize or to integrate into European structures but they welcome business opportunities. Thus, Russia is interested in curtailing the supply of Caspian gas to the EU, since that would hinder Russia's economic interests[56] and to some extent compete with Russia's gas exports. Russia promised Azerbaijan "serious consequences" for its participation in the EaP and the Nabucco pipeline project and by buying the gas intended for Nabucco basically left the pipeline without supply.[57] While seemingly a more profitable deal for Azerbaijan, selling large amounts of gas to Russia has the potential of endangering the former's export diversification plans and decreasing its bargaining power against Russia.[58]

How did Russia counteract EaP in Armenia?

Since its independence from the Soviet Union, Armenia has welcomed democracy promotion efforts and committed to the regional policies of the EU and the US, including democracy promotion. The expulsion of Russian military bases from Georgia after the 2008 conflict and their move to Armenia made the latter the last remaining stronghold of Russian military power in the region. The entire spectrum of Russia's instruments in counteracting democracy promotion or for that matter any EU/US policy deemed as challenging were particularly evident in the case of Armenia's 2013 "U-turn"[59] from the EU AA to Russia's Customs Union. The case of Armenia demonstrates that Russia is most prone to counteract the EU and the US when faced with imminent effectiveness of democracy promotion supported by local actors or when faced with challenges to its geostrategic interests. As Delcour and Wolczuk show in this special issue, this logic also applies to Russia's actions in Georgia and Ukraine. By the employment of economic and military instruments and through the promotion of alternative regional institutions, Russia counteracted EU policy, which has also been supported by the US. Thus, Russian efforts for counteracting the initiatives within the EaP peaked with success in September 2013: Armenia turned to the Eurasian Customs Union and in November 2013 Ukraine withdrew from initialling the AA despite a wave of domestic protests in both countries.[60]

Energy, more specifically gas, and the protracted conflicts are the main pressure points used by Russia in Eastern Europe and the South Caucasus. Devoid of natural energy resources and with a protracted conflict at hand, Armenia makes a compliant target for Russia's energy and military pressures. In the mid-2000s Russia successfully blocked the diversification of Armenia's gas sources by imposing restrictions on the pipeline from Iran.[61] Regular Armenian concessions in terms of infrastructure and cooperation with other neighbours secured comparatively lower gas prices. However, after Armenia concluded the sixth round of DCFTA negotiations leading to the initialling of the AA, in July 2013 Russia threatened to increase gas prices by 60%, while suggesting that the costs may be subsidized and not increase in the next five years should Armenia join the Customs Union.[62] Consequently, Armenia entered negotiations for an 18% rise. It allowed Russian gas-monopoly Gazprom to acquire the remaining 20% of shares of the gas procuring company ArmRusGazprom, which had previously belonged to the Armenian government. Russian media, which is also widely viewed in Armenia, publicized a number of preferential agreements and possible subsidies promised by Putin to Armenia's President Serzh Sargsyan in return for joining the Customs Union. In addition, Russia promised larger investments into prolonging the exploitation of the Armenian nuclear power plant and other factories, regarded as obsolete or environmentally hazardous by the EU and the US.[63]

Besides economic threats, Russia has also been taking advantage of the protracted conflict between Armenia and Azerbaijan over Nagorno Karabakh region. While Azerbaijan's energy industry has allowed it to exponentially multiply its military budget, Armenia has been largely reliant on Russia for its security against possible military actions by Azerbaijan. While Armenia showed growing interest in its partnership with the EU and did not attend a June 2013 meeting of the Russian-led Collective Security Treaty Organization, Russia subsequently increased its arms export to Azerbaijan by US$1 billion.[64] This move served as a clear warning to Armenia that Russia may no longer support it in the framework of the conflict. Regularly playing two sides of the conflict against each other using the promise or threat of arms sales, Russia has managed to keep the South Caucasus divided and hindered regional projects of the EU and the US.

Armenia backpedalled on AA after two years of preparations and previously expressed confidence by the Armenian authorities that "the AAs with some partner countries, including Armenia, will be initialled" in November 2013.[65] The EU delegation in Armenia confirmed that the latter was on track for signing the AA. Former Prime Minister Tigran Sarkisian also repeatedly argued against Armenian entry into the Customs Union, due to the lack of common borders with Russia, Belarus, or Kazakhstan.[66] Thus, the decision to reject initialling the AA bewildered both the EU and the Armenian public, which took to the streets in protest (even if with limited coverage by Western media). Given the pressures coming from the Kremlin, Armenian officials attempted to frame the decision in pragmatic terms, calling Russia the "military security choice" and the DCFTA the "economic choice", since "in terms of security, Armenia is tied to Russia".[67] However, while the Armenian government and the Kremlin have attempted to present the Customs Union as a better economic and trade choice for Armenia,[68] the benefits of joining it are hardly identifiable. Due to its closed borders with Azerbaijan and Turkey, and lack of a border with Russia, Armenia conducts most of its trade through Georgia. Since Georgia signed the DCFTA in summer 2014, these two neighbouring countries will now have to abide by different tariffs and agreements, further straining Armenia's already weak economy.

Conclusions

The stagnation of democracy in post-Soviet countries has been the result of a set of factors, such as low resonance of democracy, high adaptation costs to democracy, protracted conflicts, weak institutions, or illiberal elites. Yet, through economic sanctions, military threats, and even through such formal institutions as the Eurasian Union, Russia has contributed to the stagnation of democratization in its near abroad. It counteracted democracy promotion or, for that matter, any other Western policies, which it considered a threat to its geostrategic interests and ambitions for restoring its great power status. At the same time, even if the level of democracy in its near abroad has gradually deteriorated, there is no evidence of Russia promoting autocracy or any other regime alternative to democracy.

Russia's actions are hardly surprising. For centuries under the direct influence of Russia, the regions of Eastern Europe, the South Caucasus, and Central Asia did not only constitute parts of the Russia-led Soviet Union but also of the earlier Russian Empire. The exposure to Western principles (along with material incentives) and democratization under the guidance of the EU or the US may potentially steer the allegiance of its near abroad away from Russia. Moreover, just as the EU and the US have continuously preferred stability over democracy,[69] Russia has also strived to maintain the status quo and safeguard its interests in its own neighbourhood. At the same time, the EU and the US currently do not match either the level of political prowess – borderline blackmail – or the type of economic or security pressures employed by Russia in its near abroad.

These observations lead to other tentative conclusions, which require further deliberation but have been beyond the scope of this article. First, democracy promotion should focus on the possibilities of strengthening bargaining powers of target countries against Russia's (or others') counteractions, especially if the target countries display willingness to embrace democratic practices promoted by the EU and the US. The examples of EaP countries and particularly Armenia demonstrate that Russia's counteraction to democracy promotion or Western policies has been effective because it has capitalized not so much on the discrepancies of EU or US policies, but on the internal issues of these countries. In the case of Armenia, and to some extent Azerbaijan, Russia has used the internal security problems created by the protracted Nagorno Karabakh conflict. Thus more active involvement of democracy promoters in issues of national importance, even if not directly democracy-related, may loosen the links these countries have with illiberal regional powers.

Second, it is not only rapid economic development or democratic values that may find emulators without active regime promotion. At the same time, it is not only transitioning countries that may stagnate in their democratizations. Being disappointed in Europe's competitiveness and democratic models,[70] former democratic frontrunners such as Hungary may openly revert to "Putinesque" practices of centralizing power and silencing dissent.

Finally, not all illiberal regimes may counteract democracy promotion for the same reasons and their drivers are likely to be lodged *inter alia* in their historical legacies and political cultures. Understanding these sometimes far-fetched drivers is likely to help democracy promoters to reframe their regional policies and ease the tensions. This special issue shows that the examined illiberal powers – China, Russia, and Saudi Arabia – are preoccupied more with their geostrategic interests than with the regime types of their neighbours. Yet, their historical legacies are likely to shape their strategies toward democratizing or westernizing countries: while Saudi Arabia is preoccupied with the survival of the House of Saud (see Hassan's article), Russia seems interested in the "return of the empire".

Acknowledgements
I also thank Thomas Risse, two anonymous reviewers, and the participants of the workshop for their insightful comments and suggestions on the earlier draft of this article.

Funding
This article has been prepared for the special issue originated in the framework of the TRANSWORLD project funded by the EU's 7th Framework Program for Socio-Economic Research (Grant agreement 290454). The Research College "Transformative Power of Europe," funded by the German Research Foundation DFG sponsored the authors' workshop on 23 May 2014.

Notes

1. Risse and Babayan, "Democracy Promotion and the Challenges of Illiberal Regional Powers."
2. Delcour and Wolczuk, "Spoiler or Facilitator of Democratization? Russia's Role in Georgia and Ukraine."
3. Risse and Babayan, "Democracy Promotion and the Challenges of Illiberal Regional Powers."
4. Bader, Grävingholt, and Kästner, "Would Autocracies Promote Autocracy?"; Cameron and Orenstein, "Post-Soviet Authoritarianism"; Melnykovska, Plamper, and Schweickert, "Do Russia and China Promote Autocracy in Central Asia?"; Tolstrup, "Studying a Negative External Actor."
5. Tsygankov, "If Not by Tanks, Then by Banks?"; Babayan, "The South Caucasus."
6. Taylor, "Is China Looking to Vladimir Putin for Tips on Suppressing Hong Kong Protests?"; Zakaria, "The Rise of Putinism."
7. Whitehead, *The International Dimensions of Democratization*.
8. Johnson, "In Pursuit of a Prosperous International System"; Russett, *Grasping the Democratic Peace*; Kegley and Hermann, "In Pursuit of a Peaceful International System."
9. Bader, Grävingholt, and Kästner, "Would Autocracies Promote Autocracy?"
10. Whitehead, *The International Dimensions of Democratization*.
11. Obydenkova and Libman, "Understanding the Foreign Policy of Autocratic Actors."
12. Burnell, "Is There a New Autocracy Promotion?"
13. Dempsey, "Europe's Response to Morsi's New Powers"; Hamid, "The Brotherhood Will Be Back."
14. Obydenkova and Libman, "Understanding the Foreign Policy of Autocratic Actors," 350.
15. Trenin, "Drivers of Russia's Foreign Policy."
16. Putin, "Russia Crossing the Millenia."
17. Lipman, "Putin's 'Sovereign Democracy.'"
18. Pavlikova, "Association with the EU Means Broadening of Gay-culture Sphere [Assotsiatsiya s ES oznachaet rasshirenie sfery gay-kulturi]."
19. Wilkinson and Langlois, "Special Issue"; Browne and Nash, "Resisting LGBT Rights Where 'We Have Won.'"
20. Trenin, "Drivers of Russia's Foreign Policy," 36.
21. The oppositional parties argue that this move intends to prolong the power of the incumbent president, Serzh Sargsyan, who is barred from running for a third consecutive term. Nevertheless, this example attests to Russia's indifference to regime particularities as long as its interests stay intact.
22. Linz, "The Perils of Presidentialism"; Przeworski et al., *Democracy and Development*.

23. Mahony, "Orban Wants to Build 'Illiberal State.'"
24. Rywkin, *Moscow's Lost Empire.*
25. Krickovic, "Imperial Nostalgia or Prudent Geopolitics?"; RIA News, "The U-Turn over the Atlantic."
26. Putin 1999 in Bullough, "Vladimir Putin."
27. Secrieru, "Russia's Foreign Policy Under Putin"; US Embassy Cable, *Russian Analysts Tell A/s Gordon Anti-Americanism Pillar of Russian Foreign Policy.*
28. Trenin, "Drivers of Russia's Foreign Policy," 36.
29. Shevtsova, "Russia under Putin."
30. Balmforth, "Levada Center, Russia's Most Respected Pollster, Fears Closure"; Goncharenko, "Rallying behind Russia's 'Foreign Agent' Levada Center."
31. Levada Center, "Russians about Ukrainian Events."
32. Levada Center, "Indice."
33. Carothers, "Barack Obama"; Chen and Kinzelbach, "Democracy Promotion and China"; Hassan, "Undermining the Transatlantic Democracy Agenda?"
34. Babayan, *Home-Made Adjustments*; Lynch, "George W. Bush," 188.
35. Rutland, "Still out in the Cold?"
36. Sakwa, "Looking for a Greater Europe."
37. Newsru, "Putin Is Unanimously Elected."
38. BBC, "Russian NGO Bill Signed into Law."
39. Cooper, "Promises of 'Fresh Start' for U.S.-Russia Relations."
40. Rosenberg, "US Agency Expelled from Russia."
41. Newsru, "Putin Is Unanimously Elected."
42. Nicola, "Europe's Pipeline War"; BBC, "Putin Pushes Forward Gas Pipeline."
43. RT, "Washington Pushing Ukraine to Conflict."
44. Rosenblum, "Twenty Years of Democracy and Governance Programs in Europe and Eurasia"; Nuland, "Toward a Transatlantic Renaissance"; Nuland, *A Pivotal Moment for the Eastern Partnership.*
45. Babayan and Braghiroli, "Il Buono, Il Brutto, Il Cattivo?"
46. ENPI Info, *Reliable and Strong, like a Bear*; Armenpress, "EU Poll Shows Armenians Have Positive Attitude toward Armenia-EU Relations."
47. RFE/RL, "Armenian Opposition Launches New Wave of Protests."
48. Migdalovitz, *Armenia Update*; RFE/RL, "Rostelekom Intends to Invest"; Elliott, *Wikileaks Cable.*
49. Lazaryan, "Medvedev."
50. Füle, "Statement on the Pressure Exercised by Russia."
51. RFE/RL, "Transdniester Deepens Ties With Russia."
52. Interfax, "Chisinau"; Moldova.org, "Russia Likely to Ban Wines from Moldova on Wednesday"; Heil, "Dour Grapes."
53. EurActiv, "Russia Hits at Ukraine with Chocolate War"; Reuters, "UPDATE 1-Russia Bans Ukrainian Dairy Imports from Six Companies."
54. Rettman, "EU and Ukraine Suspend Trade Pact."
55. Council of the European Union, *EU Sanctions against Belarus Extended*; US Treasury Department, "Belarus Sanctions."
56. Zaynalov, "Azerbaijan-Gazprom Agreement."
57. US Embassy Cable, *Azerbaijan*; Zaynalov, "Azerbaijan-Gazprom Agreement."
58. Niftiyev, "Gazprom-SOCAR Gas Deal."
59. Bildt, "Armenia U-Turn."
60. Gevorgyan, "Putin Protest"; Bank, "Russia Pressures Armenia."
61. Socor, "Iran-Armenia Gas Pipeline: Far More than Meets the Eye."
62. Movsisian, "Russian-Armenian Gas Deal Ratified Amid Parliament Turmoil, Protests"; Stepanyan, "The Issue of Gas Price."

63. Harutyunyan, "Russian Utility Seeks Early End to Armenian Nuclear Plant Management."
64. Grove, "Russia Starts Delivering $1 Billion Arms Package to Azerbaijan."
65. RFE/RL, "Yerevan Confident About Association Agreement With EU."
66. Banks.am, "We Should Find the Formula of Interaction with Customs Union, Tigran Sargsyan Says"; Hayrumyan, "Customs Union Is Ransom for Tigran Sargsyan."
67. PanArmenian.Net, "NSC Chief."
68. Lazaryan, "Medvedev."
69. Magen, Risse, and McFaul, *Promoting Democracy and the Rule of Law*; Babayan and Risse, *So Close but Yet So Far*.
70. Orban, "Viktor Orbán's Speech."

Notes on contributor

Nelli Babayan is a senior researcher at the Center for Transnational Relations, Foreign and Security Policy at the Otto Suhr Institute of Political Science, Freie Universität Berlin. She is the author of *Democratic Transformation and Obstruction: EU, US and Russia in the South Caucasus* (Routledge, 2015).

References

Armenpress. "EU Poll Shows Armenians Have Positive Attitude toward Armenia-EU Relations." Armenpress, 2014. http://armenpress.am/eng/news/776950/eu-poll-shows-armenians-have-positive-attitude-toward-armenia-eu-relations.html

Babayan, Nelli. *Home-Made Adjustments? US Human Rights and Democracy Promotion.* TRANSWORLD Working Paper, 2013a. http://www.transworld-fp7.eu/?p=1151

Babayan, Nelli. "The South Caucasus." In *Alternatives to Democracy: Non-Democratic Regimes and the Limits of Democracy Diffusion in Eurasia*, edited by Elena Baracani and Roberto Di Quirico, 189–208. Florence: European Press Academic Publishing, 2013b.

Babayan, Nelli, and Stefano Braghiroli. "Il Buono, Il Brutto, Il Cattivo? Assessing Imperialist Aspirations of the EU, Russia and the US." *Central European Journal of International and Security Studies* 5, no. 2 (2011): 79–104.

Babayan, Nelli, and Thomas Risse. *So Close but Yet So Far: European and American Democracy Promotion.* TRANSWORLD Working Paper, 2014. http://www.transworld-fp7.eu/?p=1565

Bader, Julia, Jörn Grävingholt, and Antje Kästner. "Would Autocracies Promote Autocracy? A Political Economy Perspective on Regime-Type Export in Regional Neighbourhoods." *Contemporary Politics* 16, no. 1 (2010): 81–100. doi:10.1080/13569771003593904

Balmforth, Tom. "Levada Center, Russia's Most Respected Pollster, Fears Closure." *RadioFreeEurope/RadioLiberty*, May 21, 2013, sec. Russia. http://www.rferl.org/content/russia-levada-center-foreign-agent/24992729.html

Bank, Stephen. "Russia Pressures Armenia to Join Customs Union." *The Central Asia-Caucasus Analyst*, 2013. http://www.cacianalyst.org/publications/analytical-articles/item/12793-russia-pressures-armenia-to-join-customs-union.html

Banks.am. "We Should Find the Formula of Interaction with Customs Union, Tigran Sargsyan Says." *Banks.am*, 2013. http://www.banks.am/en/news/newsfeed/7827/

BBC. "Putin Pushes Forward Gas Pipeline." *BBC*, December 30, 2011, sec. Europe. http://www.bbc.co.uk/news/world-europe-16367396

BBC. "Russian NGO Bill Signed into Law." *BBC News*, 2012. http://www.bbc.com/news/world-europe-18938165

Bildt, Carl. "Seems as If Armenia Will Break Talks on Free Trade Agreement with EU and Integrate with Russia Instead. U-Turn." Microblog. *@carlbildt*, September 3, 2013. https://twitter.com/carlbildt/status/374921434499653632

Browne, Katherine, and Catherine J. Nash. "Resisting LGBT Rights Where 'We Have Won': Canada and Great Britain." *Journal of Human Rights* 13, no. 3 (July 3, 2014): 322–336. doi:10.1080/14754835.2014.923754

Bullough, Oliver. "Vladimir Putin: The Rebuilding of 'Soviet' Russia." *BBC News*, 2014. http://www.bbc.com/news/magazine-26769481

Burnell, Peter. "Is There a New Autocracy Promotion?" *FRIDE Working Paper*, no. 96 (2010). http://www.fride.org/download/WP96_Autocracy_ENG_mar10.pdf

Cameron, David R., and Mitchell A. Orenstein. "Post-Soviet Authoritarianism: The Influence of Russia in Its 'Near Abroad.'" *Post-Soviet Affairs* 28, no. 1 (January 1, 2012): 1–44. doi:10.2747/1060-586X.28.1.1

Carothers, Thomas. "Barack Obama." In *US Foreign Policy and Democracy Promotion: From Theodore Roosevelt to Barack Obama*, edited by Michael Cox, Timothy J. Lynch, and Nicolas Bouchet, 196–213. New York: Routledge, 2013.

Chen, Dingding, and Katrin Kinzelbach. "Democracy Promotion and China: Blocker or Bystander?" *Democratization* 22, no. 3 (2015): 400–418.

Cooper, Helene. "Promises of 'Fresh Start' for U.S.-Russia Relations." *The New York Times*, April 2, 2009, sec. International / Europe. http://www.nytimes.com/2009/04/02/world/europe/02arms.html?_r=1&hp

Council of the European Union. *EU Sanctions against Belarus Extended*. Brussels: European Union, 2013. http://www.consilium.europa.eu/uedocs/cms_Data/docs/pressdata/EN/foraff/139261.pdf

Delcour, Laure, and Kataryna Wolczuk. "Spoiler or Facilitator of Democratization? Russia's Role in Georgia and Ukraine." *Democratization* 22, no. 3 (2015): 459–478.

Dempsey, Judy. "Europe's Response to Morsi's New Powers." *Carnegie Europe*, 2012. http://carnegieeurope.eu/strategiceurope/?fa=50124

Elliott, Susan. *Russia Plays Its Cards In Armenia, Azerbaijan, Turkey 10MOSCOW60*. US Embassy Cables. Embassy Moscow (Russia), January 14, 2010. http://www.cablegatesearch.net/cable.php?id=10MOSCOW60

ENPI Info. *Reliable and Strong, like a Bear: Poll Finds Armenians at Ease with Its Neighbour, the European Union*. EU Neighbourhood Info Centre, 2010. http://www.enpi-info.eu/maineast.php?id=23526&id_type=1&lang_id=450

EurActiv. "Russia Hits at Ukraine with Chocolate War." Text. *EurActiv | EU News & Policy Debates, across Languages*, 2013. http://www.euractiv.com/europes-east/russia-hits-ukraine-chocolate-wa-news-529804

Füle, Štefan. "Statement on the Pressure Exercised by Russia on Countries of the Eastern Partnership." European Commission, 2013. http://europa.eu/rapid/press-release_SPEECH-13-687_en.htm

Gevorgyan, Siranuysh. "Putin Protest: Russian President Arrives in Gyumri as Protesters Rally in Yerevan." *ArmeniaNow.com*, 2013. http://www.armenianow.com/news/50548/vladimir_putin_serzh_sargsyan_customs_union_protest

Goncharenko, Roman. "Rallying behind Russia's 'Foreign Agent' Levada Center." *DW.DE*, 2013. http://www.dw.de/rallying-behind-russias-foreign-agent-levada-center/a-16849225

Grove, Thomas. "Russia Starts Delivering $1 Billion Arms Package to Azerbaijan." *Reuters*. June 18, 2013. http://www.reuters.com/article/2013/06/18/us-russia-azerbaijan-arms-idUSBRE95H0KM20130618

Hamid, Shadi. "The Brotherhood Will Be Back." *The New York Times*, May 23, 2014. http://www.nytimes.com/2014/05/24/opinion/more-democratic-less-liberal.html

Harutyunyan, Sargis. "Russian Utility Seeks Early End to Armenian Nuclear Plant Management," November 29, 2011, sec. in English. http://www.azatutyun.am/content/article/24401196.html

Hassan, Oz. "Undermining the Transatlantic Democracy Agenda? The Arab Spring and Saudi Arabia's Counteracting Democracy Strategy." *Democratization* 22, no. 3 (2015): 479–495.

Hayrumyan, Naira. "Customs Union Is Ransom for Tigran Sargsyan." *Lragir.am*, 2013. http://lragir.am/index.php/eng/0/comments/view/30259

Heil, Andy. "Dour Grapes: Russia Bans Moldovan Wine, Again." *RadioFreeEurope/RadioLiberty*, September 11, 2013, sec. Transmission. http://www.rferl.org/content/moldova-wine-russia-import-ban/25102889.html

Interfax. "Chisinau Says Signing DCFTA with EU Poses No Threat to Russian-Moldovan Economic Ties." *Interfax News Wire*, 2013. http://www.interfax.co.uk/ukraine-news/chisinau-says-signing-dcfta-with-eu-poses-no-threat-to-russian-moldovan-economic-ties-2/

Johnson, Juliet. "In Pursuit of a Prosperous International System." In *Exporting Democracy: Rhetoric Vs. Reality*, edited by Peter J. Schraeder, 31–52. Boulder, CO: Lynne Rienner Pub, 2002.

Kegley, Charles W., and Margaret G. Hermann. "In Pursuit of a Peaceful International System." In *Exporting Democracy: Rhetoric Vs. Reality*, edited by Peter J. Schraeder, 15–29. Boulder, CO: Lynne Rienner Pub, 2002.

Krickovic, Andrej. "Imperial Nostalgia or Prudent Geopolitics? Russia's Efforts to Reintegrate the Post-Soviet Space in Geopolitical Perspective." *Post-Soviet Affairs* 0, no. 0 (0): 1–26. doi:10.1080/1060586X.2014.900975

Lazaryan, Tatevik. ""Medvedev: The Customs Union Will Create Additional Opportunities for Armenia [Medvedev. Maksayin miutyuny Hayastani hamar lratsutsich hnaravorutyunner ksteghtsi]." *Radio Free Europe/Radio Liberty*, 2013. http://www.azatutyun.am/content/article/25100739.html

Levada Center. "Indice." *Levada Center*, 2014a. http://www.levada.ru/indeksy.

Levada Center. "Russians about Ukrainian Events [Rossiyane Ob Ukrainskikh Sobitiyakh]," 2014b. http://www.levada.ru/06–05–2014/rossiyane-ob-ukrainskikh-sobytiyakh?fb_action_ids=10202850835885341&fb_action_types=og.likes&fb_source=other_multiline&action_object_map=5B6916894075630395D&action_type_map=5B22og.likes225D&action_ref_map=5B5D

Linz, Juan. "The Perils of Presidentialism." *Journal of Democracy* 1, no. 1 (1990): 51–69.

Lipman, Masha. "Putin's 'Sovereign Democracy.'" *The Washington Post*, July 15, 2006, sec. Opinions. http://www.washingtonpost.com/wp-dyn/content/article/2006/07/14/AR2006071401534.html

Lynch, Timothy J. "George W. Bush." In *US Foreign Policy and Democracy Promotion: From Theodore Roosevelt to Barack Obama*, edited by Michael Cox, Timothy J. Lynch, and Nicolas Bouchet, 179–195. New York: Routledge, 2013.

Magen, Amichai, Thomas Risse, and Michael McFaul. *Promoting Democracy and the Rule of Law: American and European Strategies*. Basingstoke, UK: Palgrave Macmillan, 2009.

Mahony, Honor. "Orban Wants to Build 'Illiberal State.'" *EUobserver.com*, 2014. http://euobserver.com/political/125128

Melnykovska, Inna, Hedwig Plamper, and Rainer Schweickert. "Do Russia and China Promote Autocracy in Central Asia?" *Asia Europe Journal* 10, no. 1 (May 1, 2012): 75–89. doi:10.1007/s10308–012–0315–5

Migdalovitz, Carol. *Armenia Update*. CRS Report for Congress. Washington, DC: Foreign Affairs, Defense, and Trade Division, 2004. http://stuff.mit.edu/afs/sipb/contrib/wikileaks-crs/wikileaks-crs-reports/RS20812.pdf

Moldova.org. "Russia Likely to Ban Wines from Moldova on Wednesday." *Moldova.org*, 2013. http://economie.moldova.org/news/russia-likely-to-ban-wines-from-moldova-on-wednesday-238778-eng.html

Movsisian, Astghik Bedevian ?? Hovannes. "Russian-Armenian Gas Deal Ratified Amid Parliament Turmoil, Protests," 2013, sec. in English. http://www.azatutyun.am/content/article/25209730.html

Newsru. "Putin Is Unanimously Elected as Presidential Candidate at United Russia Session. [Na Sjezde Edinoi Rossii Putin Edinoglasno Vybran Kandidatom v Prezidenty]." *Newsru.com*, 2011. http://www.newsru.com/russia/27nov2011/edro.html#6

Nicola, Stefan. "Europe's Pipeline War." *UPI*, February 5, 2008. http://www.upi.com/Business_News/Energy-Resources/2008/02/05/Analysis-Europes-pipeline-war/UPI-24561202258576/

Niftiyev, Efgan. "Gazprom-SOCAR Gas Deal: Should Azerbaijan Commit to a Long-Term Contract?" *Today's Zaman*, 2010. http://www.todayszaman.com/newsDetail_getNewsById.action;jsessionid=AB83ECA7EBC13D25B15B3DB7F37252C5?newsId=207061

Nuland, Victoria. *A Pivotal Moment for the Eastern Partnership: Outlook for Ukraine, Moldova, Georgia, Belarus, Armenia, and Azerbaijan*. Testimony. Washington, DC: Subcommittee on European Affairs of the Senate Foreign Relations Committee, November 14, 2013a. http://www.state.gov/p/eur/rls/rm/2013/nov/217576.htm

Nuland, Victoria. "Toward a Transatlantic Renaissance: Ensuring Our Shared Future." Remarks|Remarks. *U.S. Department of State*, November 13, 2013b. http://www.state.gov/p/eur/rls/rm/2013/nov/217560.htm

Obydenkova, Anastassia, and Alexander Libman. "Understanding the Foreign Policy of Autocratic Actors: Ideology or Pragmatism? Russia and the Tymoshenko Trial as a Case Study." *Contemporary Politics* 20, no. 3 (May 14, 2014): 347–364. doi:10.1080/13569775.2014.911500

Orban, Viktor. "Prime Minister Viktor Orbán's Speech at the 25th Bálványos Summer Free University and Student Camp." *Government*, 2014. http://www.kormany.hu/en/the-prime-minister/the-prime-minister-s-speeches/prime-minister-viktor-orban-s-speech-at-the-25th-balvanyos-summer-free-university-and-student-camp

PanArmenian.Net. "NSC Chief: Customs Union Offers More Benefits than DCFTA." *PanARMENIAN.Net*, 2013. http://www.panarmenian.net/eng/news/169665/

Pavlikova, Olga. "Association with the EU Means Broadening of Gay-culture Sphere [Assotsiatsiya s ES oznachaet rasshirenie sfery gay-kulturi]." *Slon.ru*, 2013. http://slon.ru/russia/assotsiatsiya_s_es_oznachaet_rasshirenie_sfery_gey_kultury-1032020.xhtml

Przeworski, Adam, Michael E. Alvarez, Jose Antonio Cheibub, and Fernando Limongi. *Democracy and Development: Political Institutions and Well-Being in the World, 1950–1990*. Cambridge: Cambridge University Press, 2000.

Putin, Vladimir. "Russia Crossing the Millenia [Rossia Na Rubezhe Tisiacheletii]." *Nezavisimaya Gazeta*, 1999. http://www.ng.ru/politics/1999-12-30/4_millenium.html

Rettman, Andrew. "EU and Ukraine Suspend Trade Pact." *EUobserver.com*, 2014. http://euobserver.com/foreign/125601

Reuters. "UPDATE 1-Russia Bans Ukrainian Dairy Imports from Six Companies." *Reuters*, 2014. http://www.reuters.com/article/2014/04/07/russia-imports-idUSL6N0MZ1BI20140407

RFE/RL. "Rostelekom Intends to Invest USD 30 Mnl into Armenia's Broadband Network [Rostelekom Nameren Investirovat $30 Mln v Shirokopolosnii Internet v Armenii]." *Radio Free Europe/Radio Liberty*, 2012. http://rus.azatutyun.am/content/article/24802515.html

RFE/RL. "Yerevan Confident About Association Agreement With EU," 2013, sec. in English. http://www.azatutyun.am/content/article/25037930.html?utm_term=%23Armenia&utm_source=twitterfeed&utm_medium=twitter

RFE/RL. "Armenian Opposition Launches New Wave of Protests." *RadioFreeEurope/RadioLiberty*, September 28, 2014a, sec. Caucasus Report. http://www.rferl.org/content/caucasus-report-armenia-opposition-protests/26610291.html

RFE/RL. "Transdniester Deepens Ties With Russia." *RadioFreeEurope/RadioLiberty*, July 3, 2014b, sec. Moldova. http://www.rferl.org/content/transniester-deeperns-ties-with-russia/25444549.html

RIA News. "The U-Turn over the Atlantic [Razvorot Nad Atlantkoi]." *RIA News*, 2011. http://ria.ru/history_comments/20110321/356280998.html

Risse, Thomas, and Nelli Babayan. "Democracy Promotion and the Challenges of Illiberal Regional Powers: Introduction to the Special Issue." *Democratization* 22, no. 3 (2015): 381–399.

Rosenberg, Steve. "US Agency Expelled from Russia." *BBC*, September 19, 2012, sec. Europe. http://www.bbc.co.uk/news/world-europe-19644897

Rosenblum, Daniel. "Twenty Years of Democracy and Governance Programs in Europe and Eurasia." Remarks|Remarks. *U.S. Department of State*, December 12, 2011. http://www.state.gov/p/eur/rls/rm/2011/187475.htm

RT. "Washington Pushing Ukraine to Conflict – Lavrov." *RT*, 2014. http://rt.com/news/169076-lavrov-usa-ukraine-conflict/

Russett, Bruce. *Grasping the Democratic Peace: Principles for a Post-Cold War World*. Princeton, NJ: Princeton University Press, 1994.

Rutland, Peter. "Still Out in the Cold? Russia's Place in a Globalizing World." *Communist and Post-Communist Studies* 45, no. 3–4 (2012): 343–354.

Rywkin, Michael. *Moscow's Lost Empire*. 1st ed. Armonk, NY: M E Sharpe Inc, 1994.

Sakwa, Richard. "Looking for a Greater Europe: From Mutual Dependence to an International Regime." *Communist and Post-Communist Studies* 45, no. 3–4 (2012): 315–325.

Secrieru, Stanislav. "Russia's Foreign Policy Under Putin: 'CIS Project Renewed.'" *UNISCI Discussion Papers*, no. 10 (2006): 289–308.

Shevtsova, Lilia. "Russia under Putin: Titanic Looking for Its Iceberg?" *Communist and Post-Communist Studies* 45, no. 3–4 (2012): 209–16.

Socor, Vladimir. "Iran-Armenia Gas Pipeline: Far More than Meets the Eye." *Eurasia Daily Monitor*, March 21, 2007. http://www.jamestown.org/single/?no_cache=1&tx_ttnews[tt_news]=32607

Stepanyan, Ruzanna. "The Issue of Gas Price Subsidies Will Be Decide within the Customs Union Framework [Vopros Subsidirovania Tseni Na Gaz Budet Reshen v Ramkakh Tamozhennogo Soyuza]." *Radio Free Europe/Radio Liberty*, 2013. http://rus.azatutyun.am/content/article/25103117.html

Taylor, Adam. "Is China Looking to Vladimir Putin for Tips on Suppressing Hong Kong Protests?" *The Washington Post*, October 3, 2014. http://www.washingtonpost.com/blogs/worldviews/wp/2014/10/03/is-china-looking-to-vladimir-putin-for-tips-on-suppressing-hong-kong-protests/

Tolstrup, Jakob. "Studying a Negative External Actor: Russia's Management of Stability and Instability in the 'Near Abroad.'" *Democratization* 16 (October 2009): 922–944. doi:10.1080/13510340903162101

Trenin, Dmitri. "Drivers of Russia's Foreign Policy." In *Russia's "Pivot" to Eurasia*, edited by Kadri Liik, 36–42. London: ECFR, 2014. http://www.ecfr.eu/page/-/ECFR103_RUSSIA_COLLECTION_290514_AW

Tsygankov, Andrei. "If Not by Tanks, Then by Banks? The Role of Soft Power in Putin's Foreign Policy." *Europe-Asia Studies* 58, no. 7 (2006): 1079–1099.

US Embassy Cable. *Azerbaijan: President's Foreign Policy Advisor Discusses Regional Issues and Nabucco #09BAKU448*. Embassy Baku (Azerbaijan): Wikileaks, June 3, 2009a. http://www.cablegatesearch.net/cable.php?id=09BAKU448

US Embassy Cable. *Russian Analysts Tell A/s Gordon Anti-Americanism Pillar of Russian Foreign Policy #09MOSCOW2371*. Embassy Moscow (Russia): Wikileaks, September 16, 2009b. http://www.cablegatesearch.net/cable.php?id=09MOSCOW2371

US Treasury Department. "Belarus Sanctions." *U.S. Department of the Treasury*, 2014. http://www.treasury.gov/resource-center/sanctions/Programs/pages/belarus.aspx

Whitehead, Laurence. *The International Dimensions of Democratization: Europe and the Americas*. 2nd ed. Oxford: OUP Oxford, 2001.

Wilkinson, Cai, and Anthony J. Langlois. "Special Issue: Not Such an International Human Rights Norm? Local Resistance to Lesbian, Gay, Bisexual, and Transgender Rights—Preliminary Comments." *Journal of Human Rights* 13, no. 3 (July 3, 2014): 249–255. doi:10.1080/14754835.2014.931218

Zakaria, Fareed. "The Rise of Putinism." *The Washington Post*, July 31, 2014. http://www.washingtonpost.com/opinions/fareed-zakaria-the-rise-of-putinism/2014/07/31/2c9711d6–18e7–11e4–9e3b-7f2f110c6265_story.html

Zaynalov, Mahir. "Azerbaijan-Gazprom Agreement Puts Nabucco in Jeopardy." *Today's Zaman*, July 16, 2009. http://www.todayszaman.com/news-181072–105-azerbaijan-gazprom-agreement-puts-nabucco-in-jeopardy.html

Spoiler or facilitator of democratization?: Russia's role in Georgia and Ukraine

Laure Delcour[a] and Kataryna Wolczuk[b]

[a]*Scientific Directorate, Maison des Sciences de l'Homme (FMSH), Paris, France;* [b]*Centre for Russian, European and Eurasian Studies, University of Birmingham, Birmingham, UK*

In the post-Soviet space, Georgia and Ukraine are broadly perceived as exceptions to the growing authoritarianism in the region owing to the far-reaching political changes triggered by the so-called Colour Revolutions a decade ago. This article examines Russia's reaction to political changes in Georgia and Ukraine in light of the interplay between the democracy-promotion policies implemented by the EU and US and domestic patterns of democratization. We argue that despite the relatively weak impact of EU and US policies vis-à-vis domestic structures, Russia has responded harshly to (what it perceives as) a Western expansionist agenda in pursuit of reasserting its own hegemonic position in the post-Soviet space. However, coercive pressure from Russia has also unintended, counterproductive effects. We argue that the pressure has actually made Georgia and Ukraine more determined to pursue their pro-Western orientation and has spawned democratization, thereby supporting the objectives of the Western democracy promoters.

Introduction

Ukraine and Georgia are two countries that illustrate the effects of Western democracy promotion in the domestic contestation against a backdrop of a powerful illiberal actor. They shed a new light on the role of external actors in shaping political developments in target countries. The influence of both democracy promoters and illiberal regional powers ("democracy challengers") is interwoven because their respective actions interact with each other while contending with diverse and shifting domestic contexts. Our article examines the effects of Russia's counteracting strategies on democratization processes in Georgia and Ukraine, in light of the intricate set of relations between the democracy-promotion policies pursued by

© 2015 The Author(s). Published by Taylor & Francis.
This is an Open Access article distributed under the terms of the Creative Commons Attribution License (http://creativecommons.org/Licenses/by/4.0/), which permits unrestricted use, distribution, and reproduction in any medium, provided the original work is properly cited.

the European Union (EU) and the United States (US) and domestic receptivity to external influences. Thereby, we focus on one of the key themes of this special issue: how do the policies of non-democratic regional powers affect domestic outcomes and democracy promotion efforts by the US and EU in target countries?

While the collapse of the Soviet Union initially raised hopes for a sustainable democratic transition, political developments in the former Soviet Union since the late 1990s have dealt a death knell to the transition paradigm.[1] Even though pursuing different reform paths, most post-Soviet countries have entered a political grey zone between authoritarianism and democratization.[2] They have been depicted as "hybrid regimes" characterized by competitive authoritarianism, where "formal democratic institutions are viewed as a means of obtaining and exercising political authority", yet "where incumbents violation of those rules means, that the regime fails to meet conventional minimum standards for democracy".[3]

Georgia and Ukraine are relative exceptions due to the far-reaching political changes that started a decade ago as a result of the so-called Colour Revolutions (the Rose Revolution in 2003 in Georgia and the Orange Revolution in 2004 in Ukraine).[4] The new elites came to power on the grounds of opposing authoritarianism and embracing democracy. The 2003–2004 revolutions also illustrated the role of external actors in domestic political changes: the public protests were supported by Western foundations mostly funded by the United States Agency for International Development (USAID) and the EU member states.[5] The emergence of elites seemingly pursuing democratization appeared to strengthen the role of external democracy promoters there.

However, political changes also triggered adverse reactions from a powerful external player – Russia. The backlash, which followed the Colour Revolutions, occurred first and foremost within Russia itself, with the imposition of controls over non-governmental organizations (NGOs), the de facto exclusion of the opposition from political life, and the shift toward the "sovereign democracy" model, indicating the fears of contagion.[6] But, above all, the events in Ukraine and Georgia were interpreted in Moscow in terms of geopolitical contestation with the West. The Rose Revolution triggered Russian concern over a loss of influence in the post-Soviet space, while the Orange Revolution exacerbated Moscow's fury at the perceived subversive role of "Western agents". This fury then shaped Russia's perception of the Maidan protests of 2013–2014, which in contrast to the earlier mass revolts, turned violent and which Russia blamed on the West.

Therefore, we argue that despite the primacy of domestic factors accounting for democratization with EU and US democracy promotion playing a secondary role, Russia primarily responds to (what it perceives as) a Western expansionist agenda in the post-Soviet space. And it is actually Russia's reaction, rather than democracy promotion *per se*, that most strongly influences domestic developments in these countries. Paradoxically, it seems to have ushered political changes (even if limited and/or unsustainable) toward democratization and resulted in a concerted push away from Russia. At the same time, Russia's reaction has also stimulated the US and EU's responses in support of the countries in question, thereby strengthening their engagement in promoting domestic change. Our argument is that Russia's coercive actions have diminished its own influence in some post-Soviet states as a "democracy spoiler" and strengthened the role of democracy promoters.

In the first section, we provide an overview of EU and US democracy promotion policies and their (limited) effects in Georgia and Ukraine. We then proceed to scrutinize when and how Russia has responded to – what it perceived as – EU and US interference in domestic affairs. Finally, we examine the paradoxical outcomes of Russia's countervailing actions and specify the conditions under which they influence democratization processes in Georgia and Ukraine. In the concluding section, we offer broader generalizations emerging from the two case studies.

Democratization – an externally-driven or a home-made process?
EU and US policies in Ukraine and Georgia: whither democracy promotion?

While in recent years the EU and the US have converged in their democracy promotion policies, the EU has been less inclined to make democracy promotion central to its strategy. This is a consequence of the EU's new emphasis on "good governance",[7] especially since the launch of the Eastern Partnership (EaP) in 2009.

The EU's policy in Eastern neighbouring countries highlights a paradox in terms of democracy promotion. Since 2011 the EU has become more vocal about promoting "deep democracy".[8] Along with existing instruments such as the European Instrument for Democracy and Human Rights (EIDHR), it has introduced new tools for this purpose (for example, the European Endowment for Democracy). These complement the instruments created under the EaP's multilateral track in 2009 to support democracy, for example, the Civil Society Forum. Yet, since its launch in 2004, democracy promotion has not been the primary objective of the European Neighbourhood Policy (ENP);[9] security and stability are. In particular, the EaP has prioritized regulatory convergence with a view toward improving good governance in the Eastern neighbourhood. Upon the EaP, the EU adopted explicit conditionality based on benchmarks only with regard to specific sectors viewed as priority areas prior to opening negotiations on Deep and Comprehensive Free Trade Areas (DCFTAs), as well as negotiations related to visa liberalization. Some argue that functional cooperation reflects a shift in the EU's approach to democracy promotion, complementing the traditional "linkage" and "leverage" strategies.[10] This is because EU sectoral policies include strongly codified democratic governance provisions.[11] Thus, while the "democratic governance approach"[12] does not target core political institutions, it indirectly promotes democracy through embedding democratic principles (transparency, accountability, participation) in sectoral cooperation and thus diffuses them in partner countries' practices.

Closer scrutiny of EU conditions under key sectoral policies reveals that the EU has only occasionally fostered the "incorporation of democratic principles into administrative rules and practices" at the sectoral level.[13] Instead, the EU has sought to export those norms guaranteeing the quality and safety of products to be traded under DCFTAs as well as anti-monopoly regulation, intellectual property rights, and so on. Likewise, under the visa liberalization process it has prioritized security-related rules at the expenses of human rights-related provisions. Furthermore, when launching the EaP, the EU accepted the political *status quo* in the partner countries (with the exception of Belarus) without making explicit political changes a precondition for closer ties, despite concerns over, for example, Azerbaijan. Democracy promotion was thus decoupled from functional aspects of integration in the neighbourhood.[14]

In Georgia, the EU has been consistent in its approach in terms of democracy promotion, as evidenced in the Country Strategy Paper. Despite significant progress in democratization since the Rose Revolution, subsequent developments highlighted its fragility. In the EU's view, the domination of the executive branch of power has prevented Georgian democracy from consolidating. Therefore, the EU has included support for democratic development as a priority in its assistance documents.[15] It has mobilized a wide range of assistance mechanisms to promote democracy in Georgia and combined different types of support, for example, support for core political institutions (for example, the parliament) under the Rapid Reaction Mechanism and Technical Assistance for the Commonwealth of Independent States (TACIS), as well as support for grass-roots organizations under the EIDHR and the Non-State Actors Local Authorities Program.

At the same time, the EU has placed a greater emphasis on good governance and institution-building under the EaP's bilateral track. Starting in 2010, the Association Agreement together with a DCFTA emerged as an overarching priority in Georgia-EU relations.[16] While the Association Agreement includes references to democracy and values,[17] during the negotiations, the overarching focus has been on legal approximation with trade-related *acqui*s.

In Ukraine, continuity rather than change characterized the EU's approach to democracy promotion during 2005–2011, despite the persistent nature of the many problems facing Ukraine. The lack of political will and capacity of the Ukrainian authorities to initiate and sustain a comprehensive reform process meant that the initial reform momentum developed in the wake of the Orange Revolution was lost by 2009–2010. While articulating its assistance priorities under the EaP, the EU did not acknowledge this deterioration sufficiently and only belatedly reacted through democratic conditionality in 2011–2013.

In terms of assistance, a shift away from democracy promotion was evident. The assistance agenda for 2011–2013 did not mention democracy as a key reform priority and focussed on constitutional reform, the rule of law, combating corruption, and improving the business and investment climate. Overall, there was a shift toward good governance in more threat-oriented areas such as justice, freedom and security, "integrated border management", and disarmament.

The EU's assistance suffered from lax benchmarking and lacked explicit connection to democratic reforms. This indicated that Ukraine was perceived as a source of threat and instability, accounting for the EU's weakened role in democracy promotion in Ukraine until 2012.

Nevertheless, the EU still conducted extensive democracy-related activities in its bilateral assistance to both countries. The EU also outsourced democracy promotion to other organizations such as the Council of Europe.[18] Importantly, two Council of Europe bodies – the Parliamentary Assembly and the Venice Commission, which provide monitoring, expertise, and advice to the government on elections, rule of law, and judiciary[19] – act as prominent external "watchdogs" premised on Ukraine's and Georgia's membership commitments. In Ukraine, Europe has remained an important source of funding for civil society and the media, a powerful role-model, and a reference point for the pro-democratic forces.

Regarding the US, democracy assistance programmes designed in the 1990s had more modest goals than suspected by Russia (that is, regime change).[20] When the Rose Revolution happened, USAID programmes concentrated on free elections, functioning political institutions, and support to civil society. However, in the years following the revolution, US assistance shifted toward supporting the government and the new authorities' priorities.[21] This led to prioritizing support for pro-government NGOs and to the termination of USAID's biggest media programme in 2005.[22] Nevertheless, the current USAID strategy for Georgia emphasizes democratic development by enhancing the government's accountability, as well as checks and balances.[23] While promoting good governance, current USAID activities are more focussed on democracy than the EU, with support for free and fair elections, independence of the media sector, and the development of civil society.[24]

In the case of Ukraine, the US followed the pattern of the EU in terms of assuming the commitment to democracy and the rule of law after the Orange Revolution. So while in 2004–2005 US democracy assistance significantly increased, since 2006 the amount of USAID democracy assistance has dropped significantly. Also, US support to non-state actors decreased by 70% between 2004 and 2007, while assistance to the governmental sector increased.[25] Thus in 2013, in contrast to 2004, the US offered less support to civil society and the media and its role in regime change is less prominent than expected and claimed by Russia.

Nevertheless, Western support for Ukraine's media and civil society remained important because, with a few exceptions, there is no local funding for these actors. Independent media, especially new media, which played a crucial role on the Maidan, is a sector where donor support was perceived as most valuable.[26]

Overall, both in Georgia and Ukraine, the EaP marked the EU's prioritization of good governance and institution-building, in contrast to the US, which pursued a more traditional approach to democracy promotion, though less focussed on non-state actors. Despite considerable efforts and resources still committed to democracy promotion in the post-Soviet countries, since 2008 the US has been much less influential under Obama's administration due to broader changes in its foreign policy, interpreted in Georgia and Ukraine as a withdrawal from the post-Soviet space.[27]

Democratization in Georgia and Ukraine: limited impact of democracy promotion

Democracy promotion is only effective when there is a receptive domestic constituency. In this respect, Georgia and Ukraine demonstrate "the ability of external actors to deal with changing local context",[28] and adjust to specific domestic conditions in each country. Despite shared Soviet-era legacies and the experience of "electoral revolutions", Georgia and Ukraine have differed in terms of democratization agendas and actors, including veto players. Yet, both the US and EU have been relatively inattentive to the domestic dynamics, reacting hesitantly and belatedly to events, despite their proclaimed aims in the region.

In Georgia, both the EU and the US have (at least initially) assumed that the Rose Revolution would be an irreversible shift toward democratization. Yet, as captured in the literature,[29] while improving in terms of governance, the country failed to build representative institutions and to ensure the participation of civil society in the policy dialogue. The wide-ranging reform process which developed after the Rose Revolution actually concentrated power in the president's hands. External democracy promoters continued to support those individuals and organizations they had supported before 2004, thus failing to fully take domestic developments into account.[30] Under Saakashvili, the EU was more outspoken on democratic setbacks and placed a greater emphasis on the need for checks and balances than the US.[31] Despite shortcomings in the democratization process, the US has unconditionally supported the Georgian president for geopolitical purposes.[32] The bulk of US assistance to Georgia was focussed on economic and military support rather than democracy promotion.[33] However, even if belatedly, the current USAID country strategy for Georgia acknowledges both the shortcomings in the democratization process under Saakashvili and the politicized use of US assistance in Georgia.[34]

More recent domestic developments in Georgia highlight persisting dilemmas for external democracy promoters. In the October 2012 parliamentary elections, President Saakashvili's United National Movement lost to the Georgian Dream of Bidzina Ivanishvili. This was welcomed by both the EU and the US as the first democratic transfer of power in Georgia in free and fair elections. Both Brussels and Washington exerted strong pressure on the president and the new prime minister to ensure a smooth transition. However, the growing polarization of political life again exacerbated tensions in the run-up to the 2013 presidential elections. In addition, the imprisonment of key political figures of the Saakashvili period (including former Prime Minister Merabishvili), the arrest of the former mayor of Tbilisi Gigi Ugulava, and the filing of criminal charges against the former president raised Western actors' concerns about the use of the judiciary as a political tool. On several occasions, EU leaders warned Georgia against selective justice. However, the EU was mainly driven by the desire to turn the EaP into a success story prior to the Vilnius Summit in November 2013. Georgia is one of the three countries which signed the Association Agreement/DCFTA and, despite concerns over the political use of the judiciary, the new authorities have been performing quite well in terms of regulatory alignment with EU *acquis*. While they significantly built upon the progress made under Saakashvili, they have also moved away from the previous authorities' liberal agenda for deregulation, something that underpinned resistance to some EU regulations.[35] Hence, EU leaders (with the exception of members of the European Parliament and some EU member states) have refrained from overly criticizing domestic developments in Georgia.

In marked contrast, in Ukraine, the deteriorating political context under President Yanukovych (2010–2014) forced the EU, even if hesitantly, to resort to democratic conditionality in the process of concluding a new legal framework for relations. In late 2011, the EU adopted a bolder position and postponed signing the Association Agreement – the only tool at its disposal – to pressure the Ukrainian authorities to address the deterioration of democratic standards. The signing of the agreement was initially put on hold owing to political prosecutions of opposition figures, with the former prime minister, Yulia Tymoshenko, being the most prominent. Moreover, the conduct of the 2012 parliamentary elections as well as harassment of the political opposition and independent media during 2012–2013 led to objections in the EU to signing the agreement. However, the EU overestimated its power of persuasion vis-à-vis the non-democratic actors and misread the domestic context in Ukraine. For example, the preoccupation with the Tymoshenko case did not resonate widely with the Ukrainian public, since many saw her as a highly populist, opportunistic figure ready to sacrifice democratization in pursuit of political power.

The EU formulated a more comprehensive list of democratic conditions in December 2012, including adoption of anti-corruption measures and reforms of the electoral code and the judicial system, for signing the Association Agreement. Symptomatically, this list failed to galvanize the ruling elites, that is, President Yanukovych and the Party of Regions, into action. Making economic integration contingent on upholding democratic standards entailed significant political costs for the Ukrainian authorities. This is because meeting EU conditions affected the prospects of remaining in power for the ruling elites, which sought to consolidate their power by rendering ineffective any domestic challenge to their rule. Therefore, with explicit political conditionality, the pursuit of association with the EU carried direct political risks for President Yanukovych and the ruling Party of Regions in the context of preparations for the 2015 presidential elections. This was recognized with the EU and democratic conditions were made more flexible in the run up to the Vilnius Summit, as the EU became concerned over "losing" Ukraine and a "Vilnius failure".[36]

Overall, at the political level, there was a palpable sense of disillusionment and fatigue in the EU and the US with Ukraine already prior to and, especially, under

President Yanukovych. The initial (and perhaps naïve) hope was that Yanukovych would actually bring stability and improvement to the chaotic "orange" regime.[37] Both the US and the EU were fatigued by Ukraine.[38] Yet while the EU's highly technocratic approach with its focus on rule-based functional cooperation helped it retain credibility as a partner, it simultaneously created a distinct perception of the EU as a disinterested and detached democracy promoter. The US had a secondary role during Yanukovych's rule with little, if any, leverage over domestic developments.

Therefore, both external actors were hardly prepared to respond to the political crisis in Ukraine when it erupted in November 2013 as a result of Yanukovych's refusal to sign the Association Agreement. There is no evidence that the EU or the US were involved in any way in instigating the mass protests or providing any material or organizational support. During the protests, the EU limited itself to welcoming the expression of support for Ukraine's European orientation and calling for a peaceful resolution to the crisis, punctuated by periodic visits by officials from EU institutions and member states. While during the protests on the *Maidan* the EU appeared passive, the US was stronger on rhetoric (and outraged with EU passivity).

Overall, in Ukraine neither the US nor the EU played a strong role, whether during the 2013–2014 protests or prior to them. In Georgia, while the EU has been more vocal on the setbacks of the democratization process (whether under Saakashvili or after), neither the EU nor the US have used political conditionality to effectively pressure the incumbent authorities. This is not unusual, especially considering the Western responses to the Arab Spring. However, the EU's initial passivity and lack of strategy vis-à-vis the protests in Ukraine have weakened its standing as a committed democracy promoter. As such, the Ukrainian protesters expressed strong support for European values – democracy, human rights, and the rule of law – rather than the policies of the EU. The annexation of Crimea by Russia in March 2014 also elicited strong condemnation but tepid and much-delayed sanctions from the EU and US.[39] In Georgia, however, it was the credibility of the US which was most weakened in the wake of its passivity during the 2008 conflict with Russia.

Therefore, our overall contention is that neither the US nor the EU has pursued democracy promotion vigorously in Ukraine and Georgia. Democratization – even if patchy and reversible – can be attributed to domestic factors, especially societal mobilization against authoritarian leaders. However, its corollary has been a pro-Western orientation of the countries, something which in turn triggered a powerful backlash from Russia.

Russia's counteracting strategies in Georgia and Ukraine

For sustained democratization, there should be no major power in the region opposing democracy, as argued by Whitehead.[40] Russia is a vivid example of such a counteracting power in the post-Soviet space, hostile to democracy promotion by Western actors in the region. We argue that the key factor triggering Russia's reaction to Western policies is its perception of partner countries' degree of integration with Western organizations such as the EU and the North Atlantic Treaty Organization (NATO), that is, the institutionalization of the pro-Western orientation.

The introduction to this special issue highlights two conditions under which illiberal powers are likely to react to Western democracy promotion policies: the perception of a threat to their own regime survival and to their geostrategic interests. In the case of Russia, these two conditions are intertwined as, in historical terms, Russia is a successor state to empires (both the Tsarist empire and the USSR) in which the political regime and geopolitical expansion were closely linked. The literature has identified the fear of democratic contagion as instrumental in Russia's opposition to democratization in neighbouring countries.[41] Indeed, after each of three revolutions in Georgia and Ukraine, out of fear of contagion, Russian authorities strengthened their control over elections, limited the freedom of expression and assembly, and circumscribed the role of foreign countries in supporting civil society.

However, while the mechanisms and effects of Russia's actions have been extensively studied, less attention has been paid to the drivers behind them. We hypothesize that Russia is driven not so much by a sense of feeling threatened by democratization taking place in neighbouring countries *per se*, but rather the Western influence which it believes underlies it (and leading to a decrease in Russia's influence). This is despite the fact that, as argued above, democratization primarily occurred as a result of domestic factors rather than as a consequence of external democracy promotion. The elites who gained power in the wake of mass protests have also been strongly pro-Western. Therefore, besides being a threat to Russia's own regime stability, democratization in Ukraine and Georgia has been deemed to undermine Russia's hegemonic position in the post-Soviet space.

In essence, for Russia democracy-promotion policies are a smokescreen for expanding the Western sphere of influence in the post-Soviet space. Democracy promotion in the post-Soviet space is therefore seen by Russia as a geopolitical tool used by the West *in contestation with* Russia. Relations of neighbouring states with NATO have long been viewed with suspicion in Russia and so has increasingly the EU's EaP, much to the EU's surprise. This is because the Association Agreements run counter to Russia's plans for close economic reintegration of the post-Soviet countries though the Eurasian Economic Union, one of the key instruments for Russia's assertion of regional hegemony.[42]

Therefore, we hypothesize that the major driver behind Russia's responses is its objection to fostering closer ties between the post-Soviet states and the West. A corollary of this is that the more advanced, wide-ranging, and tangible integration is in institutional terms, the more threatening it will be perceived as by Russia, leading to stronger countervailing responses. The Russian government can more easily and rapidly utilize a broader array of instruments (economic, political, or military) than the West,[43] and demonstrated its readiness to do so, that is, to resort to hard power and coercion to achieve its aim of containing the Western influence.

In Georgia, relations with Russia significantly worsened immediately after the Rose Revolution. Russia actually viewed the political changes that led to the ousting of President Shevardnadze as a *coup d'état*. The pro-Western orientation of President Saakashvili only exacerbated Russia's irritation, triggering increasingly harsher reactions as Georgia got closer to NATO. Between 2004 and 2008 Russia scaled up pressure on Georgian authorities to hinder integration with Western structures. For example, to undermine Georgia's territorial integrity, Russian passports were offered (*pasportizatsiya*) to citizens of the two breakaway regions: Abkhazia and South Ossetia. In 2006, when relations between Georgia and Russia abruptly deteriorated, trade and migration flows were disrupted. Georgia was also subjected to Russian trade embargos, with Georgian wines, water, and vegetables being banned and transport connections between Moscow and Tbilisi being suspended. Following the autumn 2006 espionage controversy, Russian authorities strengthened administrative controls over Georgian migrants living in Russia and deported a significant number of Georgians. Ultimately, Russia intervened militarily a few months after the NATO Bucharest Summit agreed that Georgia would become a NATO member (even though no actual mechanism for realizing this prospect was outlined).

While Russia initially claimed it was using its prerogatives as a peacekeeper under the Dagomys agreement to intervene in South Ossetia, the fact that the Russian army went significantly beyond the breakaway regions and into Georgian territory indicated its stance on the prospect of NATO's accession.[44] The recognition of Abkhazia and South Ossetia's independence in August 2008 created a "point of no return" in Georgian-Russian relations. While trade flows and transport connections had already stopped since 2006, Russia's move put an end to the diplomatic relations between the two countries – while also triggering a break in Georgia's rapprochement with NATO. Therefore, since 2008 Russia has primarily tried to influence Georgia indirectly, for example, through supporting, including militarily, the breakaway regions.

Like in Georgia, Russia's role in Ukraine has been multi-faceted and highly adaptive to a rapidly changing context. First, the strategy centred on short-term cross-conditionality to undermine the attractiveness of the EU and responsiveness to EU's democratic conditionality. In doing so, Russia exploited the weaknesses of the EU strategy in the context of growing authoritarian tendencies and the resulting isolation of the Ukrainian authorities during Yanukovych's presidency. The EU's approach has been premised mostly on the long-term benefits of functional integration into the single market. However, this emphasis on long-term benefits required lengthening time horizons of the political class in the neighbouring countries. Enlargement created a favourable framework for lengthening time horizons of the political elites in the accession countries: the prospect of EU membership stretched the time framework for decision-making on ambitious, comprehensive, and costly reforms in East-Central Europe.[45] But the EU lacks similar leverage under the neighbourhood policy.

This dearth becomes especially significant in the context of Russia's role in the region: In late 2013, the economic crisis and high energy prices proved highly conducive to a shortening of time horizons for the Ukrainian ruling elites under Yanukovych. Faced with Russia's economic and political pressure combined with significant incentives, Yanukovych did not sign the Association Agreement during the Vilnius Summit in November 2013.[46] Shortly after, he accepted the Russian offer of a financial bailout of 15 billion dollars, in the context of a growing fiscal crisis in Ukraine and the forthcoming presidential elections of 2015. Providing economic support to authoritarian leaders who become increasingly isolated from the West is a noted Russian strategy.[47] By providing immediate, large-scale economic support to Yanukovych, vastly exceeding anything the Western institutions were willing to offer, Russia offered a lifeline to his increasingly authoritarian regime.

Following the regime change (as a result of violent clashes and Yanukovych's escape), Russia responded to the coming to power of pro-Western leaders in Ukraine with a punitive, hard-power reaction. In addition to economic and energy-related pressure, Russia has sought to undermine Ukrainian statehood. This was most dramatically evidenced in the annexation of Crimea in March 2014. Then, in the second phase, Russia's strategy centred on repeating a similar scenario in south-eastern Ukraine, a region with historical links to Russia (labelled "Novorossiya" even though the name has little resonance and hence low mobilizing potential in Ukraine itself).[48] But it only succeeded in Donbass, where Russia supported separatist forces, depicting them as part of a bottom-up local rebellion, denying any involvement. This "hybrid warfare" deliberately blurs the boundaries between state-controlled regular armed forces and the rogue local and mercenary forces. It is effective owing to the porous border between the Donbass region and Russia (the demarcation of the Ukrainian-Russian border has long been opposed by Russia), easy transportation routes, and ready volunteers within and from beyond Ukraine. This subterfuge has failed and the conflict transformed into a Ukrainian-Russian war.[49] This is because with a new impetus provided by the election of President Poroshenko in May 2014, the growing success of the Ukrainian armed forces against the separatists during the summer prompted Russia to provide more explicit support to the separatists, including weaponry and personnel.[50] At the same time, Russia's policy vis-à-vis Ukraine has been wrapped up in a historical narrative whereby Ukraine has been re-conceptualized as forming an "integral" part of Russia owing to linguistic, historical, cultural, and religious ties, thereby justifying Russia's aggressive actions against Ukraine's sovereignty.[51]

Our analysis indicates that the greater the perception of threat by Russia, the harsher its response has been. Russia tends not to explicitly counteract Western efforts at democracy promotion *per se* but, rather, at first, promotes and supports pro-Russian actors whenever possible inside the countries, and, failing that, moves to undermine the capacity of the "target countries" to pursue integration with the West. However, in Georgia and Ukraine, Russia's role as a spoiler comes at different times in terms of both domestic political changes and the integration with Western structures. The differences in timing result in diverse consequences for democratization and also trigger diverse reactions from the West.

The effects of Russia's response: spoiling or unintentionally favouring democratization?

In this section we examine the outcomes of Russia's counteracting policies and specify the conditions under which they influence democratization processes in Georgia and Ukraine. In doing so we confirm the assumptions presented in the introduction to this special issue, yet also bring important nuances. The introduction posits that the outcome of external actors' policies depends upon their influence on the domestic balance of power between liberal and illiberal elites and citizens, which is in turn conditioned by economic and security linkages and by the leverage which the external actors have over domestic forces.

In both countries, by posing a major security threat and promoting challenges to territorial integrity, Russia could be seen as just taking attention away from domestic reforms, including democratization. Yet, having failed to sway the countries by peaceful means, Russia has challenged their statehood in order to jeopardize the linked processes of democratization and integration with the Western organizations. This is because the territorial integrity of the state, control over means of coercion, and secure/stable borders are essential prerequisites to democratization. Tolstrup has shown how Russia is able to affect the neighbouring countries' "effective power to rule", by using economic leverages or supporting secessionist entities.[52] Yet, by showing how Russian attempts at destabilizing partner countries subvert their democratization, the literature focuses exclusively on Russia's role as a negative (and effective) actor. By emphasizing the spoiling effects, the literature omits the positive (though unintended) effect of Russia's actions on strengthening democracy in the "contested neighbourhood".

We argue that such effects occur because Russia's initiatives to undermine both countries' statehood actually weaken linkages and reduce the regional power's leverage over domestic elites and societies.[53] In fact, Russia's actions have united the national elites and population (outside the "breakaway" regions) around sovereignty, democracy, and integration with the West.

In the case of Georgia, for example, there was little Russia could do in 2009– 2012 to hinder Georgia's progress toward EU integration, since breakaway regions were de facto occupied and Georgia had diversified its trade flows as a result of the Russian 2006 embargo. Following the 2012 elections in Georgia, the new authorities have sought to normalize ties between the two countries and have adopted a less confrontational stance vis-à-vis Moscow.[54] This new approach provided Russia with renewed leverage over the country.

On the one hand, Russia has continued to exploit breakaway regions as its main instrument of pressure, for example, through promoting "borderization" (that is, the construction of barricades along the administrative borderline of South Ossetia and actually expanding the territory of the breakaway region) and strongly influencing the selection of leaders there (for example, the ousting of the Abkhaz de facto President Aleksandr Ankvab, who resisted Russian pressure on several occasions and adopted a softer stance vis-à-vis the

Georgian population in Abkhazia).[55] Russia's proposed "alliance and integration" treaty to Abkhazia, however, goes beyond the destabilization tactics which had been used since 2008 and envisages a merger of military forces, coordination of police, and an alignment with the Russia-led Eurasian Economic Union.[56] It is perhaps unsurprising that the proposal was tabled in a context of enhanced contacts between Georgia and NATO.

On the other hand, the re-opening of trade flows, in particular, has triggered new expectations in Georgia vis-à-vis the Russian market. While this has resulted in increased trade flows between the two, this increases the number of trade instruments, including embargos that Russia can utilize. It is perhaps unsurprising that the trade leverage was soon used again after the EU-Georgia Association Agreement was signed, when Russia drafted a decree suspending the Russian-Georgian Free Trade Agreement signed in February 1994.[57]

Yet, Russia's behaviour has so far yielded opposite effects from those intended in both cases. By threatening the sovereignty and existence of Georgia and Ukraine, Russia's policies induced both countries to make substantial efforts in terms of democratization, in compliance with US and especially EU recommendations and requirements.

Despite polarization in Georgian domestic politics, a broad consensus on integration with Western structures has so far persisted. There are very few actors that Russia can mobilize to divert the country's geopolitical orientation away from the EU and NATO. For instance, only two small political parties oppose EU integration while advocating closer links with Russia.[58] True, the Georgian Orthodox Church strongly opposes some of the measures (for example, anti-discrimination legislation) demanded by the EU as part of the visa liberalization process – it is not however challenging integration. However, even if prompted by the sharply deteriorating political climate inside the ruling coalition rather than inspired by Russia, the dismissal and resignation of key ministers in charge of defence, foreign affairs, and Euro-Atlantic integration in November 2014 may affect the country's actual integration with both the EU and NATO.

In Ukraine, Russia succeeded in exerting pressure on illiberal elites by dissuading President Yanukovych from signing the Association Agreement. Yet mass protests ensued. Even though very few protestors were actually familiar with the content of the Association Agreement, for them Europe symbolized democracy, human rights, and the rule of law – precisely the principles sorely lacking in Ukraine under Yanukovych.[59] For the protesters, moving closer to Russia offered more of the same: deteriorating democratic standards and governance, suppression of the opposition, media, civil society, and corruption. While Russia would work effectively with the "pliant", self-interested, and short-thinking elites, it had no similar purchase over the public, as indicated by a Maidan slogan "we won't sell our freedom for gas".

Inadvertently, Russia's policies have actually facilitated compliance with EU demands. By propping up authoritarian leaders in Ukraine and then engaging in a military conflict in Ukraine and Georgia, Russia has given a powerful push to the pro-Western orientation not only at the elite but also societal levels. As former president of Poland, Aleksander Kwasniewski, who acted as an emissary of the European Parliament to Ukraine during 2012–2013, put it in July 2014:

> [Putin] can fail because of societal attitudes. There never has been such a high level of anti-Russian feelings in Ukraine. It could turn out that even when faced with an economic catastrophy, the Ukrainian people will proclaim that our dignity and soveregnty are more important than pacts with Putin. Russia still believes that destabilisation, pressure, propaganda and money will turn Ukraine back to Moscow.[60]

Nevertheless, it can also be hypothesized that by undermining both countries' statehood and territorial integrity, Russia has also made democratization more difficult. Since the shift of power at the end of 2012, Russia has indirectly fuelled the growing polarization of political life in Georgia.[61] Despite a broad consensus on the prioritization of Euro-Atlantic integration, Russia has emerged as a divisive issue in the domestic political debate. The then Prime Minister Ivanishvili has repeatedly criticized the former authorities on their strategy vis-à-vis Russia and, conversely, the normalization sought with Moscow has been fiercely opposed by the former president's allies. Since 2012, the policy shift toward Russia has remained rhetorical rather than substantive, yet Russia's growing presence in the political discourse has contributed to increasing tensions between the authorities and the opposition (as shown, for instance, by the reactions to Ivanishvili's statement on the need for Georgia to consider the Eurasian option).[62] The break-up of the Georgian Dream coalition in November 2014 does not only add political instability to the sharply polarized political climate. It also makes Euro-Atlantic integration more complex (especially the implementation of the Association Agreement and DCFTA) and offers new opportunities for Russia to manipulate domestic politics.

The emergence of Russia as a direct security threat to Ukraine since 2014 has served to consolidate Ukraine's pro-Western orientation, underpinned by a strong commitment to democracy amongst civil society and the political elites that came to power in 2014. Russia's undeclared war against Ukraine diminished the influence it was able to exert through language, culture, and religion, even in Russian-speaking south-eastern Ukraine. However, Ukraine's ability to pursue wide-ranging democratization, including institution-building, has so far been severely circumscribed by the crippling conflict in eastern Ukraine and a prioritization of security issues amidst a deep economic crisis. Contrary to Russia's discourse, the country is not a "failed state": if anything, the conflict in Donbass has galvanized society and state structures (which became notoriously weak) in the face of unprecedented external threats providing the push for reforms. However, a sense of insecurity and vulnerability also fuels frustration and impatience with formal political processes and carries the risk of growing populism and radicalization.

In sum, Russia has endeavoured to destabilize Ukraine and Georgia by jeopardizing their territorial integrity. Yet, by undermining their statehood, Russian actions has consolidated the political and foreign policy courses in both countries.

So far this is clearly the most direct and unintended effect of Russia's policies. At the same time, by supporting breakaway regions, Russia has also undermined Ukraine's and Georgia's "effective power to rule",[63] thereby indirectly affecting their capacity to conduct reforms, including democratization.

Conclusions

In both Georgia and Ukraine political developments have been far from linear, illustrating the complex political trajectories of even the most pro-Western countries in the post-Soviet space. The push for democracy came from domestic actors: the Rose Revolution, the Orange Revolution, and the Maidan were not so much the result of the efforts of the EU and US, but rather combined bottom-up and intra-elites' pressures to oust the incumbent regimes. Yet, oblivious to domestic demands for democracy, Russia regards these domestic changes as resulting from "Western interventions" which aimed to promote pro-Western geopolitical realignment in the post-Soviet space. In response to such a perceived Western "plot", Russia felt compelled to simultaneously "punish" the countries and prevent their integration with the West.

For the West, almost six years after the conflict in Georgia, the annexation of Crimea and the hybrid war in eastern Ukraine turned out to be a rude awakening regarding Russia's ends and means. The EU and the US neglected Russian sensitivities and interpretations of their motives and actions, let alone the multiple dependencies that Russia could exploit vis-à-vis the target countries. Thus, the EU and US failed to grasp Russia's sheer determination to prevent a pro-Western orientation of the neighbouring countries and they have not been able (and willing) to promptly respond with adequate countermeasures to shore up democracy and sovereignty of those countries.

However, (so far) Russia has not prevailed: the influence of the EU and US has arguably increased as a result of Russia's actions. Russia's biggest strengths – economic pressure and military might – have been utilized in a way counterproductive to Russia's proclaimed interests. Instead of bringing Ukraine and Georgia back in to the fold, the use of force made them ever more mindful of the threat presented by Russia and, as a result, ever more determined to integrate with Western structures. Thus, the biggest paradox from the Russian perspective is that its policies have inadvertently imbued the EU and the US with disproportionate levels of influence.

Four broader conclusions can be drawn.

The first one relates to the drivers behind illiberal powers' actions and confirms one of the assumptions presented in the introduction to this special issue: geopolitical interests (rather than fear of democratic contagion) drive illiberal power's objections to any developments that are perceived as weakening its leverage over the "target countries". Our article points to the correlation between, on the one hand, Georgia and Ukraine's increased linkages and integration with Western structures, and, on the other hand, Russia's countervailing responses.

Second, as noted in the introduction, the West's agenda of democracy promotion does not correspond to actual policies toward individual countries. Nevertheless, even when democracy promotion is weak and/or ineffective, illiberal powers can blame Western democracy promotion for democratic changes in target countries. This means that democratic breakthroughs that occur in countries targeted by democracy promotion (even when they do not necessarily result from democracy promotion as such) can be interpreted by illiberal powers as "meddling" and "intervention" and trigger reaction from illiberal powers to counteract geopolitical implications of such "interventions".

The third conclusion focuses on the mechanisms used by illiberal powers to counter democracy promotion. As suggested in the introduction to this special issue, illiberal powers countervail democracy promotion through empowering illiberal groups in neighbouring countries. Supporting authoritarian incumbent elites through political, economic, and security means is indeed the simplest and most effective way to secure loyalty. However, when the authoritarian elites are replaced by pro-Western leaders, as has been the case in Georgia and Ukraine, illiberal powers can no longer rely upon non-democratic domestic players inside the countries. Yet, with few domestic constraints, illiberal powers are free to activate a broad array of tools, ranging from political and economic ones to coercion and force, and are able to deploy them at will. This readiness has been an unwelcome surprise for democracy promoters.

Finally, the effects of the actions by illiberal powers on domestic democratization deserve closer scrutiny. By undermining their statehood and violating their territorial integrity, illiberal powers inadvertently push the target countries toward the West, increasing the influence of democracy promoters and thereby strengthening the prospects for democratization. However, at the time of writing, this democratization outcome is not certain, especially with regard to Ukraine. Russia's actions are likely to provide further evidence not only on the extent to which illiberal powers can affect the capacity to conduct reforms, including democratization in the target countries, but also how far democracy promoters are willing to shore up democratization when faced with a belligerent illiberal power.

Acknowledgements

We would like to thank the two anonymous reviewers and the editors of the special issue and *Democratization* for their editorial guidance.

Funding

The preparation of this manuscript was facilitated by a collaborative research project conducted by the co-authors and entitled "Exploring the Role of the EU in Domestic Change in the Post-Soviet States" jointly funded by the ESRC (UK) and the ANR (France) research grant (RES-360-25-0096, ANR-10-ORAR-014-01). See http://euimpacteast.org.

DEMOCRACY PROMOTION AND THE CHALLENGES

Notes

1. Carothers, "The End of the Transition Paradigm."
2. Ibid., 9.
3. Way and Levitsky, "The Rise of Competitive Authoritarianism," 52.
4. The Colour Revolutions are also called "electoral revolutions." See Bunce and Wolchik, "Favorable Conditions." In both countries they are intrinsically associated with democratization for two reasons. First, free and fair elections were a core demand of protesters in Tbilisi and Kyiv, where movements developed in the wake of elections (parliamentary in Georgia, presidential in Ukraine) marred by electoral fraud. Second, in both countries the protests resulted in a change of power that spurred democratic reforms.
5. Muskhelishvili and Jorjoliani, "Georgia's Ongoing Struggle"; Stewart, "The Interplay of Domestic Contexts and External Democracy Promotion."
6. Ambrosio, *Authoritarian Backlash*; Horvath, "Putin's 'Preventive Counter-Revolution'"; Carothers, "The Backlash against Democracy Promotion."
7. Good governance is more concerned with the effectiveness of government than its legitimacy. Stewart, "The Interplay of Domestic Contexts and External Democracy Promotion."
8. According to the EU's High Representative, together with free election, "deep democracy" includes: respect for the rule of law and human rights, freedom of speech, an independent judiciary, and impartial administration. Speech on main aspects and basic choices of the Common Foreign and Security Policy and Common Security and Defence Policy, Strasbourg, 11 May 2011. http://europa.eu/rapid/press-release_SPEECH-11-326_en.htm
9. Ghazaryan, *The European Neighbourhood Policy*.
10. Lavenex and Schimmelfennig, "EU Democracy Promotion," 887.
11. Freyburg et al., "Democracy Promotion."
12. Lavenex and Schimmelfennig, "EU Democracy Promotion."
13. Freyburg et al., "Democracy Promotion."
14. Ghazaryan, *The European Neighbourhood Policy*.
15. European Commission, ENPI Country Strategy Paper for Georgia, 2007–2013, Brussels, 2006; ENPI National Indicative Programme for Georgia, 2011–2013, Brussels, 2010.
16. This required strengthening key institutions, primarily those involved in the negotiation and the implementation of the future agreement, for example, the Office of the State Ministry for Euro-Atlantic Integration.
17. The Preamble refers to the "common values on which the European Union is built – democracy, respect for human rights and fundamental freedoms, and the rule of law," and indicates that these values are shared by Georgia. EU-Georgia Association Agreement, http://eeas.europa.eu/georgia/assoagreement/pdf/ge-aa-preamble_en.pdf.
18. Some EU democracy funds are implemented through an EU–Council of Europe (CoE) Joint Programme financed up to 90% by the EU. For example, the CoE run joint projects on media, judiciary, women's and children's rights, and anti-corruption.
19. Shapovalova, "Assessing Democracy Assistance: Ukraine."
20. Mitchell, *Uncertain Democracy*, 1.
21. Ibid., 129.
22. Lazarus, "Neoliberal State Building," 19.
23. USAID, *Country Development Strategy, Georgia*.
24. USAID, "Democracy, Human Rights and Good Governance," http://www.usaid.gov/georgia/democracy-human-rights-and-governance.
25. Shapovalova, "Assessing Democracy Assistance: Ukraine."
26. Ibid.; and Stewart, "Power Relations."

27. Wilson, *Ukraine Crisis*, 9.
28. Stewart, "The Interplay of Domestic Contexts and External Democracy Promotion," 804.
29. Muskhelishvili and Jorjoliani, "Georgia's Ongoing Struggle"; Siroky and Aprasidze, "Guns, Roses and Democratization."
30. Stewart, "Democracy Promotion," 650.
31. The EU provided support to those institutions which may counterbalance the executive branch of power, for example, the parliament and the judiciary.
32. Mitchell, "Democracy in Georgia."
33. See Sasse, "Linkages and the Promotion of Democracy," 589.
34. USAID, *Country Development Strategy, Georgia*, 8–9.
35. Delcour, "Meandering Europeanisation."
36. Interviews with EU officials, Kyiv, September 2013 and June 2014.
37. Authors' interviews with EU officials in Brussels and Kyiv, December 2009 and January 2011.
38. Delcour and Wolczuk, "Eurasian Economic Integration."
39. MacShane, "Eurosphere has lost Ukraine."
40. Whitehead, *The International Dimensions of Democratization*.
41. Ambrosio, *Authoritarian Backlash*; Horvath, "Putin's 'Preventive Counter-Revolution'"; Carothers, "The Backlash against Democracy Promotion."
42. Dragneva and Wolczuk, *Eurasian Economic Integration*.
43. Tolstrup, "Negative External Actor," 929.
44. Cornell and Starr, *The Guns of August 2008*.
45. Jacoby, "Inspiration, Coalition, and Substitution," 623.
46. In the summer of 2013, Russia started the so-called "trade war" by imposing an embargo on Ukrainian goods and lengthy customs checks in order to persuade Ukraine to join the Customs Union and dissuade Ukraine from concluding the Association Agreement.
47. Ambrosio, *Authoritarian Backlash*.
48. Hava, "IstoriaNovorossiyi ta EtnichnohoSkladu XIX Stolittia." See also Halyshko, "Malorossiya: KrainaYaka Ne Vidbulasia."
49. Wilk and Konończuk, "Ukrainian-Russian War."
50. Wolczuk, "How-Far-Were-Russias-Little-Green-Men-Involved."
51. Menkiszak, "The Putin Doctrine."
52. Tolstrup, "Negative External Actor," 936.
53. Levitsky and Way, "Linkage versus Leverage."
54. Gordadze, "Georgia."
55. Ibid.
56. "Russia to Pocket Abkhazia?," http://www.eurasianet.org/node/7048, 16 October 2014.
57. RFE/RL, "Russia Hits Back At Georgia Over Trade Agreement With European Union," 2 August 2014.
58. Kapanadze, "Georgia's Vulnerability."
59. Wilson, *Ukraine Crisis*, Chapter 3.
60. "Interview with Aleksander Kwaśniewski: jest ryzyko wygranej Kaczyńskiego," *Gazeta Wyborcza*, 6 August 2014.
61. Muskhelishvili and Jorjoliani, "Georgia's Ongoing Struggle"; Siroky and Aprasidze, "Guns, Roses and Democratization."
62. Rettman, "Georgia PM says 'Why Not?' on Eurasian Union."
63. Tolstrup, "Negative External Actor," 932.

Notes on contributors

Laure Delcour is Senior Research Fellow and Scientific Coordinator of the EU-FP7 Project CASCADE "The Democracy-Security Nexus in the Caucasus", at la Maison des Sciences de l'Homme (FMSH), Paris. She holds a BA in History (Paris IV-Sorbonne), an MA in Political Science and a PhD from Sciences-Po Paris. Her publications include: *Shaping the Post-Soviet Space? EU Policies and Approaches to Region-Building* (Farnham: Ashgate, 2011).

Kataryna Wolczuk is Reader in Politics and International Studies, Centre for Russian, European and Eurasian Studies, University of Birmingham in the United Kingdom. She holds an MA in Law from the University of Gdansk, Poland and an MSocSc and a PhD from the University of Birmingham. Her publications include: R. Dragneva and K. Wolczuk (eds), *Eurasian Economic Integration: Law, Policy, and Politics* (Cheltenham: Edward Elgar, 2013).

Bibliography

Ambrosio, Thomas. *Authoritarian Backlash: Russian Resistance to Democratization in the Former Soviet Union*. Farnham: Ashgate, 2009.

Bunce, Valerie, and Sharon L. Wolchik. "Favorable Conditions and Electoral Revolutions." *Journal of Democracy* 17, no. 4 (2006): 5–18.

Carothers, Thomas. "The End of the Transition Paradigm". *Journal of Democracy* 13, no. 1 (2002): 5–21.

Carothers, Thomas. "The Backlash against Democracy Promotion." *Foreign Affairs*, 85 no. 2 (2006): 55–68.

Cornell, Svante, and Frederick Starr. *The Guns of August 2008. Russia's War in Georgia*. New York: M.E. Sharpe, 2009.

Delcour, Laure. "Meandering Europeanisation. EU Policy Instruments and Patterns of Convergence in Georgia under the Eastern Partnership." *East European Politics* 29, no. 3 (2013): 344–357.

Delcour, Laure, and Kataryna Wolczuk. "Eurasian Economic Integration and Implications for the EU's Policy in the Eastern Neighbourhood." In *Eurasian Economic Integration: Law, Policy, and Politics*, edited by Rilka Dragneva, and Kataryna Wolczuk, 179–203. Cheltenham: Edward Elgar, 2013.

Dragneva, Rilka, and Kataryna Wolczuk (eds). *Eurasian Economic Integration: Law, Policy, and Politics*. Cheltenham: Edward Elgar, 2013.

Freyburg, Tina, Sandra Lavenex, Frank Schimmelfennig, Tatiana Skripka, and Anne Wetzel. "Democracy Promotion through Functional Cooperation? The Case of the European Neighbourhood Policy." *Democratization* 18, no. 4 (2009): 1026–1054.

Ghazaryan, Nariné. *The European Neighbourhood Policy and the Democratic Values of the EU*. Oxford and Portland: Hart Publishing, 2014.

Gordadze, Thornike. "Georgia." *Geopolitics of Eurasian Integration*. Special Report SR019. London: London School of Economics, 2014: 54–59.

Halyshko, Kyryl. "Malorosiya: Kraina Yaka Ne Vidbulasia." *Ukrainska Pravda*, 10 December 2012.

Hava, Oleh. "Istoria Novorosiyi ta Etnichnoho Skladu XIX Stolittia." *Ukrainska Pravda*, 7 May 2014.

Horvath, Robert. "Putin's 'Preventive Counter-Revolution': Post-Soviet Authoritarianism and the Spectre of Velvet Revolution." *Europe-Asia Studies,* 63, no. 1 (2011): 1–25.

Jacoby, Wade. "Inspiration, Coalition, and Substitution. External Influences on Postcommunist Transformations." *World Politics* 58, no. 4 (2006): 623–651.

Kapanadze, Sergi. "Georgia's Vulnerability to Russia's Pressure Points." *ECFR Policy Memo* (2014): 43–58.

Lavenex, Sandra, and Frank Schimmelfennig. "EU Democracy Promotion in the Neighbourhood: From Leverage to Governance?" *Democratization* 18, no. 4 (2011): 885–909.

Lazarus, Joel. "Neoliberal State-Building and Western 'Democracy Promotion': The Case of Georgia." Paper presented at the 7th Pan European Conference on International Relations, 2010.

Levitsky, Steven, and Lucan A. Way. "Linkage versus Leverage. Rethinking the International Dimension of Regime Change." *Comparative Politics* 38, no. 4 (July 1, 2006): 379–400.

MacShane, Denis. "Eurosphere Has Lost Ukraine." *Kyiv Post*, 10 May 2014.

Menkiszak, Marek. "The Putin Doctrine: The Formation of a Conceptual Framework for Russian Dominance in the Post-Soviet Area." *Commentary* No. 131, Centre for Eastern Studies, 28 March 2014.

Mitchell, Lincoln. "Democracy in Georgia since the Rose Revolution." *Orbis* 50, no. 4 (2006): 669–676.

Mitchell, Lincoln. *Uncertain Democracy. US Foreign Policy and Georgia's Rose Revolution*. Philadelphia: University of Pennsylvania Press, 2008.

Muskhelishvili, Marina, Jorjoliani, Gia. "Georgia's Ongoing Struggle for a Better Future Continued: Democracy Promotion through Civil Society Development." *Democratization* 16, no. 4 (2009): 682–708.

Rettman, Andrew. "Georgia PM says 'Why Not?' on Eurasian Union." *EUObserver*, 4 September, 2013. https://euobserver.com/foreign/121315

Sasse, Gwendolyn. "Linkages and the Promotion of Democracy: The EU's Eastern Neighbourhood." *Democratization* 20, no. 4 (2013): 553–591.

Shapovalova, Natalia. "Assessing Democracy Assistance: Ukraine." *Project Report: Assessing Democracy Assistance*. FRIDE, May 2010.

Siroky, David S., and David Aprasidze. "Guns, Roses and Democratization: Huntington's Secret Admirer in the Caucasus." *Democratization* 18, no. 6 (2011): 1227–1245.

Stewart, Susan. "Democracy Promotion before and after the 'Colour Revolutions.'" *Democratization* 16, no. 4 (2009a): 645–660.

Stewart, Susan. "The Interplay of Domestic Contexts and External Democracy Promotion: Lessons from Eastern Europe and the South Caucasus." *Democratization* 16, no. 4 (2009b): 804–824.

Stewart, Susan. "Power Relations Meet Domestic Structures: Russia and Ukraine." In *The Substance of EU Democracy Promotion Concepts and Cases*, edited by Anne Wetzel and Jan Orbie. London: Palgrave Macmillan, 2015.

Tolstrup, Jakob. "Studying a Negative External Actor: Russia's Management of Stability and Instability in the 'Near Abroad.'" *Democratization* 16 (October 2009): 922–944.

USAID. *Country Development Strategy, Georgia. Fiscal Years 2013–2017* (2012).

Way, Steven, and Levitsky Lucan. "The Rise of Competitive Authoritarianism." *Journal of Democracy* 13, no. 2 (2002): 52–65.

Whitehead, Laurence. *The International Dimensions of Democratization: Europe and the Americas*. 2nd ed. Oxford: Oxford University Press, 2001.

Wilk, Andrzej, and Wojciech Konończuk. "Ukrainian-Russian War under the Banner of Anti-terrorist Operation." *Analyses*, Centre for Eastern Studies, 6 August 2014.

Wilson, Andrew. *Ukraine Crisis. What It Means for the West*. New Haven and London: Yale University Press, 2014.

Wolczuk, Kataryna. "How-Far-Were-Russia's-Little-Green-Men-Involved-in-the-Downing-Of-Malaysia-Airlines-Flight-Mh17." *The Conversation* (2014).

Undermining the transatlantic democracy agenda? The Arab Spring and Saudi Arabia's counteracting democracy strategy

Oz Hassan

Politics and International Studies, The University of Warwick, Coventry, UK

Saudi Arabian foreign policy is often declared to be countering the possible democratic transitions of the Arab Spring. As such, Saudi Arabia has been cast as a "counter-revolutionary" force in the Middle East and North Africa. This article explores the extent to which this has been the case in Egypt and Bahrain, and the extent to which Saudi foreign policy has challenged United States and European Union democracy promotion efforts in those countries. The article highlights how the transatlantic democracy promotion strategy is complicated by a conflict of interests problem, which leads them to promote democracy on an ad hoc and incremental basis. As a result, their efforts and larger strategic thinking are undermined by Saudi Arabia in Egypt. However, in Bahrain, transatlantic democracy promotion is itself muted by the strategic interest in containing Iran. As a result, Saudi Arabia can be seen as a regional countervailing power but this is implicitly in line with transatlantic policy. Tensions with Saudi foreign policy in Bahrain are over how best to manage the uprisings and maintain the status quo, rather than a conflict over political transition.

The United States (US) and the European Union (EU) have been slow and uncertain in their reactions to the political unrest in the Middle East and North Africa (MENA). Indeed, there has been a great deal of strategic confusion from the transatlantic partners, as events have outpaced policymakers' ability to produce cohesive strategies. Compounding this is the complexity of national interests that both the US and the EU have in the region. Whilst democracy promotion has been seen as a pragmatic national interest, which was most prominently expressed

---

© 2015 The Author(s). Published by Taylor & Francis.
This is an Open Access article distributed under the terms of the Creative Commons Attribution-NonCommercial-NoDerivatives License (http://creativecommons.org/Licenses/by-nc-nd/4.0/), which permits non-commercial re-use, distribution, and reproduction in any medium, provided the original work is properly cited, and is not altered, transformed, or built upon in any way.

after 11 September 2001, both transatlantic partners have a "conflict of interests" problem.[1] In addition to promoting democracy, the US and EU, to greater and lesser extents, also seek to secure the free flow of energy into the global market, the movement of military and commercial traffic through the Suez Canal, to secure business contracts throughout the region, cooperation on immigration, military, counter-terrorism, and counter-proliferation policies, the security of regional allies such as Israel, and to contain hostile regimes such as Iran. This is a wide array of national security interests, of which democracy promotion is only one amongst many, and which often conflicts with these other more near-term interests and a desire for regional stability.[2] Democracy promotion policies ask governments to relinquish power across state institutions and to their citizenry, whilst these other security interests often entail the cooperation of regional governments. This is the paradox at the centre of US and EU relations with the MENA, which has been exacerbated by political unrest, rather than reduced.

With the conflict of interests problem being at the heart of many US and EU bilateral relations with countries across the MENA, it is unsurprising that the tone and texture of those relations differ. However, nowhere in the MENA region is this conflict of interest problem more pronounced and one-sided towards near-term interests than in transatlantic relations with the Gulf, and in particular with the regional hegemon Saudi Arabia. This dimension of transatlantic relations has been well-documented, and clearly shapes Western powers' bilateral relationships with the Kingdom. Yet, in the context of the unfolding political unrest in the region, questions need to be asked regarding how the transatlantic–Saudi Arabian security nexus is affecting wider regional relationships as Saudi Arabia has become more assertive? On shallow first appearances this nexus would appear to be under strain. Official US and EU narratives profess a desire for democracy and human rights to take hold in the MENA, whilst Saudi Arabia has developed a reputation for "pushing back" against political transitions with the adoption of countervailing strategies throughout the region.[3] This simplistic impression is, however, deeply problematic and fails to appreciate the complexities and nuances on both sides. What this article reveals is that, in spite of the tremendous political upheaval across the region, the US and EU have largely continued to prioritize immediate security interests over promoting democracy. As a result, there is in fact little direct or immediate tension between transatlantic policies and Saudi Arabian foreign policy. Tensions persist over strategy, and not the wider objective of regional stability and the maintenance of the status quo.

To elucidate this argument, this article outlines the nature of the US and EU's relationships with Saudi Arabia to provide a wider context. It demonstrates that the US–Saudi relationship is broadly based on a wide variety of interests and security guarantees, and the EU–Saudi relationship is mainly based on trade without a strategic partnership. Second, this article outlines two case studies through the lens of US, EU, and Saudi policy in Egypt and Bahrain. The Egyptian and Bahraini cases are important because of the significant domestic involvement of Saudi Arabia and the transatlantic partners in the aftermath of their political unrest, and also because they provide the clearest cases of a complex "conflict of interests" problem. With regard to the Egyptian case, it is shown that Saudi Arabia is undermining long-term efforts to promote democratic reform by challenging the model of democracy promotion at the heart of US and EU policies in the region. However, this does not involve the Kingdom directly confronting or clashing with the US and EU. Indeed, the US and EU themselves are all too ready to abandon this model when it proves expedient. Evidently, Saudi Arabian foreign policy in Egypt is less of a perspicuous reaction to a well-implemented transatlantic democracy agenda and more of an attempt to secure Saudi Arabia's own long-term national security interests.

Similarly, in the case of Bahrain, Saudi Arabia has supported the status quo in an effort to protect the Kingdom's national interests. However, rather than this being contrary to US and EU democracy promotion efforts in Bahrain, the tension between the US, EU, and Saudi Arabia is over how best to reform the al-Khalifa regime and maintain the status quo in an effort to contain Iranian influence in the Gulf. Bahrain's continued political unrest has not altered strategic calculations or the convergence of interests between the transatlantic partners and Saudi Arabia. Accordingly, the empirical account presented below supports the hypotheses that first, illiberal regional powers react to US and EU democracy promotion efforts if this is a threat to the illiberal states' geostrategic interests, or threatens the regime's survival; but second, Western democracy promoters will only react to countervailing policies by illiberal regimes if and when they prioritize democracy and human rights goals over stability and security goals.

Transatlantic relations with Saudi Arabia

Saudi Arabia is an ally and trading partner of both the US and EU. For the US, "Saudi Arabia's unique role in the Arab and Islamic worlds, its possession of the world's largest reserves of oil, and its strategic location make its friendship important to the United States". The US openly declares that it shares "common concerns and consult[s] closely on [a] wide range of regional and global issues". This is buttressed with the assertion that "Saudi Arabia is also a strong partner in regional security and counterterrorism efforts, providing military, diplomatic, and financial cooperation". Indeed, for the US it is clear that this close working relationship is based on "safeguarding both countries' national security interests".[4] Within this context, the US has long provided Saudi Arabia's ruling House of Saud with a security guarantee against both external and internal threats.[5] There was a subtle shift in this position following the terrorist attacks on 11 September 2001 and the onset of President George W. Bush's Freedom Agenda. However, whilst over the last decade the US has been engaged in diplomatic efforts aimed at persuading Saudi Arabia to liberalize and focus on human rights issues by holding elections, releasing political prisoners, and allowing free expression and rights for women, this was never done at the expense of abandoning a long-term ally and undermining regional stability.[6] Simply put, the US favours stability and security goals rather than prioritizes democracy and human rights. This is significant for

US democracy promotion in the region. The overall relationship with Saudi Arabia, emphasizing security and stability, shapes the US reaction to the Kingdom's countervailing policies that have emerged as a result of the Arab revolutions.

The nature of the US–Saudi alliance structures the EU's relationship with the Kingdom. With the House of Saud being supported by the US and buttressed by its vast resource revenues, the EU is unable to exert any significant influence over the Kingdom. Instead, the EU largely engages with the Gulf Cooperation Council (GCC), whilst Saudi Arabia's foreign policy elite views the EU as little more than an inconsequential partner of the US. Nevertheless even the EU's position is tempered by considerations of stability and security goals. The EU maintains that Saudi Arabia's human rights record remains "dismal" and that there is a gap between "international obligations and ... implementation". Nevertheless, the EU all too often stresses that "a large number of EU companies are investors in the Saudi economy, especially in the country's petroleum industry" and that Saudi Arabia is "an important market for the export of EU industrial goods in areas such as defence, transport, automotive, medical and chemical exports".[7] Moreover, the EU, in line with the US, accepts Saudi Arabia's importance for the maintenance of traditionally conceived security issues. For the EU, Saudi Arabia is "an influential political, economic and religious actor in the Middle East and the Islamic world, the world's leading oil producer, and a founder and leading member of the Gulf Cooperation Council ... and of the G-20 group", which makes it an "important partner for the EU".[8] As such, the EU emphasizes the common challenges it faces with the Kingdom, "such as a rapidly changing economy, migration, energy security, international terrorism, the spread of weapons of mass destruction (WMD) and environmental degradation".

Given the broad range of national security interests both the US and the EU maintain with Saudi Arabia, it is little wonder that transatlantic policies elevate stability in the Gulf as a top priority. The maintenance of the House of Saud and Saudi Arabia's strategic cooperation are seen as two sides of the same coin necessary for the pursuit of transatlantic interests. However, whilst Saudi national interests largely converge with the transatlantic powers, they do not always fully align. Within the wider complexities of the region, the geopolitical orientation and political nature of other Arab states affect Saudi Arabia more directly. As a result, Saudi Arabia has become more active in asserting its national interests in the region. This is particularly the case when the Kingdom's foreign policy elite views such action as necessary for their geostrategic interests and their survival. This creates a complex geostrategic landscape in which US and EU democracy promotion programmes need to operate, which at times, converge and diverge with the interests of their allies in the Gulf, which is highly evident in the case of Egypt and Bahrain.

Transatlantic democracy promotion and Saudi–Egyptian relations

US and EU values and professed objectives of promoting democracy converged with the removal of Egyptian President Hosni Mubarak in January 2011.

However, the transatlantic approach to Egypt initially diverged from that of its allies in the Gulf, creating considerable public disquiet from the Saudi foreign policy elite. For the Saudi regime, the US was willing to quickly abandon long-term partners and security guarantees if it proved expedient, whilst also allowing the rise of the Muslim Brotherhood. This was significant for Saudi Arabia, because Egypt's size and stature in the region could make it a potential rival, and if led by the Muslim Brotherhood could offer an alternative model for the relationship between Islam and the state. Consequently, the political direction of Egypt is perceived, by the Kingdom's foreign policy elite, as having direct consequences for Saudi Arabia's national interests and the continuation of the House of Saud. It is within this context that the Saudi regime was persistent in its declarations that events in Egypt were the product of "external" forces, and Saudi Arabia was eager to enlist US security guarantees on behalf of the Egyptian regime.[9]

Nevertheless, after considerable hesitation and the realization that events on the ground had led to a tipping point for Mubarak to leave, the US moved towards backing a democratic transition in Egypt. This was in direct conflict to personal pleas made by King Abdullah that the Obama administration protect the Mubarak regime and quash the uprising. Over the coming months, the Obama administration made clear assertions that the US would "promote reform across the region, and ... support transitions to democracy".[10] This was in addition to launching the Middle East Response Fund (MERF), creating a new US–Egyptian Enterprise Fund, in principle relieving Egypt of up to $1 billion in debt, providing Overseas Private Investment Corporation (OPIC) loan guarantees of up to $1 billion, supporting job creation through small and medium-sized enterprise (SME) development, and providing letters of credit. In addition to this economic assistance, the US also sought to boost trade with Egypt through the MENA Trade and Investment Partnership (MENA-TIP), stimulate greater private sector growth and activity, and expand exports through Qualifying Industrial Zones (QIZs).[11] The US also mobilized the Middle East Partnership Initiative (MEPI) and other instruments for the distribution of democracy support funding, targeted at civil society organizations, political parties, and elections, along with providing technical and governance assistance to prepare for parliamentary and presidential elections.

Similar tools were adopted by the EU, seeking to exert leverage through its trade liberalization and development policies. In an effort to gain closer political relations, stabilize the Egyptian economy, and sooth regional unrest, the EU turned to the European Neighbourhood Policy (ENP). This emphasized "more for more" in an attempt to promote "deep democracy" along the theme of the "3Ms"; "Money, Markets and Mobility".[12] Accordingly, to boost economic assistance, development, and reforms, the EU institutionalized the SPRING programme to provide additional funding for the transitions, whilst refocusing the European Neighbourhood Partnership Instrument (ENPI), and expanding Europe Investment Bank (EIB) and Neighbourhood Investment Facility (NIF) activity. Additionally, the EU was active in providing macro-financial assistance (MFA), and promoting

SME activity through direct investment, microcredit and job creation and training. Having identified a serious gap in its available instruments to support democracy in the region, the EU also created the European Endowment for Democracy (EED), whilst expanding the European Initiative for Democracy and Human Rights (EIDHR), it created a new Civil Society Facility (CSF), and emphasized capacity building, electoral assistance, and education programmes.[13]

The convergence between the US and the EU approach to post-Mubarak Egypt is evident in their emphasis on economic incentives and attempts to stabilize the Egyptian economy. This is significant at a policy level, as it has allowed for greater transatlantic cooperation, and, more importantly, the institutionalization of that cooperation in, for example, the Deauville Partnership. Moreover, whilst the US and EU have not yet reached the level of strategic coordination, they are operating with the same vision of how democratization processes come to fruition; namely through processes outlined in modernization theory instigated by economic liberalization.[14] This provided part of the strategic background for engaging the Muslim Brotherhood with mainly economic incentives rather than, as Greenfield, Hawthorne, and Balfour illustrate, pushing too hard on democracy and human rights issues.[15] Yet, relying on economic statecraft as a modus operandi for large parts of democracy support programming is not without its problems, and is undermined by Saudi Arabia.

For the US, its democratization strategy has long been tied to what those who institutionalized the Freedom Agenda called a "competitive liberalization strategy".[16] That is to say, the US has long sought to make assaults on protectionism in the region, motivated more by geopolitical and security considerations and less by economic concerns. The rationale was that countries in the MENA who were eager for greater access to US markets would vie for Washington's attention and approval, and in return for liberalizing their economies MENA governments would avoid legitimation crises by diffusing popular dissatisfaction. The theory portrayed in Washington was that this closer access would allow slow and stable processes of modernization to take place and over decades would lead to the democratization of the region. Indeed, this was the framework under which the G.W. Bush administration sought to create a Middle East Free Trade Area (MEFTA), and it has also been a core component of MEPI and the Broader Middle East and North Africa (BMENA) initiative programming.[17] Moreover, despite the political upheaval in Egypt, the Obama administration has continued utilizing this policy paradigm with its emphasis on economic assistance, trade, and investment. President Obama's MENA-TIP is merely an extension of much of the thinking behind President G.W. Bush's MEFTA.

The EU's democratization strategy in Egypt, and across the Mediterranean, shares this emphasis on modernization through economic liberalization, and is a "competitive liberalization strategy" in all but name. Indeed, a core basis of the 1995 Euro-Mediterranean Partnership (EMP) was that the EU perceived some of its most pressing security concerns as emanating from the region. Consequently, it was concluded that the region needed to modernize. The strategic thinking behind this was that economic liberalization would spill over into political liberalization, and as a result the EU emphasized the need for a Euro-Mediterranean Free Trade Area. This stressed the need for the region to remove trade barriers, strengthen the private sector, develop regulatory and legal frameworks, and develop macro-economic policies. This was designed to create a "zone of peace and stability".[18] The EU merely extended the same policy paradigm, after the political unrest in the MENA started, with its articulation of "more for more", "deep democracy", and "Money, Markets and Mobility".[19] Indeed, notions of "normative power Europe" have long relied on attracting and shaping partners through economic statecraft and access to the European market. As such, the greatest difference between the US and EU position is the latter's significant emphasis on conditionality.

The transatlantic emphasis on democratization through economic modernization is deeply significant with regard to Saudi Arabia's ability to counter democracy promotion efforts in Egypt. Whilst the US and EU both have a plethora of programmes on the ground supporting civil society and providing political party and election assistance, Saudi Arabia does not need to challenge these directly to undermine the wider transatlantic approach to external democracy promotion. The US and EU envisage democracy promotion in the MENA as a long-term objective that can be socially and economically engineered. Within this context there are programmes that emphasize the importance of elections, political liberalization, and the role of civil society, but at the core of the strategy is economic liberalization.[20] It is through the latter that external democracy promotion strategies seek to create an independent middle class, which in turn sets into motion wider political and economic modernization processes. With this form of modernization thesis underlying both the US and EU external democracy promotion strategies in the MENA, Saudi Arabia's willingness to financially support the Egyptian state can be seen to undercut these efforts. That is to say, that to stymie transatlantic democracy promotion's long-term efforts of promoting democracy, Saudi Arabia targets these modernization processes. In turn, this also undermines the US and EU's leverage over Egypt's political elites; effectively undermining transatlantic efforts to institutionalize their competitive liberalization strategies. Saudi Arabia's ability to undercut the US and EU's economic leverage, and plans to promote modernization, are therefore a direct challenge to the transatlantic external democracy promotion agenda. For example, how can the EU institutionalize conditionality and "more for more" if Egypt is more financially reliant on Saudi Arabia for immediate economic support? With the US and EU facing fiscal constraints, it is Saudi Arabia that has provided a less conditional financial "carrot" to Egyptian elites willing to act as a bulwark against the Muslim Brotherhood and align themselves with the Kingdom's national interests. Undertaking such a task has been central to the development of Saudi Arabia's bilateral relationship with Egypt following the 2011 revolution, and the Kingdom has found a willing partner in Egypt's military elites following their 2013 counter-revolution against the Muslim Brotherhood.

Following the fall of President Mubarak, multiple high-level meetings were held between Saudi and Egyptian officials, as the Egyptians sought to provide reassurances and maintain bilateral relations. Indeed, Prime Minister Essam Sharaf, who was asked to form a government by the Supreme Council of the Armed Forces (SCAF) in March 2011, asserted that "we are tied with the G.C.C. countries by historic relations and interference in their affairs is a red line".[21] Moreover, Cairo was eager to reassure Riyadh that its apparent rapprochement with Iran, most visibly evident in two Iranian war ships sailing through the Suez Canal in February 2011, would not interfere with Egyptian–GCC relations. Bilateral relations between Egypt and Saudi Arabia remained stable, with joint military exercises taking place along with a $500 million grant to support the Egyptian budget, the commitment of a $3.75 billion aid package, 48,000 tons of liquefied petroleum gas, and discussions of a further $1.5 billion aid package commitment through the Saudi Development Fund.[22]

With the election of the Muslim Brotherhood's Mohammad Morsi to presidential office on 24 June 2012, the certainty of having the SCAF rule Egypt was removed. Saudi Arabia received initial reassurances when Morsi's first foreign visit was undertaken to Riyadh in July.[23] This was, however, short-lived. President Morsi visited Tehran the following month, being the first Egyptian leader to do so since relations were severed in 1980. This sent a deeply troubling signal to Riyadh. Not only was President Morsi refusing to accept the long-held Iranian containment policy put in place by the US, the EU, and the GCC, but in doing so he was demonstrating Egypt's potential to rival Saudi Arabia's hegemony across the Arab world. Moreover, Egypt's ability to upset the region's geopolitical rivalries aside, the democratic election of the Muslim Brotherhood itself also posed a problem to some in Riyadh. It created a democratically elected Islamist rival to claims of Saudi Arabia being the protector of Islam, and offered a potentially dangerous exemplar in the region that could well have undermined the kingdom's legitimacy in the long term.[24] As a result, following the military coup on 3 July 2013, Saudi Arabia has been deeply supportive of the Egyptian military, which has led to openly strained relations with Turkey, Qatar, the US, and the EU.

The form of Saudi support for the military coup has been evident in the financial backing Riyadh has provided. Just days after the coup, Saudi Arabia announced a $5 billion aid package, along with an additional $3 billion from the United Arab Emirates (UAE) and $4 billion from Kuwait.[25] Yet, in addition to this, the Saudi regime has been extremely vocal in its support of the Egyptian military's crackdown on the Muslim Brotherhood and its efforts to fight "terrorism, falsehood and sedition". In a rare display of open diplomatic gesturing with the US and EU, King Abdullah also warned "against those who try to tamper with Egypt's domestic affairs".[26]

With close ties between the Saudi regime and Egypt's Field Marshal Abd-al-Fattah al-Sisi, it is clear that Saudi Arabia is actively backing autocratic rule in Egypt through financial and diplomatic support designed to buy influence in the country. Moreover, the interests of the Egyptian military and Saudi Arabia align to the extent that they seek to maintain the status quo and economic stability. This provides Saudi Arabia with a partner and purchase for internal interference in Egyptian affairs. Saudi interests rest on countering the Muslim Brotherhood across the region and, therefore, in supporting the counter-revolution. Thus, although the Egyptian military are ultimately responsible for countering democratic reforms in Egypt, the Saudi foreign policy elite has been backing their efforts, and undermining US and EU democratization and liberalization strategies. This is not to argue that the US and EU have a consistent track record of promoting democracy in Egypt, but rather to suggest that the transatlantic partners have a larger strategic vision of how to incrementally transform the Egyptian state, which is being challenged by Saudi foreign policy. Moreover, whilst the transatlantic partners maintain the same incremental vision for other states in the region this is itself weakened depending on the urgency and priority of other strategic interests. Indeed, this is highly visible in Bahrain where democracy promotion efforts emphasize reform rather than transition, and transatlantic interests align with those of the Saudi foreign policy elite.

Transatlantic democracy promotion and Saudi–Bahraini relations

With protesters occupying Manama's Pearl Roundabout in February 2011, it was clear that the Arab Spring had reached Bahrain, threatening the first Gulf monarchy. As the protesters attempted to create a cross-sectarian politics and appeal to a national consciousness, calls were limited to political reform. However, as demands began to grow, calls for the Sunni House of al-Khalifa to put an end to the discrimination against the 60% Shia Muslim population emerged. These calls were seized upon by hardline members of the ruling al-Khalifa regime and interpreted through a sectarian discourse. As a result, they were branded by the regime as attempts by Iran to gain influence in the country and expand Iranian influence in the region. This discursive move was easily done, drawing on notions that the Shia population represents a "fifth column" under Iranian authority. Under this discursive umbrella, Bahraini security forces surrounded the Pearl Roundabout protesters on 17 February, and used tear gas and baton rounds to remove the protesters. Further protests on 18 February, were met with the same coercive response. However, Bahraini security forces later pulled back, and allowed protesters to reoccupy the Pearl Roundabout and hold the largest demonstrations in Bahraini history on 22 February and 25 February. In turn, the ruling al-Khalifa regime announced plans for a national dialogue, whilst releasing 308 Bahraini prisoners, and removing two al-Khalifa family members from cabinet posts.[27]

With key parties unwilling to accept the al-Khalifa offer of a national dialogue, the spread of the Sunni-Shia clashes, and Manama's financial district threatened by a protester blockade, Bahrain turned to the GCC for support. Having stymied the "Day of Rage" in its own country, and feeling more domestically stable, Saudi Arabia led the GCC's efforts to secure key sites within Bahrain. The manner in which Saudi Arabia actively supported the status quo in Bahrain and helped maintain the power of the monarchy significantly contributed to the wider conception that Saudi Arabia is "blocking democracy" and engaged in a "counter-revolution" across the region. Indeed, on 14 March, Saudi Arabia sent 1200 armed forces personnel across the King Fahd Causeway that joins the two countries.[28] Bahraini officials argued that the Peninsular Shield force was there to protect government facilities, rather than to intrude in the internal affairs of the country itself.[29] Nevertheless, the presence of the Peninsular Shield force coincided with Bahraini security forces once again clearing the demonstrators from the Pearl Roundabout and demolishing the Pearl Monument. This put an end to protests in downtown Manama, and led to more limited and sporadic protests throughout the country. Saudi Arabia had significantly contributed to preventing the overthrow of the al-Khalifa regime, in line with its policy of not allowing a majority Shia population to come to power. For the Saudi foreign policy elite, this urgent action was needed to prevent the political aspirations of its own Shia population in the Eastern Province, but also those of Shia minorities across the GCC, coming to fruition. Moreover, supporting the al-Khalifa regime was a fundamental part of the long-held Saudi policy of containing Iranian influence.

Saudi Arabia's heightened commitment to the security of the al-Khalifa regime, following the quelling of the initial protests, came in the form of a bilateral donation of at least $500 million to boost the Bahraini economy. Further still, Saudi Arabia sought to renew closer political and security unity within the GCC. On 14 May 2011, Saudi Arabia and Bahrain announced a plan for greater political and military union in the Riyadh Declaration. This unequivocally signalled that Bahrain maintained Saudi backing, and was intended as a deterrent against further protests. Whilst other members of the GCC, in particular Oman, have opposed political unity plans, the GCC agreed a collective security agreement in December 2012. In Bahrain, these efforts are directly intended to prevent a majoritarian Shiite government from emerging with the downfall of the House of al-Khalifa. Saudi intervention in Bahrain can therefore be seen as a countervailing strategy adopted by an illiberal regime seeking to prevent political transition. The rationale for this is two-fold; first, for geostrategic reasons designed to prevent Iran gaining influence throughout the region, and second, to stop unrest spreading further in its own Eastern Province, which could threaten the Saudi regime's survival. This is particularly fecund as both conditions are outlined as "triggers" in Risse and Babayan's[30] hypothesis explaining why illiberal regional powers push back against US and EU democracy promotion efforts. The US and EU have had to adapt to this push back due to all three of conditions Risse and Babayan outline as determinants of where democracy promotion and human rights fit into the foreign policy agenda. First, there is a transatlantic preference in the Gulf for stability and security over democracy and human rights, second, Saudi Arabia is deemed too strategically important in its regional hegemonic role, and third, internal considerations of democracy promotion within the US and EU undermine the agenda.

DEMOCRACY PROMOTION AND THE CHALLENGES

At a superficial level, Saudi Arabia's actions in Bahrain are in direct competition with the US and EU's espoused democratization policies in the country. The US has long-established democracy support programmes in the country through MEPI, which has conducted media training, promoted legal and judicial reform, and sought to bolster non-governmental organizations and civil society activity.[31] The US and Bahrain also signed a Free Trade Agreement in 2004 under the auspices of MEFTA. This came into effect in January 2006 and was part of the competitive liberalization rationale held by the G.W. Bush administration. Moreover, under the Obama administration, the US was eager during the protests to urge Bahraini security forces to pull back from targeting protesters with coercive force, to compromise and maintain a dialogue, and it also halted some arms sales that could potentially have been used against the protesters.[32] Yet, the Obama administration never called for a political transition or the start of a democratization process. This is because the maintenance of the regime is tied to the US's strategic interests in the region, which are also aligned with those of Saudi Arabia.

The US is Bahrain's primary Western partner and maintains an extensive security relationship, with the small Gulf state being home to the US naval headquarters in the region for over 60 years. The US and Bahrain, since 1991, have also been committed to a Defence Cooperation Agreement (DCA), and Bahrain is designated as a "major non-NATO ally". In spite of Bahrain's considerable unrest, and its willingness to use coercive force against protesters, the US has maintained these agreements and continued its partnership. Indeed, the military side of this relationship has been expanded since the uprisings with expanding US military facilities in Bahrain.[33] For the US the emergence of a Shiite-led government in Bahrain could provide Iran with greater influence in the Gulf and undermine the current US–Bahraini security relationship, and therefore lead to the agreement over US use of military facilities being withdrawn. As such, there is a conflict of interests problem at the heart of the US–Bahraini relationship, where US democracy promotion efforts are in tension with other US security interests.

As a result of the conflict of interests problem, US's calls for democracy in the country are mitigated to pronouncements for reform and dialogue. These are intended to promote slow incremental change under the existing regime, and not revolutionary action that could undermine other US interests. This was not only the dominant approach adopted under the Freedom Agenda and its competitive liberalization strategy in the 2000s, but has also been evident in the Obama administration's approach to the Arab awakening in Bahrain. Thus, whilst the Obama administration was critical of the Saudi-led GCC intervention, it emphasized the need for a political reform process that maintained the status quo. As Secretary of State Clinton argued, at length, on 19 March 2011:

> The United States has an abiding commitment to Gulf security and a top priority is working together with our partners on our shared concerns about Iranian behaviour

> in the region. We share the view that Iran's activities in the Gulf, including its efforts to advance its agenda in neighbouring countries, undermines peace and stability ... Bahrain obviously has the sovereign right to invite G.C.C. forces into its territory under its defence and security agreements ... violence is not and cannot be the answer. A political process is.[34]

Within this context it is clear that the stated US "top priority" of containing Iranian influence is in line with Saudi national interests, and calls for democracy had been relegated down the political agenda. The tension between the US and Saudi Arabian foreign policy, therefore, is over how the status quo in Bahrain is maintained whilst observing human rights norms, and not if the regime should be maintained. Indeed, even as the Bahraini state and media has pushed back against MEPI activity, the US response has been to emphasize how MEPI provides "direct support to the work of local partners, helping them to network and partner with like-minded colleagues from the United States and the region", rather than "alter the internal politics" of the state itself. In turn the US stresses the importance of implementing the recommendations of the Bahrain Independent Commission of Inquiry (BICI) and the need for "trade liberalization and economic diversification in the country". As the US argues, it is through these activities that it is "committed to supporting the Government of Bahrain's efforts to achieve its economic, development, and reform goals".[35] This is envisioned as a long and distant "democracy promotion" strategy in "partnership" with the al-Khalifa regime, and not one that seeks the empowerment of Bahrain's Shiite majority population.

EU–Bahraini relations share the same conflict of interests problem as their transatlantic partner. The EU is a tertiary actor in Bahrain compared to the US and Saudi Arabia, and its normative agenda is stymied by many of the same factors that limit its influence throughout its relations with other GCC states. However, the EU's limited response to the uprising in Bahrain, stopping at declaratory policy, should also be understood by virtue of Britain, France, and Germany objecting to the potential of greater Iranian influence in the region. As Tobias Schumacher argues,

> the E.U. stressed the need for reforms and demanded that the Bahraini regime engage in comprehensive and inclusive dialogue. Yet, it stopped short of defining more precisely the character of reforms and the challenges it refers to and calling for a transition and therefore the resignation of King Hamad bin Isa Al Khalifa and his ruling family ... numerous member states' governments ... fear that such a development would help those Iranian factions that conceive of Bahrain as Iran's fourteenth province.[36]

As a result of the conflict of interests problem, the EU Foreign Affairs Council was unable to achieve more than a vague declaratory policy on the situation in Bahrain, and did not seize opportunities to condemn the Bahraini regime when they presented themselves. Indeed, British Prime Minister David Cameron expounded the differentiation being made between the regional uprisings when he declared that "Bahrain is not Syria".[37] This is deeply problematic given that within the EU, Britain enjoys the closest relationship with Bahrain because of its colonial legacy and arms sale relationship. Moreover, Robert Cooper, a special adviser to the EU's High Representative for Foreign Affairs and Security Policy, simply declared that "accidents happen" when briefing Members of European Parliament about the use of force against Bahraini protesters.[38] The timidity of the EU's response to the uprising in Bahrain undermines its normative agenda. This has led some analysts to highlight the relationship between European arms sales and the EU's willingness to confront regimes in the Gulf.[39]

Evidently, Saudi Arabia has provided instrumental support to the Bahraini regime and is a countervailing power against domestic pressures for political transition. However, the notion that this has conflicted with the US and the EU's democracy promotion policy is deeply problematic. At best the conflict is over how best to manage the uprisings in Bahrain and maintain the existing regime. At worst, "the US and the EU have implicitly condoned the sectarianism used by the Bahraini and Saudi governments to subdue protesters" and the transatlantic partners have been "complicit in creating a sectarian Gulf, which is in line with its strategic goal of keeping the Gulf monarchies in power to help counter Iran".[40] Although in the case of Bahrain it is clear that Saudi Arabia has sought to block the emergence of democracy, there is little by way of tension with the transatlantic approach to the small Gulf island and their democracy promotion efforts.

Conclusion

The assertion that illiberal regional powers respond to Western efforts at democracy promotion in third countries if they perceive challenges to their geostrategic interests and/or the survival of their regime is clearly the case with regard to Saudi Arabian foreign policy in Egypt and Bahrain. Moreover, the observation that Western democracy promoters only react to countervailing policies when they prioritize democracy and human rights over security in the target country is not challenged with regard to US and EU foreign relations with Egypt or Bahrain. Evidently, the empirical evidence presented above supports Risse and Babayan's hypothesis, and Western and Saudi policies appear to correspond to the main propositions about motives and policies they set out. The US and EU have varied interests across the MENA region, and these influence the extent to which they pursue their democratization agendas. Within the Gulf region other strategic interests are elevated above those of promoting democracy and Saudi Arabia can therefore act as a countervailing power. Yet, even in Egypt, where the US and EU had a window of opportunity for promoting democracy, this was not seized and the counter-revolution was straightforwardly institutionalized with the implicit approval of the US and EU. Instead, the transatlantic partners relied on a policy paradigm that emphasized modernization and political liberalization as a cautious long-term approach. Without expanding their foreign policy tools beyond this policy paradigm, the transatlantic approach has been undermined by Saudi Arabia's ability to buy influence and undermine Western leverage for political reforms. The evidence suggests that the incremental and cautious transatlantic approach has not changed much since it was developed in the 2000s and has certainly not adapted to "pushback" from countervailing powers. This is in and of itself remarkable given the profound nature of change sweeping across the region. Whilst it is clear that the geopolitical and geostrategic landscape of the region is changing, the transatlantic approach is not. It is little wonder therefore that Saudi Arabia has been able to adapt and pursue its interests, at the expense of any serious transatlantic democracy promotion agendas.

Funding

Economic and Social Research Council (ESRC) [grant number ES/K001167/1].

Notes

1. This term was adopted from Wittes, *Freedom's Unsteady March.*
2. See Hassan, *Constructing America's Freedom Agenda for the Middle East.*
3. For an analysis of "push back" as a global phenomenon, see Carothers and Brechenmacher, "Closing Spaces."
4. Bureau of Near Eastern Affairs, "U.S. Relations With Saudi Arabia."
5. Weisman, "Reagan Says U.S. Would Bar a Takeover in Saudi Arabia That Imperiled the Flow of Oil"; also see Hassan, *Constructing America's Freedom Agenda for the Middle East.*
6. Weisman, "Rice Urges Egyptians and Saudis to Democratize."
7. European Parliament Committee on Foreign Affairs, *On Saudi Arabia, Its Relations with the EU and Its Role in the Middle East and North Africa.*
8. Ibid.
9. Saudi News Agency, "Saudi King Telephones Egyptian President, Slams 'Malicious Sedition'."
10. Obama, "Remarks by the President on the Middle East and North Africa."
11. See Danya and Balfour, *Arab Awakening.*
12. Archick and Mix, *The United States and Europe.*
13. Greenfield and Balfour, *Arab Awakening.*
14. See Hassan, *Constructing America's Freedom Agenda for the Middle East*; Bridoux and Kurki, *Democracy Promotion*, 76–85.
15. Danya, Hawthorne, and Balfour, *US and EU*, 2.
16. Hassan, *Constructing America's Freedom Agenda for the Middle East.*
17. Ibid.
18. Youngs, *The European Union and Democracy Promotion*, 47–93.
19. The "3M's" were "money," to provide resources for the transitions, support civil society, and meet economic needs; "markets," to give advantages to the region for trade; and "mobility," to allow people to move around, especially business people to enable all of them to be more effective.
20. Hassan, "Bush's Freedom Agenda."
21. Saudi News Agency, "Egyptian Premier Praises Saudi Ties, Says Gulf Security 'Red Line'."
22. Saudi News Agency, "Saudi Arabia Details Support to Egypt after Complaint."
23. Mossavat, "Hosting Morsi's First Foreign Trip Is a Coup for Saudi Arabia."
24. Hearst, "Why Saudi Arabia Is Taking a Risk by Backing the Egyptian Coup."

25. Peel and Hall, "Saudi Arabia and UAE Prop up Egypt Regime with Offer of $8bn"; and Nordland, "Saudi Arabia Promises to Aid Egypt's Regime."
26. Saudi News Agency, "Saudi King Declares Support for Egypt against 'Terrorism'."
27. Katzman, *Bahrain*.
28. Ibid.
29. Lessware, "State of Emergency Declared in Bahrain."
30. Risse and Babayan, "Democracy Promotion and the Challenges of Illiberal Regional Powers."
31. US Department of State, "MEPI in Barhrain."
32. Katzman, *Bahrain*.
33. Ibid.
34. Clinton, "Press Availability at Chief of Mission Residence."
35. US Embassy Bahrain, "Statement from the U.S. Embassy Concerning MEPI."
36. Schumacher, "Gulf Cooperation Council (GCC) Countries and Yemen."
37. Wearing, "Bahrain May Not Be Syria, but That's No Reason for Activists to Turn a Blind Eye."
38. BBC, "EU Envoy Defends Bahrain Police amid Unrest."
39. Matthiesen, "EU Foreign Policy towards Bahrain in the Aftermath of the Uprising."
40. Ibid.

Notes on contributor

Oz Hassan is an assistant professor at the University of Warwick, UK, and a visiting scholar at the Carnegie Endowment for International Peace, Washington DC, USA. He has authored multiple articles and reports on US and EU foreign policy, democracy promotion, and the Middle East, and is the author of the book *Constructing America's Freedom Agenda for the Middle East*. He is also the primary investigator on the ESRC-funded project *Transatlantic Interests and Democratic Possibility in a Transforming Middle East* which has supported this research.

Bibliography

Archick, Kristin, and Derek E. Mix. *The United States and Europe: Responding to Change in the Middle East and North Africa*. Report Number R43105. Washington, DC: Congressional Research Service, 2013.

BBC. "EU Envoy Defends Bahrain Police amid Unrest." *BBC News*, 2011. http://www.bbc.co.uk/news/world-europe-12829401.

Bridoux, Jeff, and Milja Kurki. *Democracy Promotion*. London: Routledge, 2014.

Bureau of Near Eastern Affairs. "U.S. Relations With Saudi Arabia." *US Department of State: Diplomacy in Action*, 2013. http://www.state.gov/r/pa/ei/bgn/3584.htm.

Carothers, Thomas, and Saskia Brechenmacher. "Closing Spaces: Democracy and Human Rights Support Under Fire", Carnegie Endowment for International Peace, February 20, 2014, http://carnegieendowment.org/2014/02/20/closing-space-democracy-and-human-rights-support-under-fire/h8ym.

Clinton, Hillary R. "Press Availability at Chief of Mission Residence." *U.S. Department of State*, 2011. http://www.state.gov/secretary/rm/2011/03/158658.htm.

European Parliament Committee on Foreign Affairs. *On Saudi Arabia, Its Relations with the EU and Its Role in the Middle East and North Africa*. Brussels, 2014. doi:A7-0125/2014.

Greenfield, Danya, and R. Balfour. *Arab Awakening: Are the US and EU Missing the Challenge?* Washington, DC: Atlantic Council, 2012.

Greenfield, Danya, Amy Hawthorne, and R. Balfour. *US and EU: Lack of Strategic Vision, Frustrated Efforts Toward the Arab Transitions*. Washington, DC: Atlantic Council, 2013.
Hassan, Oz. "Bush's Freedom Agenda: Ideology and the Democratization of the Middle East." *Democracy and Security* 4, no. 3 (November 18, 2008): 268–89. doi:10.1080/17419160802473430.
Hassan, Oz. *Constructing America's Freedom Agenda for the Middle East: Democracy and Domination*. New York: Routledge, 2013.
Hearst, David. "Why Saudi Arabia Is Taking a Risk by Backing the Egyptian Coup." *The Guardian*. August 20, 2013.
Katzman, Kenneth. *Bahrain: Reform, Security and U.S. Policy*. Report Number 95–1013. Washington, DC: Congressional Research Service, 2014.
Lessware, Jonathan. "State of Emergency Declared in Bahrain." *The National*. March 16, 2011.
Matthiesen, Toby. "EU Foreign Policy towards Bahrain in the Aftermath of the Uprising." In *The Gulf States and the Arab Uprisings*, edited by Ana Echagüe, 77–85. Spain: Fride & Gulf Research Centre, 2013.
Mossavat, Shahab. "Hosting Morsi's First Foreign Trip Is a Coup for Saudi Arabia." *Al Monitor*. July 11, 2012.
Nordland, Rod. "Saudi Arabia Promises to Aid Egypt's Regime." *The New York Times*. 19 August, 2013. http://www.nytimes.com/2013/08/20/world/middleeast/saudi-arabia-vows-to-back-egypts-rulers.html?pagewanted=all&_r=0
Obama, Barack. "Remarks by the President on the Middle East and North Africa." *The White House*, 2011. http://www.whitehouse.gov/the-press-office/2011/05/19/remarks-president-middle-east-and-north-africa.
Peel, Michael, and Camilla Hall. "Saudi Arabia and UAE Prop up Egypt Regime with Offer of $8bn." *Financial Times*. July 10, 2013. http://www.ft.com/cms/s/0/7e066bdc-e8a2-11e2-8e9e-00144feabdc0.html#axzz31pM65QQH.
Risse, Thomas, and Nelli Babayan. "Democracy Promotion and the Challenges of Illiberal Regional Powers: Introduction to the Special Issue." *Democratization* 22, no. 3 (2015): 381–399.
Saudi News Agency. "Egyptian Premier Praises Saudi Ties, Says Gulf Security 'Red Line'." *BBC Monitoring Service*. April 25, 2011.
Saudi News Agency. "Saudi Arabia Details Support to Egypt after Complaint." *BBC Monitoring Service*. February 29, 2012.
Saudi News Agency. "Saudi King Declares Support for Egypt against 'Terrorism'." *BBC Monitoring Service*. August 16, 2013.
Saudi News Agency. "Saudi King Telephones Egyptian President, Slams 'Malicious Sedition'." *BBC Monitoring Service*. January 29, 2011.
Schumacher, Tobias. "Gulf Cooperation Council (GCC) Countries and Yemen." In *The European Union and the Arab Spring*, edited by Joel Peters, 109–126. New York: Lexington Books, 2012.
US Department of State. "MEPI in Barhrain." *Where We Work*, 2014. http://mepi.state.gov/where-we-work2/bahrain.html.
US Embassy Bahrain. "Statement from the U.S. Embassy Concerning MEPI." *U.S. Embassy of the United States*, 2014. http://bahrain.usembassy.gov/pas-61717.html?utm_source=Project+on+Middle+East+Democracy+-+All+Contacts&utm_campaign=d85a3a3e99-Bahrain_Weekly_Update_Nov_1_2012&utm_medium=email&utm_term=0_75a06056d7-d85a3a3e99-215944925.
Wearing, David. "Bahrain May Not Be Syria, but That's No Reason for Activists to Turn a Blind Eye." *The Guardian*, 2012. http://www.theguardian.com/commentisfree/libertycentral/2012/may/08/bahrain-syria-activists-human-rights.

Weisman, Steven R. "Reagan Says U.S. Would Bar a Takeover in Saudi Arabia That Imperiled the Flow of Oil." *The New York Times*. October 2, 1981. http://www.nytimes.com/1981/10/02/world/reagan-says-us-would-bar-a-takeover-in-saudi-arabia-that-imperiled-flow-of-oil.html.

Weisman, Steven R. "Rice Urges Egyptians and Saudis to Democratize." *The New York Times*. June 21, 2005.

Wittes, Tamara Cofman. *Freedom's Unsteady March*. Washington, DC: Brookings Institution, 2008.

Youngs, Richard. *The European Union and Democracy Promotion*. Oxford: Oxford University Press, 2004.

Local actors in the driver's seat: Transatlantic democracy promotion under regime competition in the Arab world

Tina Freyburg[a] and Solveig Richter[b]

[a]Department of Politics and International Studies (PAIS), University of Warwick, Coventry, Great Britain; [b]Willy Brandt School of Public Policy, University of Erfurt, Erfurt, Germany

> In studies of political transition, scholars started to explore the effect of competition between foreign policies of antipodal regimes on the political trajectories of transition countries, notably between traditional Western donors such as the European Union and the United States of America and regional authoritarian powers such as Saudi Arabia. Drawing on existing accounts, this article studies the conditions under which external actors can effectively steer local elite towards democratic reforms despite illiberal regional powers' potential counteractions. We argue that the reform-oriented political elites in the recipient country are the ultimate judges in this competition for influence. If democracy promotion is credible, they will decide in favour of democratization, but only if the expected costs and benefits of democratic engagement resist solicitation by authoritarian powers. A study of post-Arab Spring democracy promotion in Tunisia supports the pivotal role of the external donors' credibility in times of complex donor constellations.

Introduction

Regime change is not an exclusively domestic affair but rather a multi-layered and highly internationalized phenomenon. While comparativists have traditionally concurred that domestic factors are decisive in any transition to and consolidation of democracy, they increasingly acknowledged the importance of international factors in the form of both structurally induced influences such as diffusion effects[1] and more direct, agency-driven influences.[2] Scholars have devoted their attention to the specification of the conditions under which external actors can effectively support local actors in their attempts to advance and consolidate democratic reforms. There appears to be agreement that external promotion activities need to resonate with internal reform attempts in order to have any democracy-fostering influence.[3] Democracy promotion then becomes characterized by a "two-fold dynamic of cooperation and change".[4]

In this article, we join this special issue's aim to study the effectiveness of external democracy promotion in situations characterized by regime competition. Existing work tends to centre on Western external actors' efforts to empower key domestic agents in order to induce democratic change in recipient countries. Yet, recent popular demands for political liberalization, equal participation, and governance reforms in countries so diverse as Egypt, Tunisia, and Ukraine happen in an environment in which non-democratic regional powers such as Russia and Saudi Arabia seek to maintain and expand their regional if not global influence. We see our specific contribution in our approaching the question of effective democracy promotion in this context from the perspective of the local actors. The rich literature on political transitions teaches us that "transitions are elite-centered. Independent of whether regime change has been initiated from above by political elites or from below by the masses, the terms of transitions are settled by emerging elites, not by the public"[5] and also typically not by the external actor. The political elite are the domestic actors whose decisions determine a country's political trajectory. They function as "gatekeepers that actively facilitate or constrain ties to external actors".[6]

Drawing on existing knowledge, we argue that the credibility of external democracy promotion determines the elite's engagement with the demanded democratic reforms. However, under regime competition, they will implement these reforms only if the expected costs and benefits resist solicitation by the authoritarian power. Importantly, and refining previous accounts, we treat credible commitments as requisite of effective external policies and focus our analysis on the link between the credibility of democracy promotion and the reform-oriented elite's (non-)cooperation (rather than effective compliance). Focusing on local responses allows us to check the theoretical assumption of the credibility-cooperation link in a setting where the local elite would have access to assistance from sources other than Western donors.

Empirically, we apply our explanatory model to European Union (EU) and United States of America (US) democracy promotion in the Middle East and North Africa (MENA), where transition processes in some countries happen in the shadow of authoritarian regimes, notably Saudi Arabia. We concentrate on the post-Arab Spring world where the "initial flavour of civic-led 'ruptured' transitions has morphed into an elite-controlled 'pacted' transition dynamic".[7] The 2011 uprisings have turned the world's most unfree region into one in which at least one country has entered an uncertain transition period: In Tunisia the political unrest can be seen as a catalyst for long-term change whose final outcome is yet to be seen. In view of the ongoing political transition and the fact that authoritarian power structures had been broken up, effective external democracy support has become more likely.

In what follows, we first outline our theoretical argument about the credibility of democracy promotion as a requisite of its effectiveness in situations of regime competition. We then explore the plausibility of our argument empirically in the case of transatlantic democracy support in Tunisia and the influence of Saudi Arabia thereon. Taking the internal-external interaction and the potential countervailing effect of regional authoritarian powers seriously is of rising importance for the very practice of supporting democratic change from the outside.

External democracy promotion under regime competition: The theoretical argument

Traditional elite-centred democracy promotion presents a leverage-based process that is built on cooperation with the incumbent political elite. Previous studies demonstrate how important the degree of political liberalization in the target country is for its effectiveness;[8] it determines the extent to which external support measures challenge the regime's domestic power base – and thus the political elite's willingness to cooperate. Specifically, democratic conditionality exerts both a direct effect on domestic outcomes by pressuring the ruling political elite, and an indirect effect by empowering the domestic oppositional elite. External actors can foster processes of democratization at the level of polity by providing incentives for the incumbent political elite to undertake democratic reforms through conditioning support.[9] They can also influence domestic outcomes through mobilization and empowerment of the domestic opposition, by giving it a seat at the negotiating table, increasing the incumbent's costs of repression, or highlighting the ruling elite's failures and inconsistencies, amongst other means.[10] In any case, effective democracy promotion needs as background condition local actors who are supportive of democratic reforms as an outcome, such as *reform-oriented political elites* on which this article focuses.

Yet, external democracy promotion in highly volatile regions often faces authoritarian powers such as Saudi Arabia, China, or Russia, which either directly oppose or indirectly discourage democratic transition in their spheres of influence.[11] Existing studies on external autocracy promotion or "democracy blocking" suggest two main causal mechanisms.[12] First, autocratic leaders use foreign policy instruments to bolster authoritarian trends or subvert democratic ones in transition countries that are similar to those used in democracy promotion, notably the granting of financial, economic, military, or security assistance. Second, a "business as usual" standpoint by regional authoritarian leaders can counteract democratization efforts in neighbouring countries. For example, a country risks cutting favourable trade regimes with former authoritarian friends (possibly jeopardizing economic growth in the short-term) if it intensifies economic partnership with democratic countries or communities such as the EU.[13] Such – intentional or unintentional – authoritarian blocking of democratic transitions can have serious implications for the effectiveness of external democracy promotion in countries at a critical juncture in their political development.

Transition periods present critical junctures, characterized by "moments of relative structural indeterminism when wilful local actors shape outcomes in a more voluntaristic fashion than normal circumstances permit".[14] Major institutional change is a possible but not automatic outcome. External actors – be they promoters of democracy or not – can limit the options available to local actors or influence their preferences regarding democratic reforms. Democracy promoters may use such a window of opportunity and support, if not reinforce, domestic reform initiatives. However, ruling pro-reform elites might then risk losing support from the autocratic regional power. At worst, strengthened through increased regional support, anti-democratic opposition forces within the country may threaten their power base. The opposition may also portray external democracy support as illegitimate interference in the internal affairs of the country.[15] In any case, external actors – democracy promoters and their antagonists – are an important factor in the cost-benefit analyses of reform-oriented yet unassertive elites. At the heart of effective external democracy promotion is the decision of local elites to cooperate, or to refrain from doing so, and to either react neutrally or side with the regional authoritarian power. Cooperation can range from mere dialogue to structured long-term exchange up to contractual relationship which all may – ultimately – result in democratic reforms and compliance with the external actor's criteria.

Our argument is based on the notion that, in view of the uncertainty and risk involved in political transitions, the reform-oriented elite is in need of external assistance. We suppose that, by default, they turn toward those external actors that offer to support their democratic reform agenda. According to Schimmelfennig and Sedelmeier's "external incentive model", the political elite will comply with democratic conditionality if (1) the rewards are tangible and sizable, (2) the conditional threats and promises are credible, and (3) the calculated benefits exceed the anticipated political costs of compliance. The "impact of these conditions, however, varies according to the context of conditionality".[16] We apply the model to the specific context of regime competition, where the policies of Western democratic donors meet alternatives from regional authoritarian powers.

Specifically, we argue that the pro-reform elite will cooperate with the external democracy promoter if the support is credible and reliable (2), but they will comply and implement the democratic reforms only if the costs and benefits associated with such reforms resist solicitation by the authoritarian power (1/3). In other words, credibility is necessary for democracy promotion to be effective, but it is not sufficient by itself. Rather, while a conjunction of all three conditions (1/2/3) is sufficient for effective democracy promotion, a favourable cost-benefit ratio (1/3) alone is unlikely to stimulate effective implementation of democratic reforms if the external support is not credible (2). Hence, credibility is a necessary part of a conjunction of conditions that is sufficient for effective democracy promotion in the context of regime competition. It determines the extent to which the pro-reform elites are actually willing to engage with democratic reforms, as called and supported by an external actor. Against this background, we seek to test the plausibility of the following proposition:

> If an external actor is credible and reliable in its efforts to foster democratic reforms, the reform-oriented political elite will cooperate on democracy promotion – despite regional authoritarian powers' counteractions.

Hence, in this article, we look at the hypothesis that credible and reliable rewards lead to cooperation; we do not explore if, in the end, benefits exceeding costs result in compliance.

Post-Arab Spring democracy promotion and Saudi Arabia: The setting

In the MENA region prior to the 2011 uprisings, the EU and the US appeared to have preferred stable and Western-oriented autocracies to the potential instability and Islamist electoral victories associated with genuine democratization processes.[17] In reaction to the Arab uprisings both actors – in particular the EU – increased the amount of aid committed to the region, as displayed in Figure 1. However, implementation proved difficult in times of economic and financial crises at home, explicit anti-Western rhetoric by newly elected Islamic elites, US' security concerns in view of attacks on diplomatic offices, or conflicting views among EU member states.[18] Moreover, along with international financial institutions and other partners including select Gulf countries, the G8 countries initiated the Deauville Partnership. The involvement of countries such as Kuwait, Qatar, and Saudi Arabia, however, watered-down this initially quite ambitious agenda and "led to weak conditionality on aid packages and a neglect of tough issues".[19]

In terms of conditionality, both actors sought to strengthen the ties of aid to political conditions, notably democracy, rule of law, and human rights. Given that the

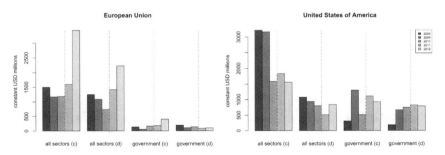

Figure 1. EU and US foreign aid before and after the Arab Spring, 2008–2012.
Note: Data is taken for all 18 MENA countries from the Creditor Reporting System (http://stats.oecd.org); "government" refers to sector 151 "Government and civil society, general". Aid activities are reported for both formal commitments (c) and actual disbursements (d). The dashed vertical line separates the pre- (2008–2010) from the post- (2011–2012) Arab Spring period.

EU offers no membership "carrot" to MENA countries (which they are not aspiring to) – the arguably most effective incentive at its disposal[20] – the EU and US are (more or less) on equal footing in terms of incentives. The EU revised its European Neighbourhood Policy (ENP) and refreshed political conditionality through new promises of "more" – in particular "money, markets, and mobility" – in return for "more" democratic progress.[21] In line with this revision, the EU started to negotiate Deep and Comprehensive Free Trade Areas (DCFTAs) and Mobility Partnerships – which simplify procedures for granting visas – with the "frontrunners" Egypt, Jordan, Morocco, and Tunisia. The Obama Administration also sought to place pressure on the new Arab transition countries, even though it is generally more reluctant to condition its support on democratic concerns.[22] In 2011, for example, by referring to national security interests Secretary of State Hillary Clinton waived a clause by the Congress which had conditioned US$1.3 billion in military aid on the protection of basic liberties.[23] Overall, the EU and US "have moved away from one-size-fits-all approaches and committed to greater differentiation and more tailor-made policies".[24]

Despite clear convergence between EU and US strategies, two main differences are noticeable, which in our view have important implications in terms of what local actors can expect from them. First, seeking primarily to foster initial political openings, the US intervenes rather early. The EU, understanding democratization as gradual evolutionary process of political and socio-economic transformation, steps in later but remains longer. As Figure 1 shows, the amount of EU foreign aid committed (and disbursed) to the region increased in 2011 but was really augmented in 2012 only. US commitments also increased in 2011 but decreased again in 2012. A similar pattern occurs with regard to democracy assistance more specifically, that is aid activities reported in sector 151 "government and civil society"[25]: both actors increased the amount of aid committed to the region. While these figures represent short-term trends only, it seems as if the US reacted quite quickly to the Arab uprisings by committing (and disbursing) a considerably higher amount of democracy-related aid in the region immediately after the uprisings whereas the EU increased its aid more gradually.

Second, EU and US democracy assistance benefits some MENA countries more than others, as shown in Figure 2. In this descriptive overview, we focus on the formal commitment of aid rather than its actual disbursement. While commitments present a good representation of the intensity of a donor's dedication in a given year, the non-disbursement of aid can be partially motivated by factors outside its intent, such as the lack of absorptive capacity in the recipient country. Out of the 18 MENA countries, seven (and the least free) receive no (democracy-related) aid at all, e.g. Bahrain. Democracy assistance committed to the remaining countries varies considerably.[26] With regard to EU assistance, the graph reflects the ENP's "more-for-more" approach: The EU increased democracy-related aid commitments to associated ENP countries in which (major) protests if not revolutions resulted in government if not regime changes, notably Algeria, Egypt, Jordan, Morocco, and Tunisia. It also suspended democracy

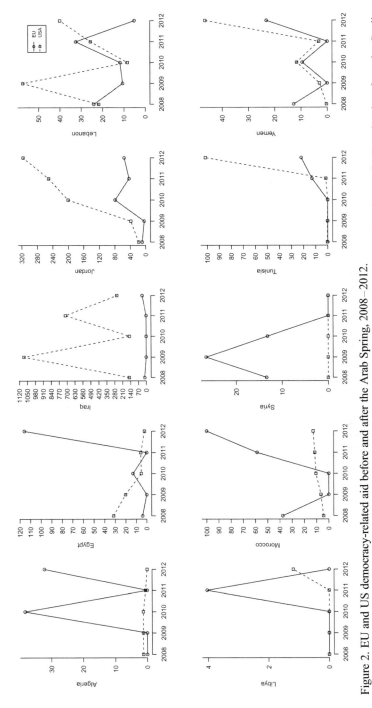

Figure 2. EU and US democracy-related aid before and after the Arab Spring, 2008–2012.
Note: US and EU democracy-related aid commitments in constant USD millions are represented by the y-axis. Data is taken from the Creditor Reporting System (http://stats.oecd.org).

assistance to countries in which violence and repression had broken out after initial protests such as in 2011–2012 Syria and Libya. Allocation of US aid, in turn, appears to be driven by security concerns. The US government was initially seeking to foster democratic change in Tunisia, as indicated by the considerable increase in aid in 2011–2012. Overall, however, the US seems to prioritize stability by favouring the countries of the conflict-prone Middle East (Jordan, Lebanon, Yemen) and targeting aid predominantly to those that are particularly marked by international conflicts (Lebanon and Libya), as also illustrated by the disproportionately high amount of democracy-related aid committed to Iraq.

Political transitions in the MENA countries are suitable terrain to study whether and how regional authoritarian powers influence the effectiveness of external democracy support. During the uprisings the most influential countervailing power was the regional hegemon Saudi Arabia, who even blocked democratization efforts by force, as was the case in Bahrain in March 2011.[27] Saudi Arabia pursues its foreign interests either unilaterally or in the context of the Gulf Cooperation Council (GCC) of which it is a founding and leading member. Most of the GCC members opposed the uprisings and sought to shape their outcomes (with the exception of Qatar and its support of the Muslim brotherhood),[28] noticeably by either directly supporting the ruling forces (Jordan, Morocco), or by brokering agreements to preserve the regime's stability even at the cost of the resignation of the president (Yemen). As "the largest Arab donor",[29] the kingdom's regional influence stems predominantly from the provision of substantial direct bilateral aid and soft loans through the Saudi development fund. Saudi Arabia provides one of the largest foreign aid programmes in the world and the largest in the MENA region. Since the eruption of the first revolts in 2010, at a time when the financial and euro zone debt crisis made financial assistance tougher for Western donors, Saudi Arabia has "pledged nearly $17.9 billion in support for fellow Arabs", out of which 3.7 billion US dollars had been distributed by September 2012.[30] In reaction to the Egyptian military's takeover in July 2013, for instance, Saudi Arabia announced "a $12 billion rescue package that dwarfs direct military and economic grants from the United States ($1.5 billion) and the European Union ($1.3 billion) combined".[31] The country also contributed to the transition fund that was established in the framework of the G8-led Deauville Partnership.

Saudi bilateral assistance is mainly unconditional and grant-based. "Even when involving loans, low interest rates and long repayment periods mean that the grant element is generally over 80 percent".[32] Saudi Arabia differs from Western donors in that it is not interested in promoting democratic governance in the recipient countries and does not participate in international debates on these issues. Yet, statistical analysis shows that a country is more likely to receive aid if it votes in tandem with Saudi Arabia in the United Nations General Assembly, among others.[33] While the US and the EU insist that aid is monitored, Saudi assistance goes directly to the political elite without oversight. Activities supported are limited to those that are non-political, such as infrastructure, economic development, basic education, and humanitarian assistance.[34] Saudi aid can thus undermine transatlantic efforts to promote democracy in transition countries, especially if the reform-oriented political elite in these countries is facing profound socio-economic and security challenges.

The link between external credibility and local elite cooperation: The analytical tasks

Does Saudi Arabian aid challenge the effectiveness of Western democracy promotion? We argue that if democracy promotion is credible, the reform-oriented local elite will prefer cooperation with the Western donors over unconditional aid from an authoritarian donor. Whether such cooperation results in the effective implementation of democratic reforms, as demanded by the Western donor, then depends on the size of political adaptation costs, in relation to the size of the incentives promised by the Western donor and the authoritarian power, respectively. In this article, however, we focus primarily on the first part of the argument and assess its plausibility using congruence analysis.[35] That is, we address the question of whether the credibility of the external actor (independent variable) and cooperation of the pro-reform local elite (dependent variable) relate in the expected positive manner. To this end, we first ascertain the value of credibility in the selected case and then explore whether the behaviour of the pro-reform local elite is consistent with our theoretical expectation. In doing so, we also consider the alternative argument of immediate influence of an authoritarian power, regardless of the Western donor's credibility.

We follow the definition of credibility that is commonly applied in studies of EU political conditionality.[36] First, conditionality is to be based on tangible incentives and credible commitment of the donor to pay or withdraw the promised reward in case of (non-)compliance. Second, the implementation of the threats and promises should not appear to impair the donor's own strategic interests. Hence, third, conditionality needs to be consistent in that rewards are explicitly and reliably linked to the fulfilment of the conditions. We then examine the behaviour of the ruling elite, notably whether or not it cooperates with the Western donor on democracy promotion (rather than turning toward the authoritarian power).

Transatlantic democracy promotion and Saudi Arabia in Tunisia: Empirical case study

The case of Tunisia is a particularly suitable empirical case. While the 2011 uprisings created critical junctures in several MENA countries, Tunisia is the "rare source of hope"[37] in the region and the only case showing some regime change. Recent reports provided by organizations such as Freedom House give a tentative prediction of preliminary transition outcomes. As Figure 3 shows, while a few examples of pro-democratic change can be identified on the basis of this information, Tunisia comes closest with a score of 63 out of 100 to the status of "free". The 2014 report of the Bertelsmann Transformation Index (BTI) comes

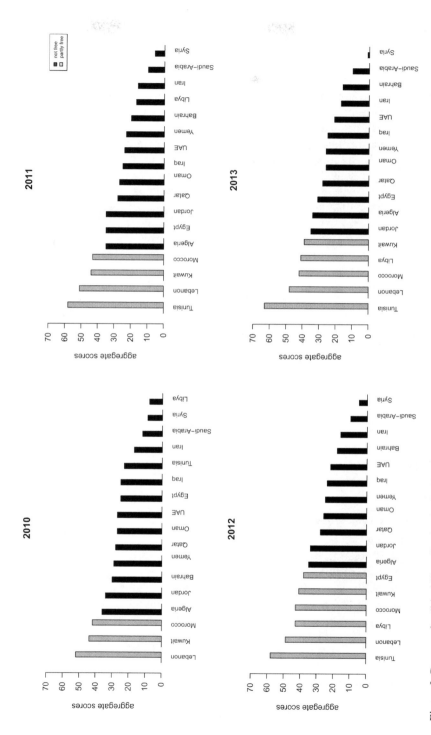

Figure 3. Degree of political liberalization in the region, 2010–2013.
Note: Freedom House "Freedom in the world" aggregated scores (political rights and civil liberties) are represented by the y-axis, with 100 = best score. Data is taken from Freedom House (http://www.freedomhouse.org/report/freedom-world-aggregate-and-subcategory-scores#.U9t-L2BwaP8).

to a similar conclusion,[38] as well as the World Bank's Governance Indicator on "voice and accountability",[39] with the latter tripling Tunisia's score between 2010 and 2012. Looking at transition trajectories more closely, only four countries experienced the dismissal of former autocratic leaders at the top level: Tunisia, Egypt, Libya, and Yemen. While in some countries local reform-oriented actors engage in pro-democratic activities, they refrain from doing so in others, or engage only half-heartedly such as in Yemen. In Egypt, Libya, and Tunisia, elections took place that qualify as free and fair, at least to a limited extent. Developments in Tunisia and Egypt initially followed a quite similar pattern, with people taking to the streets and ousting Ben Ali and Mubarak, respectively. However, while Tunisia has entered calmer waters and started to implement major reforms, we see restoration of autocratic military dictatorship in Egypt.

Tunisia has been undergoing a remarkable political development in the past three years. It is the country where the Arab upheavals started in December 2010 with the self-immolation of street trader Mohammed Bouazizi. Tunisia is also the country where the popular protests left the strongest footprint throughout the whole region in terms of democratic change. However, Tunisia's reform path was and is far from assured even though democratic elections in 2014 demonstrate that the transition "has remained broadly on track".[40] However, at least temporarily, the dramatic changes came with political instability, leading to violence and societal polarization. Similar to other countries in the region, the economic situation aggravated and created frustration and further social hardship.[41] At the same time, Tunisia has received substantial aid from several (international) partners after the revolution, including the EU, the US, World Bank, and the International Monetary Fund (IMF), but also Qatar and Saudi Arabia.[42] In brief, if we were to find any influence of international democracy promoters under competing external influences, then it would be in Tunisia. Tunisia can thus serve as plausibility probe to demonstrate the empirical relevance of our theoretical proposition.[43]

Transatlantic democracy promotion in Tunisia

Tunisia initially benefited from high-level US support to democratic reforms including a 10-fold increase in the amount of bilateral financial assistance, up to US$300 million. In line with the above-outlined regional trends and motivated by the Salafist attacks on diplomatic buildings, the US government reduced its democracy support from US$34 million in 2011 to 8.5 million in 2012[44] and prioritized security sector reforms, as exemplified by the US$22.5 million investment in police restructuring.[45] Moreover, the drawdown in embassy personnel caused the suspension or delay of many aid programmes; encouragement for democratic reforms became predominantly rhetorical. Next to security issues, US assistance focused on economic support. The 2013-launched Tunisian-American Enterprise fund, for instance, intends to help small and medium enterprises.[46] Yet, trade negotiations were postponed after 2012 and cooperation has fallen short of meaningful results since then. While the US did not act as major democracy promoter after 2012, it also did not run counter to EU policies. Against this background, in what follows, we will concentrate on EU democracy support in Tunisia.

The EU was the dominant external actor trying to shape the country's reform path. Right after Ben Ali had left the country, it set up a task force, the first one in the region, in order to bring together different stakeholders relevant to relations with Tunisia, including other international donors.[47] It also doubled the allocation of bilateral assistance for 2011. Overall, more than half of Tunisia's aid was coming from the EU and its member states.[48] "Between 2011 and 2013, Tunisia received €485 million, and it was the first recipient of additional funds under the SPRING [Support for Partnership, Reforms and Inclusive Growth] programme".[49] Specifically, the EU played a particularly important role by assisting the organization of the 2011 elections for a Constituent Assembly and ensuring that the new constitution includes no discriminatory elements concerning the rights of women and religions other than Islam. To this end, it granted additional €2 million to help prepare the elections and to strengthen civil society through the Instrument for Stability. In addition to financial assistance, EU incentives include improved market access opportunities, visa facilitation agreements, and increased opportunities for higher education cooperation. For instance, large amounts of financial assistance have been provided to Tunisia in the framework of economic and/or enterprise cooperation such as the 2012-launched Enterprise Europe Network and through other agencies such as the European Investment Bank.[50]

Credibility of EU democracy promotion

Initially, Tunisians are said to have had no positive image of the EU, in particular due to its slow reactions and (the French and Italian governments') rather unconditional support for Ben Ali. After he had left the country, and the EU froze his and his family/collaborators' assets, it was seen as more earnest supporter of the reform processes.[51] Both the PEW Global Attitudes survey and the EU Neighbourhood Barometer demonstrate that the EU was, overall, perceived positively in Tunisia.[52] According to the latter, 52.4% had a "very positive" or "fairly positive" image and 24% had neither a positive nor negative image of the EU over the period of 2012 to 2014. Today the EU is the most trusted external actor in Tunisia.[53] While at the regional level the EU is said to have had only limited success in enforcing democratic reforms, in particular due to a "mismatch between stated commitments and the will to deliver on them",[54] it gets better marks when it comes to Tunisia more specifically. Indeed, EU democracy support was more credible in Tunisia than in any other MENA country.

As to our first criterion of credibility, the EU's incentives are tangible and sizeable. Tunisia's economy is highly dependent on cooperation with the EU, notably their access to the European market. The EU is Tunisia's first trading partner: Exports to the EU were 72.1% of the country's total exports while representing only 0.6% of EU imports in 2010.[55] Tunisia is very much interested in the economic incentives offered, notably agricultural liberalization and greater economic cooperation eventually leading to participation in the Single Market.[56] Another important incentive is the Mobility Partnership, intended to make population movement easier for some citizens through visa liberalization. Given the emigration pressures in Tunisia, augmented by the post-Arab Spring economic downturn, and the demands on the part of Europe to cooperate in preventing irregular migration, incentives in the field of mobility and migration management are clearly important, too. Overall, the generally asymmetric relationship provided the EU with high leverage.

Second, the EU did not face any serious conflict of interests. While in the rest of the Arab world "security concerns often trump concern for democracy",[57] similar considerations were of minor importance in Tunisia.[58] The control of migration would be the only issue likely to undermine the credibility of EU democracy support.[59] Yet, the EU seeks to link its own "soft security interests" to incentives for reform, such as visa facilitations under the Mobility Partnership-framework. Overall, a consistent policy of democracy promotion and human rights protection was not going against the EU's own interests.

Finally, the EU's pronounced rhetorical commitment to support democracy under the revised ENP was followed by actual rewards for reforms. Further benefits were granted to acknowledge the progress made, notably the promulgation of a new, democratic constitution and the smooth establishment of a caretaker government till elections.[60] Based on an assessment of the country's progress in the context of the SPRING programme, Tunisia received additional €160 million for 2011–2013. The EU also granted Tunisia the status of "privileged partner" in 2012, agreed upon a Mobility Partnership and a new Action Plan, and initiated preparations for a DCFTA. Moreover, it has agreed on additional funding to further develop the modernization and internationalization of higher education under the Erasmus Mundus/Tempus programmes. Admittedly, "progress on disbursements and on negotiating the various incentives has been slow",[61] largely due to Tunisia's administrative incapacities.[62] By and large, however, EU conditionality appeared rather consistent and reliable. In view of both the reactions of the European public to initial support for Ben Ali and Mubarak and the financial constraints due to the economic crisis it is likely to be strengthened.

Cooperation on democracy promotion

While the overthrow of the old regime was caused by only loosely connected civil society groups, the establishment of the new one is largely influenced by emerging pro-reform elites. The Islamist party Ennahda won the 2011 free and fair elections, organized by the High Commission for the Realization of Revolutionary Goals representing most of the opposition forces, and governed the country until 2014 parliamentary elections. Ennahda, presenting itself as moderate-conservative party,[63] did not install an anti-democratic government based on radical Islamic ideas but formed a coalition government with two leftist-secular parties. Despite disagreement within this "democratic coalition" on crucial issues, notably the role of political Islam, the influence of radical Salafist groups, and a new constitution,[64] there was no political stagnation. Instead, all major political forces agreed on a constitution in January 2014,[65] celebrated as "hope and example for other countries" (European Council President Herman van Rompuy).[66] The Ennahda leaders "committed its considerable resources to the construction of a new plural democratic political system"[67] and pursued a foreign policy driven by pragmatism rather than ideological bonds. While Tunisia's structural conditions were (relatively) favourable, in particular due to a large middle class, diversified economy, ethnic homogeneity, and secular tradition,[68] they faced the tremendous task of building-up democratic institutions from scratch in a highly volatile environment and under deteriorating socio-economic conditions. Together with the elites' pragmatism and pro-democratic reform agenda, this opened up channels for external actors to influence developments from the outside.

The EU's democracy promotion policy is the "prototype of a 'cooperative' approach that aims for the active engagement of the target regimes".[69] In contrast to the pre-Arab Spring government, for which cooperation with the EU on democracy matters proved to be extremely difficult,[70] the Ennahda government engaged in cooperation. Association Council meetings have taken place on an annual basis and the attending partners have spent considerable time on discussing matters related to democracy. The meeting on 19 November 2012, was particularly important in this regard due to the creation of a Privileged Partnership, which is structured along political cooperation, economic and social integration. A new Action Plan embodies this partnership with objectives related to democracy and human rights, i.e. commitments to improve fundamental liberties, women's and refugee rights, to reform the Justice as well as to respect international conventions related to human rights. It represents an important political step for the Tunisian Government to implement reform strategies jointly defined with the EU. The clear commitment became visible when the President of the National Constituent Assembly (NCA) Ben Jaafer requested the Venice Commission of the Council of Europe to comment on the then draft constitution of Tunisia, in the framework of a programme that is supported by the EU through the €4.8 million scheme "Strengthening democratic reform in the Southern Mediterranean". Further evidence is the interim government's invitation to the EU to observe the legislative and presidential elections in 2011 and 2014, respectively.[71] Given that countries have traditionally guarded elections as a strictly domestic affair and a sacred hallmark of sovereignty, and in view of the fact that "domestic and international media listen to [the EU's] statements, as do governments around the world",[72] these invitations signal the authorities' willingness to actively engage in the EU's democracy promotion efforts.

The Tunisian authorities' willingness to cooperate on democratization is also expressed in the number of democracy-related projects, bilateral and multilateral ones, for which commonly financing agreements are to be signed. Next to the above-mentioned SPRING programme, the EU ran also the €5 billion 4-year programme Euromed Justice III that aimed to strengthen the development of the institutional and administrative capacity and good governance, including improved access to justice. At the level of bilateral projects,[73] a number of Twinning projects have been agreed upon to implement the Action Plan objectives, targeting issues such as the reform of the electoral law.

Finally, EU political conditionality is based on agreements. Despite the EU's leverage, partner countries such as Tunisia can decide whether or not to accept the conditions of the EU. The EU and Tunisia agreed on a new Privileged Partnership Action Plan at the 2012 EU-Tunisia Association Council, which provides the strategic framework for the EU's support to reforms and the democratic process in Tunisia. Overall, Tunisia has been "forthcoming in accepting EU policies and international advice".[74]

Influences of regional authoritarian powers

EU-Tunisia cooperation happens in the shadow of the Gulf powers. Most of the foreign-funded infrastructure projects in the country are supported by the Gulf States, specifically Saudi Arabia and Qatar.[75] Yet, Saudi Arabia is rivalling in particular with Qatar to influence the political transformations, both to advance geopolitical interests and to prevent popular uprisings at home. In light of this regional rivalry, the generous Saudi involvement in funding the Tunisian transition government appears to be less about the country's political developments and more about "challenging or appearing to challenge the great power with whom they are supposedly allied".[76] Moreover, while Ennahda's success is often attributed to "an infusion of Qatari petro-dollars",[77] Saudi Arabia heavily opposed the party's government.[78] Rather than welcoming the then Ennahda-prime minister al-Ghannouchi, the Saudis granted political asylum to the deposed dictator Ben Ali. Such support of the old regime largely discredited the country's policy in the eyes of the oppositional forces and then new-elites. In 2013, 31% of the adult population in Tunisia expressed a very unfavourable opinion of Saudi Arabia.[79] Overall, Saudi aid is unlikely to substantially influence the cost-benefit analyses of the ruling elite in Tunisia. Consequently, Saudi Arabia's efforts to counteract international democracy promotion may remain without results. In general, due to the limited engagement of the US after 2012 and Saudi Arabia's decision to express solidarity with the old elite, the EU can be seen as the dominant external actor in Tunisia.

However, the mere fact that the EU and Tunisia cooperate on democratic reforms would not suffice to assure an influence on the country's actual implementation of democratic change. While this question calls for further research, it appears that adaptation costs were rather moderate. In particular, potential veto players did not have enough political influence to threaten the power base of the ruling, reform-oriented elite. The military played a rather cautious role. After the uprisings, army forces withdrew from the streets back to the barracks and have since remained "apolitical".[80] The political police, a tool of the old regime, was also disbanded and could not disturb the reform process.[81] Seeking to impose radical religious norms and condemning liberal democratic ideas,[82] radical Islamist forces, notably the Salafist, have by far the highest "spoiling potential". Initially, the government was reluctant to enforce state authority and to strongly condemn them. Only after Salafists stormed the American embassy in 2012 and assassinated opposition leaders in 2013 did Ennahda take a firmer stance.[83] In general, the "Salafists remain largely outside the political arena".[84] Since "[t]here are no institutional veto powers or political enclaves" in the country,[85] "democratically elected political representatives have considerable [...] power to govern".[86] Hence, we would expect credible external democracy promotion to be rather effective in steering the political elite towards democratic reforms in Tunisia, rendering counteraction by regional powers, here Saudi Arabia, rather inconsequential.

Conclusion

When Arab citizens took to the streets to oust their authoritarian leaders, they envisioned but hardly expected a "fourth wave of democratization". While the US quickly engaged in supporting activists, it also quickly returned to business as usual and continued to pursue its security interests at the cost of democracy promotion. The EU reacted only slowly to the developments in the MENA region. Its policy innovations were predominantly rhetorical "bluff" packages of the same approach. Yet, both Western donors were facing rivalry in the battle field of external aid – regional authoritarian leaders such as Saudi Arabia supported directly or indirectly autocratic stability in the neighbourhood. This article studied whether external democracy promoters can have an impact on domestic democratization processes under the condition of regime competition.

In essence, we argued that external democracy promotion can substantially influence the decision of pro-reform local actors to engage with democratic reforms but only if it is credible, and the costs and benefits associated with democratic reforms are not outweighed by authoritarian support. Focusing predominantly on EU democracy promotion in Tunisia, we demonstrated that local elites in situations of uncertainty cooperated on democracy promotion once the EU's support was credible. While Tunisia's successful reform path can mostly be explained by domestic dynamics, the EU managed to decrease the risks the governing coalition associated with structural reforms and offered a realistic choice to avoid economic despair and instability. Indeed, today's Tunisia is the EU's prime partner in the region. Neither the US, as the other major democracy promoter, nor Saudi Arabia, the regional authoritarian power, could reach the same level of cooperation and, thus, had substantially less influence on its political trajectory.

What, then, can we learn from Tunisia with regard to external democracy promotion policy in the Arab world? In contrast to worst-case scenarios which were forecasting only a minor role for Western powers in post-Arab Spring transitions, we can give a more positive outlook: If an external actor supports democracy in reliable and credible manner, it can make a difference – even in regions characterized by regime competition with authoritarian powers such as Saudi Arabia.

However, in order to be effective, external assistance requires a certain degree of liberalization and/or the existence of pro-reform oriented elites. Against this, almost forgotten transition cases such as Yemen might obtain a new impetus if European policy makers engage wholeheartedly in the promotion of democratic values.

However, two caveats are worth making here. First, the analysis aimed at assessing the relevance of our argument taking a specific case. Yet, even if the EU or US succeed in designing credible democracy promotion policies based on consistent criteria and reliable rewards, this policy might still be perceived as incredible in the eyes of the local elite. Future research needs to carefully explore the pro-reform elite's perception of external influences, and their decision-making processes at choice-points. In order to establish a causal relationship between the behaviour of pro-domestic and external actors – be they democracy promoters or not – scholars would thus need to invest in process-tracing.

Second, the Tunisian elite are rather exceptional in their orientation. Tunisia is not only trade-dependent on the EU, considerable parts of the new elite also reject Salafi and Saudi ideology. Despite generous financial support, Saudi Arabia's model and influence did not appeal to them. Rather, the Saudis' rejection of Ennahda made the elite's decision for a more democratic/European path rather easy. In other words, Tunisia presents a most-likely-case to test the plausibility of the suggested link between external credibility and cooperation of local actors. Future research is encouraged to investigate the argument in more complex settings such as the Egyptian case where the elite appear to play Western donors and the Saudis off against each other, realizing that the US, at least, is not that serious about democracy promotion in a key strategic country.

Acknowledgments

We wish to thank the editors of the special issue, Peter Burnell, Paul Kubicek, and the Democratization referees for their extremely helpful comments. We are also grateful to Hanna Wheatley for her careful language editing.

Notes

1. Brinks and Coppedge, "Diffusion Is No Illusion."
2. Schmitter, "International Context."
3. Lavenex and Schimmelfennig, "EU Democracy Promotion"; Burnell and Schlumberger, "Promoting Democracy."
4. Van Hüllen, "Europeanisation", 118.
5. Welsh, "Political Transition", 382; see also Rustow, "Transitions"; Higley and Burton, "Elite Variable."
6. Tolstrup, "External Actors", 716.
7. Youngs, "From Transformation to Mediation", 11.
8. Kubicek, *The European Union*; Schimmelfennig et al., *International Socialization*; Van Hüllen, "Europeanisation."

9. Ethier, "Democracy Promotion"; Grabbe, *Transformative Power*; Schimmelfennig et al., *International Socialization*.
10. Vachudova, *Europe Undivided*; Donno, *Defending Democratic Norms*.
11. Risse and Babayan, "Democracy Promotion."
12. Ambrosio, *Authoritarian Backlash*; Bader et al., "Autocracies"; Burnell, "Autocracy Promotion"; Erdmann et al., "International Cooperation."
13. Ambrosio, *Authoritarian Backlash*.
14. Mahoney, *Legacies of Liberalism*, 7; cf. Collier and Collier, *Political Arena*, 9.
15. Burnell and Schlumberger, "Promoting Democracy", 8.
16. Schimmelfennig and Sedelmeier, "Governance", 663.
17. Gillespie and Whitehead, "European Democracy Promotion", 196; Youngs, "European Union", 42; Jünemann, "Security-Building", 7.
18. Greenfield et al., *US and EU*; Scott and Carter, "Cold War."
19. Greenfield et al., *US and EU*, 37.
20. Schimmelfennig and Scholtz, "EU Democracy Promotion", 188.
21. Burnell, "Democratisation", 842; European Commission, "EU and Tunisia Establish their Mobility", 5.
22. Berger, "Missing Link."
23. Huber, "US and EU", 108.
24. Greenfield and Balfour, *Arab Awakening*, 27.
25. OECD, "Reporting Directives", 18. Aid allocated to this purpose contains institutional support to the state, electoral assistance, and support to various forms of civil society. Given our focus on intergovernmental cooperation, we concentrate on publicly channelled aid that is first implemented by public sector institutions including central, state or local government departments.
26. We excluded the Palestinian Territories due to the Israel-Palestine conflict.
27. Holmes, "Military Intervention"; Hassan, "Transatlantic Democracy Agenda."
28. Kholaif, "GCC"; Albogami, "GCC."
29. IMF, "Saudi Arabia."
30. Al Arabiya, "Saudi Aid."
31. Nordland, "Saudi-Arabia Promises."
32. IMF, "Saudi Arabia", 52.
33. Neumayer, "Bilateral Sources."
34. Barakat and Zyck, "Gulf State."
35. Blatter and Blume, "In Search"; George and Bennett, *Case Studies*, 181–204.
36. Schimmelfennig and Scholtz, "EU Democracy Promotion"; Richter, "Two at One Blow"; Böhmelt and Freyburg, "Temporal Dimension."
37. Freedom House, "Freedom in the World."
38. With the exception of Egypt as data had been collected prior to July 2013.
39. World Bank, "Country Data Report for Tunisia."
40. The Guardian, "Tunisia Election Results."
41. BTI, "Regional Report", 8.
42. BTI, "Tunisia", 39.
43. Levy, "Case Studies", 6–7.
44. Greenfield et al., *US and EU*, 15.
45. Ibid., 14.
46. Ibid., 11/13.
47. Balfour, "EU Conditionality", 23; European Commission, "EU/Tunisia Task Force."
48. Burke, "Running", 8.
49. Whitman and Juncos, "Challenging", 164.
50. Greenfield et al., *US and EU*, 29.
51. Dandashly, "Building", 25; Chrisafis, "Sarkozy."

52. For both the EU Neighbourhood Barometer and the PEW Research Global Attitude Project about 1000 adults each had been interviewed in Tunisia through face-to-face interviews. For the EU survey in autumn and spring between July 2012 and June 2014 see http://euneighbourhod.eu; for the Pew survey in March/April 2012 and 2013 see http://www.pewglobal.org/.
53. PEW Research Global Attitude Project, http://www.pewglobal.org/.
54. Greenfield et al., *US and EU*, 2; see also Burke, "Running."
55. European Commission, "European Union."
56. Dandashly, "Building", 9.
57. Burke, "Running", 1.
58. Landolt and Kubicek, "Opportunities", 19.
59. Isaac, "Rethinking", 44.
60. Barroso, "Declaration."
61. Greenfield et al., *US and EU*, 33.
62. BTI, "Tunisia", 39.
63. Its model for a modern Islamist party has not been the Muslim Brotherhood but rather the Turkish Justice and Development Party (AKP). However, scepticism still persists as to how far Ennahda profoundly reformed, see Landolt and Kubicek, "Opportunities."
64. BTI, "Tunisia", 2.
65. Al-Ali and Romdhane, "New Constitution."
66. Al Jazeera, "Foreign Leaders."
67. Cavatorta and Merone, "Moderation", 862; BTI, "Tunisia", 13.
68. Landolt and Kubicek, "Opportunities", 11; Dworkin, "Struggle."
69. Van Hüllen, "Europeanisation", 119.
70. Ibid., 122/3.
71. European Commission, "EU EOM."
72. Kelley, *Monitoring*, 5.
73. A list of bilateral projects can be found at the website of the EU delegation in Tunisia, http://eeas.europa.eu/delegations/tunisia/projects/list_of_projects/projects_fr.htm.
74. Balfour, "EU Conditionality", 27.
75. Burke, "Running", 8; BTI, "Tunisia", 14.
76. Smith, "Democracy", 638; see also Salloukh, "Arab Uprisings", 44.
77. Cafiero, "Arab Awakening"; but see Kausch, "Foreign Funding", 6.
78. ICG, "Tunisian Exception."
79. PEW Research Global Attitude Project, http://www.pewglobal.org/.
80. BTI, "Tunisia", 13.
81. Landolt and Kubicek, "Opportunities", 11.
82. BTI, "Tunisia", 5; Cavatorta and Merone, "Moderation", 861.
83. BTI, "Tunisia", 5; Freedom House, "Freedom in the World."
84. Dworkin, "Struggle", 25.
85. BTI, "Tunisia", 8.
86. Ibid.

Notes on contributors

Tina Freyburg is an Assistant Professor in the Department of Politics and International Studies (PAIS) at the University of Warwick, Great Britain.

Solveig Richter is a Junior Professor for International Conflict Management at the Willy Brandt School of Public Policy, University of Erfurt, Germany.

Bibliography

Al Arabiya. "Saudi Aid to Arab Spring Countries $3.7 Billion: IMF." *Al Arabiya.* 18 September 2012.
Al-Ali, Zaid, and Donia Ben Romdhane. "Tunisia"s New Constitution: Progress and Challenges to Come." *openDemocracy*, 16 February 2014.
Albogami, Mansour Almarzoqi. "GCC: The Arab Spring spoilers." *Al Jazeera*, 13 January 2014.
Al Jazeera. "Foreign Leaders Hail Tunisia"s Constitution." *Al Jazeera*, 7 February 2014.
Ambrosio, Thomas. *Authoritarian Backlash: Russian Resistance to Democratization in the former Soviet Union.* Farnham: Ashgate, 2009.
Bader, Julia, Jörn Grävingholt, and Antje Kästner. "Would Autocracies Promote Autocracy? A Political Economy Perspective on Regime-type Export in Regional Neighbourhoods." *Contemporary Politics*, 16, no. 1 (2010): 81–100.
Balfour, Rosa. "EU Conditionality After the Arab Spring", Euromesco PapersIEMed no. 16 (2012).
Barakat, Sultan, and Steven Zyck. "Gulf State Assistance to Conflict-affected Environments." *LSE Centre for the Study of Global Governance Research Paper* (2010).
Barroso, Manuel. "Déclaration du Président Barroso suite à sa rencontre avec Monsieur Mehdi Jomaa, Premier Ministre de Tunisie, European Commission." SPEECH/14/486, June 2014.
Berger, Lars. "The Missing Link? US Policy and the International Dimensions of Failed Democratic Transitions in the Arab World." *Political Studies* 59 (2011): 38–55.
Bertelsmann Stiftung [BTI]. "Tunisia Country Report." 2014.
Bertelsmann Stiftung [BTI]. "Regional Report. Middle East and North Africa." 2014.
Blatter, Joachim, and Till Blume. "In Search of Co-variance, Causal Mechanisms or Congruence? Towards a Plural Understanding of Case Studies." *Swiss Political Science Review* 14, no. 2 (2008): 315–56.
Böhmelt, Tobias, and Freyburg, Tina. "The Temporal Dimension of the Credibility of EU Conditionality and Candidate States Compliance with the Acquis Communautaire, 1998–2009." *European Union Politics* 14, no. 2 (2014): 250–272.
Brinks, Daniel, and Coppedge, Michael. "Diffusion Is No Illusion. Neighbour Emulation in the Third Wave of Democracy." *Comparative Political Studies* 39, no. 4 (2006): 463–89.
Burke, Edward. "Running into the Sand? The EU"s Faltering Response to the Arab Revolutions." *Centre for European Reform Report (2013).*
Burnell, Peter. "Is there a New Autocracy Promotion?." *FRIDE working paper* no. 96. Madrid (2010).
Burnell, Peter, and Oliver Schlumberger. "Promoting Democracy–Promoting Autocracy? International Politics and National Political and Regimes." *Contemporary Politics* 16, no. 1 (2010): 1–15.
Burnell, Peter. "Democratisation in the Middle East and North Africa: Perspectives from Democracy Support." *Third World Quarterly* 34, no. 5 (2013): 838–55.
Cafiero, Giorgio. "Arab Awakening Triggers Saudi-Qatari Rivalries." *The Palestine Chronicle,* October 2012.
Cavatorta, Francesco, and Fabio Merone. "Moderation through Exclusion? The Journey of the Tunisian Ennahda from Fundamentalist to Conservative Party." *Democratization* 20, no. 5 (2013): 857–75.
Chrisafis, Angelique. "Sarkozy admits France made mistakes over Tunisia." *The Guardian* 24 January 2011.
Collier, Ruth Berins, and David Collier.: *Shaping the Political Arena. Critical Junctures, the Labor Movement, and Regime Dynamics in Latin America.* Princeton: Princeton University Press, 1991.

Dandashly, Assem. "Building a Security Community in the Neighbourhood. Zooming in on EU–Tunisia Relations." *Norwegian Institute of International Affairs Working Paper* no. 836 (2014).

Donno, Daniela. *Defending Democratic Norms: International Actors and the Politics of Electoral Misconduct*. Oxford: Oxford University Press, 2013.

Dunne, Michele, and Richard Youngs. "Europe and the US in the Middle East: A Convergence of Partiality." *FRIDE Policy Brief* no. 149 (2013).

Dworkin, Anthony. "The Struggle for Pluralism after the North African Revolutions." *ECFR Pluralism Report* no. 74 (2013).

Erdmann, Gero, André Bank, Bert Hoffmann, and Thomas Richter. "International Cooperation of Authoritarian Regimes: Toward a Conceptual Framework." *GIGA Research Working Paper* no. 229 (2013).

Ethier, Diane. "Is Democracy Promotion Effective? Comparing Conditionality and Incentives." *Democratization* 10, no. 1 (2003): 99–120.

European Commission. "EU EOM deployed in Tunisia", *Press Release* 140919/02. Brussels, 19 September 2014.

European Commission. "EU and Tunisia Establish their Mobility Partnership", *Press Release* IP/14/208. Brussels, 03 March 2014.

European Commission. "European Union, Trade in goods with Tunisia", Directorate-General for Trade, [http://trade.ec.europa.eu/doclib/docs/2006/september/tradoc_122 002.pdf] (27 August 2014.

European Commission. "A Partnership for Democracy and Shared Prosperity with the Southern Mediterranean", COM(2011)200final. Brussels, 8 March 2011.

European Commission. "EU/Tunisia Task Force Agrees Concrete Assistance for Tunisia"s Transition", *Press Release* IP/11/1137." Brussels, 29 September 2011.

European Commission. "The EU's Response to the "Arab Spring"", *Memo* 11/918. Brussels, 16 December 2011.

Freedom House. "Freedom in the World. Tunisia." *Freedom House Country Report* (2014).

George, Alexander, and Andrew Bennett. *Case Studies and Theory Development in the Social Sciences*. Cambridge: MIT Press, 2004.

Gillespie, Richard, and Laurence Whitehead. "European Democracy Promotion in North Africa: Limits and Prospects." In *The European Union and Democracy Promotion: The Case of North Africa*, edited by Richard Gillespie and Richard Youngs, 192–206. London: Cass, 2002.

Grabbe, Heather. *The EU's Transformative Power. Europeanization through Conditionality in Central and Eastern Europe*. New York: Palgrave Macmillan, 2006.

Greenfield, Danya, Amy Hawthorne, and Rosa Balfour. *US and EU: Lack of Strategic Vision, Frustrated Efforts toward the Arab Transitions*. Washington, DC: Atlantic Council, September 2013.

Greenfield, Danya, and Rosa Balfour. *Arab Awakening: Are the US and EU Missing the Challenge?*. Washington, DC: Atlantic Council, June 2012.

Hassan, Oz. "Undermining the Transatlantic Democracy Agenda? The Arab Spring and Saudi-Arabia"s Counteracting Democracy Strategy." *Democratization* 22, no. 3 (2015): 479–495.

Higley, John, and Michael Burton. "The Elite Variable in Democratic Transitions and Breakdowns." *American Sociological Review* 54, no. 1 (1989): 17–32.

Holmes, Amy Austin. "The Military Intervention that the World Forgot. Saudi and Emirati Forces Continue to Police Bahrain." *Al Jazeera*, 29 March 2014.

Huber, Daniela. "US and EU Human Rights and Democracy Promotion since the Arab Spring. Rethinking its Content, Targets and Instruments." *The International Spectator* 48, no. 3 (2013): 98–112.

International Crisis Group [ICG]. "The Tunisian Exception: Success and Limits of Consensus." *Middle East and North Africa Briefing* no. 37 (2014).
International Monetary Fund [IMF]. "Saudi-Arabia: Selected Issues." *IMF Country Report* no. 12/272 (2012).
Isaac, Sally Khalifa. "Rethinking the New ENP: A Vision for an Enhanced European Role in the Arab Revolutions." *Democracy and Security* 9, no. 1/2 (2013): 40–60.
Jünemann, Anette. "Security-Building in the Mediterranean After September 11." *Mediterranean Politics* 8, no. 2 (2003): 1–20.
Kausch, Kristina. "Foreign Funding in Post-revolution Tunisia", *FRIDE working paper* (2013).
Kelley, Judith. *Monitoring Democracy: When International Election Observation Works, and Why It Often Fails*. Princeton, NJ: Princeton University Press, 2012.
Kholaif, Dahlia. "Will the GCC survive Qatar-Saudi rivalry?." *Al Jazeera*. 18 March 2014.
Kubicek, Paul, ed. *The European Union and Democratization*. London: Routledge, 2003.
Landolt, Laura, and Paul Kubicek. "Opportunities and Constraints: Comparing Tunisia and Egypt to the Coloured Revolutions." *Democratization* 21, no. 6 (2014): 984–1006.
Lavenex, Sandra, and Frank Schimmelfennig. "EU Democracy Promotion in the Neighbourhood: From Leverage to Governance?" *Democratization* 18, no. 4 (2011): 885–909.
Levy, Jack. "Case Studies: Types, Designs, and Logic of Inference." *Conflict Management and Peace Science* 25 (2008): 1–18.
Mahoney, James. *The Legacies of Liberalism: Path Dependence and Political Regimes in Central America*. Baltimore: Johns Hopkins University Press, 2001.
Neumayer, Eric. "Arab-related Bilateral Sources of Development Finance: Issues, Trends, and the Way Forward." *World Economy* 27, no. 2 (2004): 281–300.
Nordland, Rod. "Saudi-Arabia Promises to Aid Egypt"s Regime." *The New York Times*, 20 August 2013.
Organisation for Economic Cooperation and Development [OECD]. "Reporting Directives for the Creditor Reporting System. Corrigendum on the Channels of Delivery." DCD/DAC(2007)39/FINAL/CORR5, 2010.
Richter, Solveig. "Two at One Blow? The EU and its Quest for Security and Democracy by Political Conditionality in the Western Balkans." *Democratization* 19, no. 3 (2012): 507–534.
Risse, Thomas, and Nelli Babayan. "Democracy Promotion and the Challenges of Illiberal Regional Powers: Introduction to the Special Issue." *Democratization* 22, no. 3 (2015): 381–399.
Rustow, Dankwart. "Transitions to Democracy." *Comparative Politics* 2, no. 3 (1970): 337–63.
Salloukh, Bassel. "The Arab Uprisings and the Geopolitics of the Middle East." *The International Spectator* 48, no. 2 (2013): 32–46.
Schimmelfennig, Frank, and Hanno Scholtz. "EU Democracy Promotion in the European Neighbourhood: Political Conditionality, Economic Development and Transnational Exchange." *European Union Politics* 9, no. 2 (2008): 187–215.
Schimmelfennig, Frank, and Ulrich Sedelmeier. "Governance by Conditionality: EU Rule Transfer to the Candidate Countries of Central and Eastern Europe." *Journal of European Public Policy* 11, no. 4 (2004): 661–679.
Schimmelfennig, Frank, Stefan Engert, and Heiko Knobel. *International Socialization in Europe. European Organizations, Political Conditionality and Democratic Change*. Basingstoke: Palgrave Macmillan, 2006.
Schmitter, Philippe. "The influence of the International Context upon the Choice of National Institutions and Policies in Neo-Democracies." In *The International Dimension of Democratization. Europe and the Americas* edited by Laurence Whitehead, 26–54. Oxford: Oxford University Press, 1996.

Scott, James, and Ralph Carter. "From Cold War to Arab Spring: Mapping the Effects of Paradigm Shifts on the Nature and Dynamics of US Democracy Assistance to the Middle East and North Africa." *Democratization*, online first, 2014.

Smith, Charles. "Democracy or Authoritarianism? Army or Anarchy? First Takes and Later Reflections on the Arab Spring." *The Middle East Journal* 67, no. 4 (2013): 633–662.

The Guardian. "Tunisia election results: Nida Tunis wins most seats, sidelining Islamists." *The Guardian*, 30 October 2014.

Tolstrup, Jakob. "When Can External Actors Influence Democratization? Leverage, Linkage, and Gatekeeper Elites." *Democratization* 20, no. 4 (2013): 716–42.

Vachudova, Milada Anna. *Europe Undivided: Democracy, Leverage and Integration After Communism.* Oxford: Oxford University Press, 2005.

Van Hüllen, Vera. "Europeanisation through Cooperation? EU Democracy Promotion in Morocco and Tunisia." *West European Politics* 35, no. 1 (2012): 117–34.

Welsh, Helga. "Political Transition Processes in Central and Eastern Europe." *Comparative Politics* 26, no. 4 (1994): 379–94.

Whitman, Richard, and Ana Juncos. "Challenging Events, Diminishing Influence? Relations with the Wider Europe." *Journal of Common Market Studies,* 52 (2014), 157–69.

World Bank. "Country Data Report for Tunisia, 1996–2012." *Worldwide Governance Indicators* (2013).

Youngs, Richard. "The European Union and Democracy Promotion in the Mediterranean: A New or Disingenuous Strategy." *Democratization* 9, no. 1 (2002): 40–62.

Youngs, Richard. "From Transformation to Mediation. The Arab Spring Reframed." *Carnegie Europe*, March 2014.

The noble west and the dirty rest? Western democracy promoters and illiberal regional powers

Tanja A. Börzel

Otto-Suhr Institute of Political Science, Freie Universität Berlin, Berlin, Germany

This conclusion summarizes the major findings of this special issue and discusses their implications for research on democratization and international democracy promotion. First, I compare the interactions between EU and US democracy promotion and the responses of non-democratic regional powers. In the cases in which Russia, Saudi Arabia, and China chose to pursue a countervailing strategy, I match the reactions of the US and the EU and explore how the combined (inter-)actions of democratic and non-democratic actors have affected efforts at democracy promotion in the target countries. The second part discusses the theoretical implications of these findings and identifies challenges for theory-building. I argue that the literature still has to come to terms with a counter-intuitive finding of this special issue, namely that non-democratic actors can promote democratic change by unintentionally empowering liberal reform coalitions as much as democracy promoters can unwittingly enhance autocracy by stabilizing illiberal incumbent regimes. I conclude with some policy considerations.

In November 2014, the world celebrated the twenty-fifth anniversary of the fall of the Berlin war, which stands for the victory of Western democracy over illiberal forms of political order.[1] After the collapse of communism in Eastern Europe and the Soviet Union, democracy promotion became an integral part of the foreign policy of Western states and established itself as a new field of action for Western international and regional organizations.[2] After the initial enthusiasm about the EU's transformative power in Central and Eastern Europe,[3] Western efforts at supporting democratic transition and stabilizing democratic consolidation have been increasingly deemed ineffective.[4] The failure of the West to bring its liberal institutions to the rest tends to be blamed on "black knights",[5] such as Russia, China, and Saudi Arabia, which yield enough hard and soft power to spoil Western attempts at international democracy promotion.[6]

This special issue challenges the conventional wisdom of the West promoting democracy and "the illiberal rest" promoting autocracy. By exploring the impact of non-democratic regional powers, such as Russia, China, and Saudi Arabia, on US and EU democracy promotion, the contributions show, first, that Western democracies do not unequivocally engage in democracy promotion. Similar to non-democratic regimes, they have a tendency to prioritize stability and security over democratic change.[7] Second, non-democratic regimes do not necessarily engage in autocracy promotion. Rather, they seek to undermine Western efforts at democracy promotion if they see their political and economic interests or their political survival at stake.[8] Third, domestic factors are much more relevant for the (in-)effectiveness of international democracy promotion than the activities of non-democratic actors.[9]

These findings resonate with more recent studies in the international democratization literature. What this special issue contributes to the state of the art is a "triangular" perspective, which focuses on the interrelated interactions between Western democracy promoters, non-democratic powers, and the target state. By exploring these three sets of interactions, it becomes clear that the domestic conditions in the target state determine how incumbent regimes respond to the incentives offered by democracy promoters and non-democratic powers to engage in or refrain from democratic change, respectively. They also shape the likelihood of whether target states accept the help of non-democratic powers in suppressing democratic opposition. Most importantly, the situation in the target country influences the attempts of non-democratic powers to countervail Western democracy promotion and the reactions of Western democracy promoters, in turn, to such spoiling strategies. Finally, domestic factors shape the effects of external democratic and non-democratic actors on democratic transition and democratic consolidation, or the lack thereof, in the target state.

This conclusion summarizes the major findings of this special issue and discusses their implications for research on democratization and international democracy promotion. It proceeds in three steps. First, I compare the interactions between EU and US democracy promotion and the responses of non-democratic regional powers. In the cases in which Russia, Saudi Arabia, and China chose to pursue a countervailing strategy, I match the reactions of the US and the EU and explore how the combined (inter-)actions of democratic and non-democratic actors have affected efforts at democracy promotion in the target countries. The second part discusses the theoretical implications of these findings and identifies challenges for theory-building. I argue that the literature still has to come to terms with a counter-intuitive finding of this special issue, namely that non-democratic actors can promote democratic change by unintentionally empowering liberal reform coalitions as much as democracy promoters can unwittingly enhance autocracy by stabilizing illiberal incumbent regimes. I conclude with some policy considerations.

Western democracy promoters, illiberal regional powers, and democracy promotion

Illiberal regional powers and western democracy promotion

After the "big bang" enlargement of the EU, which marked the end point of the successful democratization of post-communist countries in Central and Eastern Europe, optimism about Western democracy promotion quickly started to fade. The post-Soviet area, which became the target of EU and US efforts at democracy promotion, has not made any significant progress towards democracy. The so called newly independent states seem to have developed rather stable hybrid regimes "in the gray zone between democracy and autocracy",[10] which have been referred to as "semi-authoritarianism",[11] "electoral authoritarianism",[12] or "competitive authoritarianism".[13] The "Arab Spring" challenged the long-time persistence of authoritarianism in the Middle East and North Africa. Yet, the EU and the US were clearly taken by surprise by the recent developments and have only reluctantly endorsed democratic change. Their support for the new regimes has done little to foster democracy; Tunisia is the only country which has seen some significant improvements in the democratic quality of its regime.[14] US and EU attempts at promoting democracy and good governance in Sub-Sahara Africa have proven equally futile.[15] While the democratization literature has always been sceptical about the role of external actors in promoting democratic transition and consolidation, the ineffectiveness of their attempts is often blamed on the presence of powerful spoilers in the region that oppose democracy.[16]

However, this special issue convincingly demonstrates that illiberal states do not make autocracy promotion an integral part of their foreign policies in the same way as the US and EU have done it with democracy promotion. Nor do they see Western democracy promotion in third countries necessarily as a threat they have to counter. While Russia, China, and Saudi Arabia quell external and domestic attempts at democracy promotion at home, the contributors to this special issue find little evidence that they seek to promote their own or any other non-democratic regime type beyond their own borders. They do not use their economic and military capabilities to induce autocratic reforms in other countries.

Interestingly, illiberal states do engage in governance export at the regional level. Regional organizations can promote autocracy by boosting the legitimacy and sovereignty of their autocratic members.[17] Moreover, the Council of Independent States, the Shanghai Cooperation Organization, the League of Arab States, and the Gulf Cooperation Council explicitly prescribe and actively promote and protect the building, modification, and respect of governance institutions in their member states. In addition, they do so by referring to democracy, human rights, or rule of law. The regional commitment of illiberal powers to liberal norms and values serves to prevent political instability in the region, attract foreign aid and trade, or deflect attempts at governance transfer by Western actors.[18] Such signalling is strategic and aims at stabilizing rather than transforming autocracy at home. However, such regional commitments would lose their credibility if illiberal powers promoted autocracy abroad.[19] Furthermore, regional organizations can also restrict illiberal powers in promoting autocracy and resisting Western democracy promotion. Russia's threat to punish Ukraine for entering a Deep and Comprehensive Free Trade Agreement with the EU by economic retaliation runs against the decision-making rules of the Eurasian Economic Union (EEU) according to which Russia cannot impose any trade restrictions against Ukraine unilaterally. The two other members of the EEU, Belarus and Kazakhstan, have already refused to support Russia in a trade war against Ukraine.[20]

Like their commitment to liberal norms and values in regional organization, responses of illiberal regional powers to Western democracy promotion are motivated by regime survival, rent-seeking, and the protection of economic and security interests.[21] The findings of this special issue largely confirm this argument. Saudi Arabia supported the violent suppression of political protest in Bahrain for fear of democratic spill-over.[22] The 2011 and 2012 elections in Russia, which were widely perceived as fraudulent, heightened Putin's concerns about the survival of his regime due to possible contagion effects emanating from public uprisings in Ukraine.[23] He has been even more concerned about the Westernization of Ukraine, Georgia, Moldova, and Armenia pulling out of Russia's traditional sphere of influence.[24] Democratization is a precondition for closer economic and security relations with the West, of which membership in the EU and NATO is the biggest incentive the EU and US have on offer for promoting democracy. Countervailing EU and US democracy promotion in its near abroad is, hence, Putin's strategy to defend Russia's sphere of influence against what he perceives as an expansion of the Western sphere of influence into the post-Soviet area.[25] Defending Russia's power over the region also helps to ensure the survival of Putin's regime by boosting his approval rates through a foreign policy that claims to restore Russia as a great power and containing the risk of democratic spill-over. China's indifference towards EU and US democracy promotion in Sub-Sahara Africa and Myanmar confirms the finding that illiberal regional powers do not take issue with Western democracy promotion as long as their strategic interests are not at stake. Angola and Ethiopia are too far away, while Myanmar is too small and too poor to have a negative effect on Beijing's geostrategic interest or regime survival. Hong Kong, by contrast, may turn into an attractive alternative model to the autocratic rule of the Chinese Communist Party threatening its exclusive grip on power at home. While it is unclear to what extent and how actively the US and EU seek to promote democracy in Hong Kong, Beijing argues that the West supports democratic protesters to reaffirm its influence in the region against China's rising power.[26] Saudi Arabia saw the Muslim Brotherhood in Egypt as a potential threat, whose model of a democratically elected Islamist regime could have challenged the legitimacy of the Saudi kingdom as the protector of Islam.[27] How far Saudi support for the Egyptian military has undermined US and EU democratization and liberalization strategies is not clear given the latter's uneasiness over the Muslim Brotherhood and their tacit approval of the military assisted coup d'état. Likewise, the EU and the US have shared Saudi Arabia's preference for stability and security in the Gulf region. Their response to Saudi financial and military assistance to the Bahraini al-Khalifa regime in suppressing Shia protests was at best "timid".[28] Since more than 70% of Bahrainis are Shia, the overthrow of the Sunni monarchy fuelled fears of Iran escalating violence to enhance its influence in the Gulf region and undermining its stability.

In sum, democratic and non-democratic actors equally pursue geostrategic interests. These interests often conflict with international democracy promotion making Western actors compromise their efforts and illiberal powers resist them. Yet, rent-seeking and securing spheres of influence may also concur with democratic change promoted by the West. Russia, for instance, welcomed the "Tulip Revolution" in Kyrgyzstan as a chance to expand its influence in Central Asia.[29] In the end, countervailing strategies appear to depend on whether democratic and non-democratic powers pursue competing interests in a region.

Western democracy promoters and illiberal regional powers

The EU and the US made democracy promotion an explicit goal of their foreign policy. Yet, they also pursue other goals, such as political stability, economic growth, energy supply, or security. While in principle these goals are seen as complementary, the democratization of (semi-)authoritarian countries entails the risk of their destabilization at least in the short run. The more unstable and the less democratic the target state is, the more difficult it is to reconcile democracy promotion with ensuring security and stability.[30] This democratization-stability dilemma largely confirms the second hypothesis of the editors that Western democracy promoters only react to countervailing policies by non-democratic regional power if they prioritize democracy and human rights goals over stability and security goals.[31] The prioritizing explains why the US and the EU ignored attempts of Saudi Arabia to undermine democratization processes in Arab Spring countries and the Gulf region.[32] Liberal and illiberal regional powers equally prioritize stability and security.[33] Ukraine is one of the few cases in which the EU and US have sought to counter the countervailing strategies of the illiberal regional power, arguably because of Russia's attempts to *de*stabilize the country. Thus, rather than prioritizing democracy over stability, Putin's strategy of "managed instability"[34] has driven the EU and the US to step up their efforts at democracy promotion supporting democratic political forces that have the greatest potential to politically and economically stabilize Ukraine.[35]

In accordance with the second hypothesis of the editors, interdependent relationships with illiberal regional powers, particularly with regard to energy and security, also make Western democracy promoters more likely to compromise their efforts at democracy promotion and tolerate countervailing strategies of illiberal regional powers.[36] The EU and US have not been prepared to make full use of sanctions in order to counter Russia's violations of Georgia's and Ukraine's territorial integrity in 2008 and 2014, respectively.[37] While Ukraine and the EU signed the Association Agreement in August 2014, the Deep and Comprehensive Free

Trade Agreement (DCFTA) has been suspended for a year amid Russia's threats of retaliatory measures against both Ukraine and the EU. The EU also signalled that is was prepared to revise parts of the DCFTA to accommodate Russia's concerns.[38] In a similar vein, the US has been unwilling to risk its alliance with its most important allies in the region over Saudi Arabia's assistance in suppressing the Shia uprising in Bahrain.[39] Finally, China is too important for both the EU and the US to openly support Hong Kong's "umbrella revolution" in its protests against Beijing's efforts to compromise the "one country two systems" doctrine by curbing political freedoms.[40]

In sum, if illiberal powers only counteract Western democracy promotion if their economic or security interests are at stake, Western democracy promoters only respond to such countervailing strategies if they see their geopolitical interests challenged.

The domestic impact of Western and illiberal regional powers

Countervailing democracy promotion is not the same as autocracy promotion.[41] Yet, the outcome of such activities may be still autocracy enhancing. This special issue explores an important distinction between intention and outcome that has not received sufficient attention in the literature. Illiberal regional powers tend to protect their strategic interests rather than block Western democracy promotion per se. The outcome of their countervailing strategies, however, may still affect the chances of democratization in the target country by changing the balance of power between democratic and anti-democratic forces.

While their overall effectiveness is limited, external democracy promoters matter if they empower liberal reform coalitions,[42] as the US and the EU have done in Ukraine and Georgia.[43] Likewise, illiberal regimes may empower illiberal forces by providing them with financial and military support.[44] Russia and Saudi Arabia do not shy away from using overt or covert military coercion supporting the suppression of political protest by force or fuelling violent ethnic conflict in breakaway regions.[45] They also use financial and security assistance as well as market access to punish pro-Western policies and reward those straying away from them.[46] By yielding to Putin's pressure and accepting his economic support, including low gas prices, Yanukovych was spared to meet the demand of the EU to free Yulia Timoshenko and adopt an anti-corruption law and an election reform as the conditions for signing the Association Agreement.[47] Likewise, Saudi Arabia's financial assistance allowed Egyptian elites to avoid US and EU democratic conditionality.[48]

Differential empowerment certainly relies on the credibility, resources, and legitimacy of external actors as hypothesized by the editors.[49] But there are at best necessary conditions.[50] The way in which external actors sway the domestic balance of power between liberal and illiberal forces mostly depends on domestic factors.[51] Economic and security interdependence may matter but is more ambivalent in its effect on the leverage external actors have over the target state.[52] The

Ukraine, Moldova, Georgia, and Armenia are equally dependent on access to Russia's market and vulnerable to its security policy. Yet, due to its own security conundrum, only Armenia yielded to Russia's pressure to join the Eurasian Customs Union. In Ukraine, Moldova, and Georgia, Putin's economic and security threats have had the opposite effect, empowering pro-Western political forces to sign Association Agreements with the EU as an important step to closer relations with the West.[53]

Due to its natural resources, Angola is less dependent on the EU and the US than Ethiopia.[54] However, while having emerged as an equally important economic partner, China cannot compensate for EU and US aid and trade to Ethiopia. This is not the only reason why China has had little do to with the failure of the EU and US to push for democratic reforms in Angola and Ethiopia.[55] If democratization threatens the survival of the regime or external incentives are limited, Western democracy promotion is unlikely to be effective, irrespective of whether the target state has alternative funding and trade options.[56]

Besides empowering illiberal forces, the contributions to this special issue shed light on two other mechanisms through which countervailing strategies can undermine democratization processes. First, Russia's "managed instability" strategy of subverting Western-oriented governments with economic sanctions and military support for pro-Russian secessionists have harmed the economy and seriously undermined the statehood of Ukraine, Georgia, and Moldova.[57] The capacity of a government to set and enforce collectively binding rules and provide public goods is not only important to win elections, it is also a precondition for free and fair elections in the first place.[58] Unsettled disputes and frozen conflicts also render these countries less attractive for foreign direct investments and undermine their prospect of closer integration with the West.[59]

Second, illiberal regional powers can provide an attractive model that is emulated by third countries.[60] Putin's "sovereign or illiberal democracy" has found supporters outside, and increasingly also inside, Europe.[61] China's developmental capitalism might be even more attractive since, unlike Russia, it combines autocracy with growing prosperity.[62] China's economy challenges the dominance of the Western model of liberal democracy. Its soft power of attraction may be much more influential in diffusing and enhancing autocracy than any direct attempts at autocracy promotion.

In sum, illiberal regional powers do not engage in autocracy promotion. However, if Western democracy promotion challenges their strategic interests, they employ countervailing strategies which can stabilize and enhance autocracy – or they can have the opposite effect depending on the domestic conditions in the target country. Russia has ultimately promoted rather than undermined democratic change in some countries of its near abroad by empowering liberal reform coalitions in their quest for democracy and closer relations with the West and strengthening the commitment of Western actors to supporting democratization.[63] The literature has paid as little attention to such paradoxical outcomes as it has to Western democracy promoters empowering non-democratic forces.

Consorted worlds? Challenges to democratization and international democracy promotion research

The EU and US failed at promoting democracy when they supported authoritarian elites in Tunisia and Egypt before they were swept away by the Arab Spring, remained silent when a democratically elected government was overthrown by the military in Egypt, and stood by when authoritarian regimes violently suppressed political opposition in Bahrain and Syria. This failure cannot be attributed to Russia, Saudi Arabia, and China promoting autocracy or blocking democracy. It results from the democratization-stability dilemma, where democracy promotion requires a transition of power that entails political uncertainty about the outcomes and often involves conflict. This dilemma is the more pronounced, the more fragile the target state is. Where the democratization-stability dilemma is less pronounced, the effectiveness of Western democracy promotion hinges on other domestic factors.[64] Differential empowerment requires the existence of reform coalitions that have internalized liberal norms and values and are strong enough to use Western trade, aid, and political support to push for democratic change.[65] Moreover, empowering domestic reformists is not enough if actors lack the necessary resources to introduce domestic change. Statehood is not only a question of administrative capacity but is often further undermined by the contestedness of borders and political authority.[66] Finally, Western actors require legitimacy to promote democratic change.[67] EU and US democratic demands meet with public resentment whenever they clash with nationalist or religious beliefs, for example regarding the role of minorities, or are perceived as attempting to control the country.

Domestic conditions severely limit the effectiveness of Western democracy promotion. This special issue shows how countervailing strategies of illiberal powers can further undermine the chances of Western democracy promotion by subverting the statehood of target states or undermining the legitimacy of Western democracy promoters. The various contributions also show that Western democracy promotion, rather than being futile, can have the opposite effect enhancing or stabilizing autocracy. The causal mechanism is domestic empowerment, however, Western aid, trade, and security cooperation may empower both liberal and illiberal forces. What has been largely overlooked by the democratization literature is that non-democratic regimes also use Western democracy promotion to advance their power and interest.[68]

The European Neighbourhood Policy (ENP) is a case in point. From its very inception, the ENP has focused on building and strengthening state institutions which are capable of fostering legal approximation with EU rules on trade, migration, or energy.[69] By promoting effective government rather than democratic governance, the EU helped stabilize non-democratic and corrupt regimes in its Southern and Eastern neighbourhood rather than transforming them.[70] Incumbent elites have aligned their political survival strategies with the EU's demand for domestic change. They fought corruption, for instance, where it helped to oust political opponents, reward political allies, deflect international criticism, and attract foreign assistance and investments.[71] The US has been less state-centred, supporting free and fair elections, an independent media, and a stronger civil society.[72] But like the EU, the US has only reluctantly backed democratic protest movements if its geostrategic interests have been at stake and refrained from putting pressure on incumbent regimes for human rights violations or democratic back-sliding.[73] Moreover, US democracy assistance is security driven prioritizing fragile states.[74]

In short, Western democracy promotion can have unintended and negative effects on democratic change in target states. It does not only empower liberal reform coalitions, to the extent that they exist in the first place, but can also boost or stabilize the power of incumbent autocratic elites. Likewise, illiberal powers may not only fail in pulling transition or democratizing countries away from Western democracy, they may end up pushing them in this very direction. Russia's countervailing strategies have empowered pro-Western democratic forces in Ukraine and Georgia and facilitated compliance with EU demands for economic and political reforms. Putin's attempts to destabilize the two countries through economic sanctions and military support for secessionist regions made the US and the EU step up their economic and political support for democratization leading to more rather than less engagement in Russia's near abroad.[75] In a similar vein, Saudi Arabia's support for Tunisia's disposed dictator Ben Ali and its opposition against the moderate Islamist Ennahda party discredited the Saudi monarchy despite the substantial, unconditional aid offered to the transition government and boosted cooperation with the EU on democracy, notwithstanding its support for the Ben Ali regime.[76]

"Crossed-over" empowerment, where illiberal regional powers strengthen liberal domestic forces and Western democracy promoters stabilize non-democratic regimes, point to a second finding of this special issue with which research on international democracy promotion has to come to terms. While acknowledging the prevalence of domestic factors, the literature still tends to adopt a "top-down" approach where domestic actors merely respond to opportunities and constraints provided by Washington, Brussels, Moscow, Beijing, or Riyadh. However, ruling elites may strategically align external incentives or persuasion efforts with their domestic incentives, political preferences, or survival strategies, so that they can use external resources to push their own political agenda, please their constituencies, and regain or consolidate their power.[77] They pick and choose from the economic and political incentives offered to them by external actors, often seeking to play off one against the other. Victor Yanukovych, for instance, was not merely a Kremlin puppet yielding to Putin's pressure when he pulled back from the Association Agreement with the EU in November 2013. While he had hoped to use closer relations with the EU to decrease Ukraine's dependence on Russia, Putin's threats provided him with a convenient excuse for not complying with EU democratic conditionality.[78] In a similar vein, Egyptian elites have been playing off the US and EU against Saudi Arabia.[79] Interestingly, African governments have largely refrained from using their trade and aid relations with China to relinquish EU and US democratic conditionality.[80]

In sum, this special issue points to the importance of a more agency-centred perspective on international democracy promotion that places the domestic actors in the target states at the heart of the analysis and pays more attention to the unintended effects of both liberal and illiberal actors and their interaction.

Conclusion

Exploring and comparing the interactions between Western democracy promoters, illiberal regional regimes, and target countries provides a fruitful approach to studying international democracy promotion and challenges some conventional wisdoms in the state of the art. First, rather than intentionally promoting autocracy or blocking democracy, illiberal powers seek to countervail Western democracy promotion in order to protect their economic, geostrategic, or political interests, which are not so different from those of Western democracy promoters. Where the two differ is that illiberal regional powers do not have to balance security and stability against democracy and human rights.

Second, this democratization-stability dilemma undermines the effectiveness of Western democracy promotion more than the countervailing strategies of non-democratic regional powers. True, if democracy promotion threatens their geopolitical and economic interests or regime survival, Russia, China, and Saudi Arabia seek to undermine democratic processes to the extent that they unfold. They offer non-democratic regimes economic, political, and military assistance and threaten democracy-minded ruling elites to withdraw it. Moreover, they may undermine the capacity of government to introduce democratic changes by destabilizing the country. Yet, with the exception of Ukraine and Georgia, democratic processes are not promoted by Western powers but mostly endogenously driven. More often than not, the EU and US share the interest of illiberal regional powers in the stability and security of a region. Not only did they fail to develop a coherent approach on how to support the Arab Spring, they were also silent on the military coup against a democratically elected government in Egypt, tolerated the Saudi-led military intervention of the Gulf Cooperation Council that assisted Bahraini security forces in detaining thousands of protesters, and stood by the massive human rights violations committed by the Assad regime in Syria.

These two findings do not only challenge the admittedly stylized juxtaposition of the "noble West" promoting democracy, and the "dirty rest" promoting autocracy. They also yield some important policy implications, particularly for the EU and the US.

For actors whose foreign policy is not only oriented towards geostrategic interests but which also seek to promote moral goals, all good things seldom go together.[81] The more unstable a target state is and the less democratic, the more difficult it will be to reconcile the protection and promotion of human rights and democracy with ensuring security and stability. The democratization-stability dilemma seems to be somewhat unavoidable and undermines the capacity of Western democracy promoters to design credible democracy promotion policies based on consistent criteria and reliable rewards. However, democratic external actors should at least acknowledge the dilemma and develop strategies on how to balance the different goals. Otherwise reproaches of double standards and hypocrisy will continue to undermine their credibility and legitimacy. Moreover, democracy promotion should focus on countries like Tunisia, which are sufficiently stable and feature pro-democratic reform coalitions that can be empowered by democratic conditionality and assistance. Where such conditions are absent, democracy promotion usually fails. Besides empowering liberal forces, Western democracy promoters should assist target states in reducing their asymmetric interdependence on illiberal regional powers.[82] Georgia used its approximation with EU energy policies to diversify its energy supply.[83] Likewise, the EU has been trying to compensate for the energy cuts imposed by Russia on Ukraine.

Finally, stabilizing autocratic regimes by providing aid and trade should find its limits where dictators engage in massive human rights violations. For all the criticism of the EU and the US for supporting Hosni Mubarak of Egypt and Ben Ali of Tunisia, both treated Muammar al-Gaddafi of Libya and Bashar al-Assad of Syria as pariahs. Only in the case of Libya did they intervene militarily, while they did little to remedy the massive human rights violations by the Assad regime.

Overall, the findings of this special issue confirm the limits of what Western democracy promoters are willing and able to do, particularly if their geostrategic interests are at stake. Rather than blaming their failure to support democracy on illiberal powers, they should develop strategies to balance their different foreign policy goals.

Acknowledgements

I thank Nelli Babayan and Thomas Risse for their helpful comments. I am also grateful to Stefan Rinnert for his help with editing the text.

Notes

1. Fukuyama, *The End of History and the Last Man*.
2. Magen and Morlino, *Anchoring Democracy*; Magen et al., *Promoting Democracy and the Rule of Law*; Pevehouse, *Democracy from Above*; McMahon and Baker, *Piecing a Democratic Quilt?*; Kelley, *Monitoring Democracy*.
3. Grabbe, *The EU's Transformative Power*; Vachudova, *Europe Undivided*.
4. Schimmelfennig and Scholtz, "EU Democracy Promotion in the European Neighbourhood"; Kelley, *Monitoring Democracy*; Börzel, "Coming Together or Drifting Apart?"
5. Levitsky and Way, *Competitive Authoritarianism*.
6. Ambrosio, *The Authoritarian Backlash*; Tolstrup, "Studying a Negative External Actors"; Levitsky and Way, *Competitive Authoritarianism*; Whitehead, *The International Dimensions of Democratization*; Bader et al., "Would Autocracies Promote Autocracy?"; Cameron and Orenstein, "Post-Soviet Authoritarianism"; Kavalski, *The New Central Asia*.
7. Jünemann, "Security Building in the Mediterranean after September 11"; Youngs, "The European Union and Democracy Promotion in the Mediterranean"; Schlumberger, "Dancing with Wolves"; Börzel et al., "Democracy or Stability?"

8. Bader et al., "Would Autocracies Promote Autocracy?"; Obydenkova and Libman, *Autocratic and Democratic External Influences in Post-Soviet Eurasia.*
9. Carothers, "The End of the Transition Paradigm"; Whitehead, *The International Dimensions of Democratization*; Linz and Stepan, *Problems of Democratic Transition and Consolidation*; Lipset, "The Social Requisites of Democracy Revisited."
10. Hadenius and Toerell, "Authoritarian Regimes"; Carothers, "The End of the Transition Paradigm."
11. Ottaway, *Democracy Challenged.*
12. Schedler, *Electoral Authoritarianism.*
13. Levitsky and Way, *Competitive Authoritarianism.*
14. Börzel et al., "The EU, External Actors, and the Arabellions"; Hassan, "Undermining the Transatlantic Democracy Agenda?"; Freyburg and Richter, "Local Actors in the Driver's Seat."
15. Magen et al., *Promoting Democracy and the Rule of Law.*
16. Levitsky and Way, *Competitive Authoritarianism*; Whitehead, *The International Dimensions of Democratization*; Ambrosio, *The Authoritarian Backlash*; Tolstrup, "Studying a Negative External Actors"; Bader et al., "Would Autocracies Promote Autocracy?"; Melnykovska et al., "Do Russia and China Promote Autocracy in Central Asia?"; Cameron and Orenstein, "Post-Soviet Authoritarianism"; Kavalski, *The New Central Asia.*
17. Söderbaum, *The Political Economy of Regionalism*; Libman, "Supranational Organizations."
18. Börzel and van Hüllen, *Governance Transfer by Regional Organizations.*
19. Babayan, "The Return of the Empire?"
20. Libman, "Supranational Organizations."
21. Ambrosio, *The Authoritarian Backlash*; Tolstrup, "Studying a Negative External Actors"; Bader et al., "Would Autocracies Promote Autocracy?"
22. Hassan, "Undermining the Transatlantic Democracy Agenda?"
23. Dannreuther, "Russia and the Arab Spring."
24. Babayan, "The Return of the Empire?"; Delcour and Wolczuk, "Spoiler or Facilitator of Democratization?"
25. Delcour and Wolczuk, "Spoiler or Facilitator of Democratization?"
26. Chen and Kinzelbach, "Democracy Promotion and China"; Hakenesch, "Not as Bad as it Seems."
27. Hassan, "Undermining the Transatlantic Democracy Agenda?"
28. Ibid.
29. Obydenkova and Libman, *Autocratic and Democratic External Influences in Post-Soviet Eurasia.*
30. Börzel and van Hüllen, "One Voice, One Message, but Conflicting Goals."
31. Jünemann, "Security Building in the Mediterranean after September 11"; Youngs, "The European Union and Democracy Promotion in the Mediterranean."
32. Hassan, "Undermining the Transatlantic Democracy Agenda?"
33. Börzel et al., "The EU, External Actors, and the Arabellions"; Freyburg and Richter, "Local Actors in the Driver's Seat."
34. Tolstrup, "Studying a Negative External Actors."
35. Delcour and Wolczuk, "Spoiler or Facilitator of Democratization?"
36. Börzel and Pamuk, "Pathologies of Europeanization"; van Hüllen, "Europeanization through Cooperation?"
37. Delcour and Wolczuk, "Spoiler or Facilitator of Democratization?"
38. Babayan, "The Return of the Empire?"
39. Hassan, "Undermining the Transatlantic Democracy Agenda?"
40. Chen and Kinzelbach, "Democracy Promotion and China."

41. Burnell, "Is There a New Autocracy Promotion?"; Obydenkova and Libman, *Autocratic and Democratic External Influences in Post-Soviet Eurasia*.
42. Schimmelfennig et al., "Costs, Commitment and Compliance"; Schimmelfennig and Sedelmeier, *The Europeanization of Central and Eastern Europe*; Vachudova, *Europe Undivided*.
43. Delcour and Wolczuk, "Spoiler or Facilitator of Democratization?"; Babayan, "The Return of the Empire?"
44. Freyburg and Richter, "Local Actors in the Driver's Seat."
45. Hassan, "Undermining the Transatlantic Democracy Agenda?"; Babayan, "The Return of the Empire?"; Delcour and Wolczuk, "Spoiler or Facilitator of Democratization?"
46. Freyburg and Richter, "Local Actors in the Driver's Seat."
47. Delcour and Wolczuk, "Spoiler or Facilitator of Democratization?"
48. Hassan, "Undermining the Transatlantic Democracy Agenda?"
49. Schimmelfennig and Sedelmeier, *The Europeanization of Central and Eastern Europe*.
50. Freyburg and Richter, "Local Actors in the Driver's Seat."
51. Carothers, "The End of the Transition Paradigm"; Whitehead, *The International Dimensions of Democratization*; Linz and Stepan, *Problems of Democratic Transition and Consolidation*; Lipset, "The Social Requisites of Democracy Revisited."
52. van Hüllen, "Europeanization Through Cooperation?"; Börzel and Pamuk, "Pathologies of Europeanization."
53. Delcour and Wolczuk, "Spoiler or Facilitator of Democratization?"
54. Hakenesch, "Not as Bad as it Seems."
55. Ibid.
56. Schimmelfennig, "Strategic Calculations and International Socialization"; Schimmelfennig and Sedelmeier, *The Europeanization of Central and Eastern Europe*.
57. Tolstrup, "Studying a Negative External Actors."
58. Siroky and Abrasidze, "Guns, Roses and Democratization"; Tolstrup, "Studying a Negative External Actors"; Delcour and Wolczuk, "Spoiler or Facilitator of Democratization?"
59. Tolstrup, "Sub-National Level."
60. Whitehead, *The International Dimensions of Democratization*.
61. Babayan, "The Return of the Empire?"
62. Chen and Kinzelbach, "Democracy Promotion and China."
63. Delcour and Wolczuk, "Spoiler or Facilitator of Democratization?"
64. Börzel and Risse, "When Europeanization Meets Diffusion"; Börzel et al., "The EU, External Actors, and the Arabellions"; Freyburg and Richter, "Local Actors in the Driver's Seat."
65. Vachudova, *Europe Undivided*.
66. Elbasani, *European Integration and Transformation in the Western Balkans*.
67. Krasner and Risse, *External Actors, State-Building, and Service Provision in Areas of Limited Statehood*.
68. Spendzharova and Vachudova, "Catching-Up"; van Hüllen, "Europeanization through Cooperation?"; Noutcheva and Aydin-Düzgit, "Lost in Europeanisation."
69. Ademmer and Börzel, "Migration, Energy and Good Governance in the EU's Eastern Neighborhood"; Börzel and Pamuk, "Pathologies of Europeanization."
70. Youngs, "European Democracy Promotion in the Middle East"; Wetzel and Orbie, "With Map and Compass on Narrow Paths and Through Shallow Waters"; Börzel and van Hüllen, "One Voice, One Message, but Conflicting Goals."
71. Börzel and Pamuk, "Pathologies of Europeanization."

72. Börzel et al., "Democracy or Stability?"; van Hüllen and Stahn, "Comparing EU and US Democracy Promotion in the Mediterranean and the Newly Independent States"; Freyburg and Richter, "Local Actors in the Driver's Seat."
73. Huber, "A Pragmatic Actor"; Hassan, "Undermining the Transatlantic Democracy Agenda?"
74. Freyburg and Richter, "Local Actors in the Driver's Seat."
75. Delcour and Wolczuk, "Spoiler or Facilitator of Democratization?"
76. Dandashly, "The EU Response to Regime Change in the Wake of the Arab Revolt"; Freyburg and Richter, "Local Actors in the Driver's Seat."
77. Ademmer, "You Make Us Do What We Want!"; Ademmer and Börzel, "Migration, Energy and Good Governance in the EU's Eastern Neighborhood"; Börzel and Pamuk, "Pathologies of Europeanization"; Spendzharova and Vachudova, "Catching-Up?"; Woll and Jacqout, "Using Europe."
78. Delcour and Wolczuk, "Spoiler or Facilitator of Democratization?"
79. Freyburg and Richter, "Local Actors in the Driver's Seat."
80. Hakenesch, "Not as Bad as it Seems."
81. Grimm and Leininger, "Not All Good Things Go Together."
82. Babayan, "The Return of the Empire?"
83. Ademmer and Börzel, "Migration, Energy and Good Governance in the EU's Eastern Neighborhood."

Notes on contributor

Tanja A. Börzel is professor of political science and holds the Chair for European Integration at the Otto-Suhr-Institut for Political Science, Freie Universität Berlin.

References

Ademmer, E. "You Make Us Do What We Want! The Usage of External Actors and Policy Conditionality in the European Neighborhood." KFG Working Paper Series 32, no. November 2011, Kolleg-Forschergruppe (KFG) "The Normative Power of Europe", Freie Universität Berlin, 2011.

Ademmer, E., and T. A. Börzel. "Migration, Energy and Good Governance in the EU's Eastern Neighborhood." *Europe Asia Studies* 65, no. 4 (2013): 581–608.

Ambrosio, T. *The Authoritarian Backlash. Russian Resistance to Democratization in the Former Soviet Union.* Burlington: Ashgate, 2009.

Babayan, N. "The Return of the Empire? Russia's Counteraction to Transatlantic Democracy Promotion in Its Near Abroad." *Democratization* 22, no. 3 (2015): 438–458.

Bader, J., J. Grävingholt, and A. Kästner. "Would Autocracies Promote Autocracy? A Political Economy Perspective on Regime-Type Export in Regional Neighbourhoods." *Contemporary Politics* 16, no. 1 (2010): 81–100.

Börzel, T. A. "Coming Together or Drifting Apart? Political Change in New Member States, Accession Candidates, and the Eastern Neighbourhood Countries." Chap., *MAXCAP Working Paper No.3, "Maximizing the Integration Capacity of the European Union: Lessons of and Prospects for Enlargement and Beyond" (MAXCAP)*. Berlin: Freie Universität Berlin, 2014.

Börzel, T. A., and Y. Pamuk. "Pathologies of Europeanization. Fighting Corruption in the Southern Caucasus." *West European Politics* 35, no. 1 (2012): 79–97.

Börzel, T. A., Y. Pamuk, and A. Stahn. "Democracy or Stability? EU and US Engagement in the Southern Caucasus." In *Democracy Promotion in the EU and the EU*

Compared, edited by A. Magen, M. McFaul, and T. Risse. Houndmills: Palgrave Macmillan, 2009.
Börzel, T. A., and T. Risse. "When Europeanization Meets Diffusion. Exploring New Territory." *West European Politics* 35, no. 1 (2012): 192–207.
Börzel, T. A., T. Risse, and A. Dandashly. "The EU, External Actors, and the Arabellions: Much Ado About (Almost) Nothing." *Journal of European Integration* 37, no. 1 (2015): 135–153.
Börzel, T. A., and V. van Hüllen. "One Voice, One Message, but Conflicting Goals. Cohesiveness and Consistency in the European Neighbourhood Policy." *Journal of European Public Policy* 21, no. 7 (2014): 1033–1049.
Börzel, T. A., and V. van Hüllen, eds. *Governance Transfer by Regional Organizations. Patching Together a Global Script.* Houndmills: Palgrave Macmillan, 2015.
Burnell, P. "Is There a New Autocracy Promotion?" *FRIDE Working Paper 96; Madrid*, 2010.
Cameron, D. R., and M. A. Orenstein. "Post-Soviet Authoritarianism: The Influence of Russia in Its "Near Abroad"." *Post-Soviet Affairs* 28, no. 1 (2012): 1–44.
Carothers, T. "The End of the Transition Paradigm." *Journal of Democracy* 13, no. 1 (2002).
Chen, D., and K. Kinzelbach. "Democracy Promotion and China: Blocker or Bystander?" *Democratization* 22, no. 3 (2015): 400–418.
Dandashly, A. "The EU Response to Regime Change in the Wake of the Arab Revolt. A Differential Implementation." *Journal of European Integration* 37, no. 1 (2015): 37–56.
Dannreuther, R. "Russia and the Arab Spring: Supporting the Counter-Revolution." *Journal of European Integration* 37, no. 1 (2015): 77–94.
Delcour, L., and K. Wolczuk. "Spoiler or Facilitator of Democratization? Russia's Role in Georgia and Ukraine." *Democratization* 22, no. 3 (2015): 459–478.
Elbasani, A., ed. *European Integration and Transformation in the Western Balkans: Europeanization or Business as Usual?* London: Routledge, 2012.
Freyburg, T., and S. Richter. "Local Actors in the Driver's Seat: Transatlantic Democracy Promotion Under Regime Competition in the Arab World." *Democratization* 22, no. 3 (2015): 496–518.
Fukuyama, F. *The End of History and the Last Man.* New York: Avon Books, 1992.
Grabbe, H. *The EU's Transformative Power – Europeanization through Conditionality in Central and Eastern Europe.* Houndsmills: Palgrave Macmillian, 2006.
Grimm, S., and J. Leininger. "Not All Good Things Go Together: Conflicting Objectives in Democracy Promotion." *Democratization* 19, no. 3 (2012): 391–414.
Hadenius, A., and J. Toerell. "Authoritarian Regimes: Stability, Change, and Pathways to Democracy, 1972–2003." *Helen Kellogg Institute for International Studies, Working Paper No. 331. Notre Dame, IN*, 2006.
Hakenesch, C. "Not as Bad as it Seems: EU and U.S. Democracy Promotion Face China in Africa." *Democratization* 22, no. 3 (2015): 419–437.
Hassan, O. "Undermining the Transatlantic Democracy Agenda? The Arab Spring and Saudi Arabia's Counteracting Democracy Strategy." *Democratization* 22, no. 3 (2015): 479–495.
Huber, D. "A Pragmatic Actor – The US Response to the Arab Uprisings." *Journal of European Integration* 37, no. 1 (2015): 57–75.
Jünemann, A. "Security Building in the Mediterranean after September 11." In *Euro-Mediterranean Relations after September 11. International, Regional and Domestic Dynamics*, edited by A. Jünemann, 1–20. London: Frank Cass, 2003.
Kavalski, E. ed. *The New Central Asia. The Regional Impact of International Actors.* Singapore: World Scientific Publishing, 2010.

Kelley, J. G. *Monitoring Democracy: When International Election Observation Works, and Why It Often Fails*. Princeton: Princeton University Press, 2012.

Krasner, S. D., and T. Risse, eds. *External Actors, State-Building, and Service Provision in Areas of Limited Statehood*, 2014.

Levitsky, S., and L. Way. *Competitive Authoritarianism: Hybrid Regimes after the Cold War*. Cambridge: Cambridge University Press, 2010.

Libman, A. "Supranational Organizations: Russia and the Eurasian Economic Union." In *Autocratic and Democratic External Influences in Post-Soviet Eurasia*, edited by A. Obydenkova and A. Libman. London: Ashgate, 2015.

Linz, J. J., and A. Stepan. *Problems of Democratic Transition and Consolidation: Southern Europe, South America, and Post-Communist Europe*. Baltimore: Johns Hopkins University Press, 1996.

Lipset, S. M. "The Social Requisites of Democracy Revisited: 1993 Presidential Address." *American Sociological Review* 59 (1994): 1–22.

Magen, A., and L. Morlino, eds. *Anchoring Democracy: External Influence on Domestic Rule of Law Development*. London: Routledge, 2008.

Magen, A., T. Risse, and M. McFaul, eds. *Promoting Democracy and the Rule of Law. American and European Strategies*. Houndmills: Palgrave Macmillan, 2009.

McMahon, E. R., and S. H. Baker. *Piecing a Democratic Quilt? Regional Organizations and Universal Norms*. Bloomfield, CT: Kumarian Press, 2006.

Melnykovska, I., H. Plamper, and R. Schweickert. "Do Russia and China Promote Autocracy in Central Asia?" *Asia Europe Journal* 10, no. 1 (2012): 75–89.

Noutcheva, G., and S. Aydin-Düzgit. "Lost in Europeanisation: The Western Balkans and Turkey." *West European Politics* 35, no. 1 (2012): 59–78.

Obydenkova, A., and A. Libman, eds. *Autocratic and Democratic External Influences in Post-Soviet Eurasia*. London: Ashgate, 2015.

Ottaway, M. *Democracy Challenged. The Rise of Semi-Authoritarianism*. Washington, D.C. Carnegie Endowment for International Peace, 2003.

Pevehouse, J. C. *Democracy from Above: Regional Organizations and Democratization*. Cambridge: Cambridge University Press, 2005.

Schedler, A. *Electoral Authoritarianism: The Dynamics of Unfree Competition*. Boulder and London: Lynne Rienner Publishers, 2006.

Schimmelfennig, F. "Strategic Calculations and International Socialization: Membership Incentives, Party Constellations and Sustained Compliance in Central and Eastern Europe." *International Organization* 4, no. 827–860 (2005).

Schimmelfennig, F., S. Engert, and H. Knobel. "Costs, Commitment and Compliance. The Impact of EU Democratic Conditionality on Latvia, Slovakia and Turkey." *Journal of Common Market Studies* 41, no. 3 (2003): 495–518.

Schimmelfennig, F. and H. Scholtz. "EU Democracy Promotion in the European Neighbourhood. Political Conditionality, Economic Development and Transnational Exchange." *European Union Politics* 9, no. 2 (2008): 187–215.

Schimmelfennig, F., and U. Sedelmeier. *The Europeanization of Central and Eastern Europe, Cornell studies in political economy*. Ithaca, NY: Cornell University Press, 2005.

Schlumberger, O. "Dancing with Wolves: Dilemmas of Democracy Promotion in Authoritarian Contexts." In *Democratization and Development. New Political Strategies for the Middle East*, edited by D. Jung, 33–60. Basingstoke: Palgrave Macmillan, 2006.

Siroky, D. S., and D. Abrasidze. "Guns, Roses and Democratization: Huntington's Secret Admirer in the Caucasus." *Democratization* 18, no. 6 (2011): 1227–1245.

Söderbaum, F. *The Political Economy of Regionalism. The Case of Southern Africa*. Basingstoke: Palgrave Macmillan, 2004.

Spendzharova, A. B., and M. A. Vachudova. "Catching-Up? Consolidating Liberal Democracy in Bulgaria and Romania." *West European Politics* 35, no. 1 (2012): 39–58.

Tolstrup, J. "Studying a Negative External Actors: Russia's Management of Stability and Instability in the "Near Abroad"." *Democratization* 14, no. 4 (2009): 922–944.

Tolstrup, J. "Sub-National Level: Russian Support for Secessionism and Pockets of Autocracy." In *Autocratic and Democratic External Influences in Post-Soviet Eurasia*, edited by A. Obydenkova and A. Libman. London: Ashgate, 2015.

Vachudova, M. A. *Europe Undivided: Democracy, Leverage and Integration after Communism*. Oxford: Oxford University Press, 2005.

Vanderhill, R. *Promoting Authoritarianism Abroad*. Boulder, CO: Lynne Rienner, 2012.

van Hüllen, V. "Europeanization through Cooperation? EU Democracy Promotion in Morocco and Tunisia." *West European Politics* 35, no. 1 (2012): 117–134.

van Hüllen, V., and A. Stahn. "Comparing EU and US Democracy Promotion in the Mediterranean and the Newly Independent States." In *Democracy Promotion in the US and the EU Compared*, edited by A. Magen, M. McFaul and T. Risse, 118–149. Houndmills: Palgrave Macmillan, 2009.

Wetzel, A., and J. Orbie. "With Map and Compass on Narrow Paths and Through Shallow Waters: Discovering the Substance of EU Democracy Promotion." *European Foreign Affairs Review* 16, no. 5 (2011): 705–725.

Whitehead, L., ed. *The International Dimensions of Democratization: Europe and the Americas*. Oxford: Oxford University Press, 2001.

Woll, C., and S. Jacqout. "Using Europe: Strategic Action in Multi-level Politics." *Comparative European Politics* 8, no. 1 (2010): 110–126.

Youngs, R. "European Democracy Promotion in the Middle East." *International Politics and Society* 4 (2004): 111–122.

Youngs, R. "The European Union and Democracy Promotion in the Mediterranean. A New or Disingenuous Strategy?" *Democratization* 2, no. 1 (2002): 40–62.

Index

Abdullah bin Abdulaziz Al Saud, King of Saudi Arabia 103, 106
Abkhazia 88, 90–1
Africa: China 5–6, 8, 12, 39–52, 141, 147 *see also* individual countries
aids, loans and direct investment: Africa 39–45, 48–9, 145, 147; Angola 43, 44–5; Arab World 120, 121–4, 144; China 26, 39–40, 42–3, 44–5; conditionality 40, 44–5; credibility 124; Egypt 103, 105, 144; Ethiopia 43, 48–9, 145; EU 103–4, 121–3, 147; human rights 149; macro-financial assistance (MFA) (EU) 103–4; Myanmar 21, 26; Russia 63, 144; Saudi Arabia 103, 105–6, 123–4, 144; soft loans 123; Tunisia 126–7, 147; Ukraine 89; United States 49, 64, 70, 82–3, 103, 126–7
Algeria 121
American Center for International Labor Solidarity 29
Angola-China relations 12, 40, 43, 44–7: aid 43, 44–5; China Export-Import Bank (EXIM), loan from 45–6, 47; civil society, support for 45, 47; civil war 43, 44, 46; conditionality 44–5; cooperation partner, China as a 43, 45–6, 51; democracy promotion strategies 43, 44–5, 46–7, 51–2, 142, 145; dominant ruling parties 43; elections 43, 44–5; energy 44, 46; infrastructure projects 46; low levels of political competition 43; media 45, 47; MPLA 43, 46; natural resources 45, 145; oil 46; political dialogue 44–6, 51; regime survival 46; transparency 44–5; UNITA 46
Ankvab, Aleksandr 90–1
Apple Daily (China) 29

Arab World 8, 12, 116–32: agency-driven influences 116–17; aid 120, 121–4; Arabellions/Arab Spring 2, 5, 7, 86, 9–12, 99–112, 118–24, 140–8; civil society 2, 121; conditionality 118–21, 123; countervailing democracy promotion 118–20; credibility of West 13, 117–20, 124; Deep and Comprehensive FTAs (DCFTA) 121; democracy promotion 5, 11, 116–32; democratization 9, 121, 131, 143; elections 120; elites 117–20, 124, 131–2; geostrategic interests 124; human rights 120–1; institutional change 119; intention 118; leverage 118; liberalization 118, 132; money, markets and mobility (3Ms) 121; opposition and protests 118–19, 121–2; regime competition 5, 116–32; Saudi Arabia 5, 12–13, 99–112, 117–18, 124–32, 140–8; stability and security 7, 120; theoretical arguments 118–20, 124, 141, 143, 146, 148; Tunisia 12–13, 117–18, 124–31, 132
Armenia-Russia relations 5, 62, 68–70, 145: democratization 65; Eastern Partnership (EaP) 5, 59, 65, 68–70; energy 68; Eurasian Customs Union 60, 145; Gazprom 68; Georgia 69; leverage 145; military bases 68; Nagorno Karabakh, conflict with Azerbaijan over 69–70; nuclear energy 69; Westernization 142
arms: embargoes 24; sales/transfers 26, 69, 109, 111
al-Assad, Bashar Hafez 148, 149
association agreements with EU: Georgia 85, 91; Russia 59–60, 65, 67–9, 85–6,

INDEX

89, 91, 145, 147; Ukraine 1–2, 85–6, 89, 91, 143–4
authoritarianism/autocracy 2, 126: Angola 40, 42–3; Arab World 117; China 22, 42–3; competition 80, 141; condoning authoritarianism 2, 61, 111; consolidated authoritarianism 61–2; defections 43; elections 141; Ethiopia 40, 43; military 43; opposition and protests 42–3; paradoxical outcomes 13, 140; stability and security 140; Tunisia 130–1
autocracy *see* authoritarianism/autocracy; autocracy promotion
autocracy promotion 5–7, 118: balance of power 2–3; China 21, 27, 33, 42, 140, 146; definition 61; democratization 2, 5, 21, 61; Egypt 106–7; human rights 141; intention 5–7, 9, 27; Myanmar 27, 33; Russia 6, 12, 59–62, 146; Saudi Arabia 106–7, 146; theoretical and policy implications 140–2, 145, 148
Azerbaijan 60, 65–70, 82

Babayan, Nelli 21, 59, 108, 111
Bader, Julia 27
Bahrain-Saudi relations 2, 100, 102, 107–11: allies of United States 7; arms sales 109; Bahrain Independent Commission of Inquiry (BICI) 110; conflicts of interest 109; Defence Cooperation Agreement (DCA) with US 109; democracy assistance 121; democracy promotion 108–9; democratization 109; Foreign Affairs Council (EU) 110–11; human rights 108; Iran 107, 109–10, 143; al-Khalifa regime 101, 107–8, 110, 143; liberalization 109; media 109–10; Middle East Free Trade Area (MEFTA) 109; military facilities provided by US 109; opposition and protests in 6 , 7, 107–11, 142, 146, 148; Peninsular Shield Force (Saudi) 108; political dialogue 109; Riyadh Declaration 108; Shia Muslims 107–10, 143–4; spillover or contagion, risk of 142; stability and security 107–9, 143; United States, ally of US as 7
balance of power 2–3, 9–11, 22, 25–6, 90, 144
Balfour, Rosa 104
Belarus 60, 65, 66–7, 69, 82, 142

Ben Ali, Zine El Abidine 126–7, 128, 147, 149
Ben Jafaar, Mustapha 129
Benn, Hilary 40
Bertelsmann Transformation Index (BTI) 124–5
Biden, Joe 29
borders 21, 28, 69, 82, 89–91, 146
Bouazizi, Mohammed 126
Broader Middle East and North Africa (BMENA) 104
Bush, George W 104, 109

Cameron, David 31, 110–11
Central and Eastern Europe 139–41
Chan, Anson 29, 31
China: Africa 5–6, 8, 12, 39–52, 141, 147; aid 39–40, 42, 147; autocracy promotion 21, 42, 140, 146; bilateral relations with West, maintenance of 22; civil society 23, 41; coercive capacity, enhancing 23; Communist Party (CCP) 12, 20–3, 30–1, 32–3, 142; competition amongst leaders 22; conditionality 147; cooperation partner, China as a 39–43; countervailing democracy promotion 21–3, 32, 118, 140–1, 146; democracy promotion 3, 40, 41–3, 142; democratization 21, 25–33; developmental capitalism 145; Document No 9 20–3, 31; economic interests 6, 8, 12, 33, 148; energy 25, 43–4, 46; geostrategic interests 5, 8, 21–2, 32–3, 70; human rights 5, 23–7, 29–30, 40, 45; leverage 21; near abroad, interests in 5, 20–33; non-interference principle 27, 33; opposition and protests 22, 42–3; political interests 6, 8, 33; pressures on authoritarian regimes 42–3;regime survival 32–3, 40, 51–2; social stability management (*weiwen*) 22–3; spillover or contagion, risk of 22, 32; stability and security 22–3, 41; Syria, blocking of action in 2; Tiananmen crisis 1989 22; top-down perspective 12; Uganda 39–40; United Kingdom 40; veto powers in Security Council 8 *see also* Angola-Chinese relations; Ethiopia-China relations; Hong Kong-China relations; Myanmar-China relations

158

INDEX

Chinese Academy of Social Sciences (CASS) 25
Civic Exchange (United States) 29
civil society *see under* main headings
Civil Society Facility (CSF) 104
Clegg, Nick 31
Clinton, Hillary 109–10, 121
Cold War 62, 65
communism, collapse of 59, 63, 139
competition: Angola 43; Arab World 5, 116–32; authoritarianism 80, 141; China 22, 28–9; liberalization 104–5; low levels of political competition 43, 46; regime competition 5, 116–32
conditionality 5–6: Africa 44–5, 147; aid 40–2, 44–5, 120–4; China 147; Egypt 105, 144; Saudi Arabia 105, 127, 128, 144; Tunisia 127, 128; Ukraine 85, 88, 144, 147
conflicts of interest 100–1, 109, 128, 143
Cooper, Robert 111
corruption 1, 82, 85, 91, 144, 146
Council of Europe (CoE) 83
Council of Independent States 141
countervailing democracy promotion 3–4, 139–45: Arab World 118–20; Bahrain 111; China 21–9, 31–2, 118, 140–1, 146; democratization 5–7, 9, 21, 26–33, 63, 65–70, 144; Hong Kong 28–9, 31, 32; human rights 4, 7, 101, 143; Myanmar 25–7, 31; Russia 59, 61, 65–9, 79–94, 118, 140–1, 147; Saudi Arabia 140; Ukraine 86–9, 147
credibility/legitimacy of West 4, 10–11: aid 124; Arab World 13, 117–20, 124; credibility, definition of 124; elite cooperation 124; Georgia 86; nationalist or religious beliefs, clash with 146; statehood and territorial integrity, undermining 146; theoretical and policy implications 141–2, 146; Tunisia 127–8; Ukraine 86
Crimea, Russia's annexation of 2, 8, 64, 86, 89, 93

Deauville Partnership 104, 120, 123
Deep and Comprehensive Free Trade Areas (DCFTA) (EU): Arab World 121; Eastern Partnership (EaP) 66–9; Egypt 121; Georgia 82, 85; revision 144; Russia 66–9, 82, 85, 142, 143–4; suspension 143–4; Tunisia 128; Ukraine 67, 142, 143–4
deep democracy 81, 103, 105
defections 43, 46–7
Defence Cooperation Agreement (DCA) between Bahrain and US 109
Delcour, Laure 59, 67–8
democracy promotion *see under* main headings
democratization: Arab World 9, 107, 109, 121, 131, 143; Armenia 65; autocracy promotion 2, 5, 21, 61; Bahrain 109; Central and Eastern Europe 140–1; China 21, 25–33; countervailing democracy promotion 5–7, 9, 21, 26–33, 63, 65–70, 144; Egypt 104–7; elections 120; elites 118; externally-driven or home-made, democratization as 81–4; fourth wave 131; Georgia 9, 79–93; grey area between democratization and authoritarianism 80; modernization theory 104; Myanmar 21, 23–7; regime survival 145; Russia 59–63, 65–7, 70, 79–94, 142; Saudi Arabia 70, 104–7, 109, 111, 123, 129–30, 143; spillover or contagion, risk of 2, 61, 87; stability and security 143; theoretical and policy implications 140, 146–8; Tunisia 129–30; Ukraine 9, 79–93
developmental capitalism 145
dos Santos, José Eduardo 45

Eastern Partnership (EaP) policy of EU 5, 59–60, 64–70, 83
economic interests 4–5, 10: Africa 6, 8, 12; China 6, 8, 12, 28, 33, 148; EU 10; Hong Kong 28; linkage-leverage model 10; Myanmar 27; Russia 67, 70, 145; theoretical and policy implications 142, 144; Tunisia 126; United States 10
Egypt; autocracy, return to 126; Deep and Comprehensive FTAs (DCFTA) 121 *see also* Egypt-Saudi relations
Egypt-Saudi relations 100–8, 111: aid 103, 105, 144; autocracy promotion 106–7; civil society 103–5; conditionality 105, 144; deep democracy 103; democracy promotion 100, 102–7; democratization 104–7; elections 103, 105; elites 105, 107, 144, 146; energy 106; Enterprise Fund (Egypt–US) 103; European Neighbourhood Policy (ENP) 103; Iran

159

INDEX

106; Islam 103, 106, 142; leverage 103, 105; liberalization 107; loan guarantees 103; macro-financial assistance (MFA) (EU) 103–4; military 105–7, 142; modernization 104–5, 111–12; Muslim Brotherhood 103–7, 123, 142; regime competition 117; regime survival 103; rival state, Egypt as a 103; Saudi Development Fund 105; small and medium-sized enterprises 103–4; stability and security 103–4, 107, 142–3; Suez Canal 100, 105

elections: Angola 43, 44–5; Arab World 120; authoritarianism 141; China 29, 43, 44–5, 47–50; democratization 120; Egypt 103, 105; Ethiopia 43, 47–9, 50; Hong Kong 29; Islam 120, 128–9; observers 61–2, 64;Russia 61–2, 64, 142; Saudi Arabia 103, 105, 126–7, 128–9; theoretical and policy implications 145, 147; Tunisia 126–7, 128–9

elites 10, 117: Arab World 105, 107, 117–20, 124, 131–2, 144, 146; credibility 124; democratization 118; Egypt 105, 107, 144, 146; European Neighbourhood Policy (ENP) 146–7; Myanmar 26–7; reform-oriented 118–20, 124; Russia 62–3, 66, 69; Saudi Arabia 102, 105, 107, 129–30, 144, 146; Tunisia 129–30, 146

energy 10, 64–9: Angola 44, 46; Armenia 68; Azerbaijan 66–7, 69; China 25, 43–4, 46; conflicts of interest 100; democracy promotion 143; diversification 64–5, 68, 149; Egypt 106; Ethiopia 43; EU 64–5, 146, 149; gas 64–8, 91, 106; Georgia 149; nuclear energy 69; oil 25, 43–4, 46, 101–2; Russia 64–9, 88–9, 91, 144;Saudi Arabia 100–2, 106; stability and security 100, 102; Ukraine 88–9, 144, 149

enlargement of EU 60, 63, 88, 140

Ennahda political party (Tunisia) 128–9, 130, 132, 147

Enterprise Europe Network 127

Erasmus Mundus/Tempus programmes 128

Ethiopia-China relations 12, 40, 43, 47–51: aid 43, 48–9, 145; China Export-Import Bank (EXIM), loan from 49–50, 51; civil society 48, 49; Civil Society Fund (CSF) (EU) 48; cooperation partner, China as a 43, 49–50, 51; Democratic Institutions Programme (DIP) 48–9; democracy promotion 43, 47–9, 51–2, 142, 145; diversification 50; elections 43, 47–9, 50; energy 43; EPRDF 43, 48; Eritrea, war with 47; human rights 48–9; Human Rights Commission, establishment of 48, 49; infrastructure programs 49–50, 51; institutions 43, 47–8; low levels of political competition 43; media 49; Millennium Development Goals (MDGs) 47–8; observation mission (EU) 49; opposition and protests 48–9, 50; political reforms, engagement with West on 48–9, 50–1; regime survival 50; ruling parties 43; USAID 49

Eritrea-Ethiopia, war between 47

EU Neighbourhood Barometer 127

Eurasian Customs Union 68, 145

Eurasian Economic Union (EEU) 66–9, 81–2, 142

Euromed Justice 130

Euro-Mediterranean Free Trade Area 105

Euro-Mediterranean Partnership (EMP) 104–5

European Endowment for Democracy (EED) 10–11, 104

European External Action Service (EEAS) 30

European Instrument for Democracy and Human Rights (EIDHR) 81, 104

European Investment Bank (EIB) 103, 127

European Neighbourhood Partnership Instrument (ENPI) 103–4

European Neighbourhood Policy (ENP) 81, 103, 121, 128, 146–7

European Union: aid 103–4, 121–3, 126–7; Angola 41, 45, 47; Armenia 5, 59, 65, 68–70; Central and Eastern Europe 139–41; Civil Society Forum, establishment of 12, 81; declaratory policy 110–11; deep democracy 81, 103; Democratic Institutions Programme (DIP) 48–9; Eastern Partnership (EaP) 5, 59–60, 64–70, 83; energy 64–5, 68, 146, 149; enlargement 60, 63, 88, 140; Ethiopia, observation mission to 49; European External Action Service (EEAS) 30; European Instrument for

INDEX

Democracy and Human Rights (EIDHR) 81, 104; Foreign Affairs Council 110–11; Georgia 81–6, 90, 144, 147–8; government incentive tranche (EU) 41, 45; Hong Kong 30–2; leverage model 2; macro-financial assistance (MFA) 103–4; Mobility Partnerships 121, 128; normative power, as 7–8; Office to Hong Kong and Macau 30; sectoral policies 82; soft power, as 2; stability and security 2, 7, 40–1, 70, 81–3, 86, 102–5, 127, 131, 139–43, 146–9; Tunisia 127–30; Ukraine 1–2, 12, 61–2, 81–6, 92, 143, 147, 149; United States, convergence with 2, 10–11, 81, 104 *see also* association agreements with EU; Deep and Comprehensive Free Trade Areas (DCFTA) (EU); human rights and EU/US

EXIM (China Export-Import Bank) 45–6, 47, 49–50, 51

Fan Hongwei 27
Foreign and Commonwealth Office (FCO) (UK) 30
France 110
Freedom Agenda (US) 104
Freedom House 8, 43, 59, 66, 124–5
freedom of expression 29, 87

al-Gaddafi, Muammar 149
gas 64–8, 91, 106
Georgia-Russia relations 21, 81–93: Abkhazia 88, 90–1; Armenia 69; association agreements 67, 85, 91; conflict with Russia 2008 61–2, 143; consolidated authoritarianism 61; contagion from West 87; Country Strategy Paper on Georgia (EU) 82; credibility 86; Dagomys agreement 88; Deep and Comprehensive Free Trade Area (DCFTA) (EU) 82, 85; democracy promotion 81–9; democratization 9, 79–93; Eastern Partnership (EaP) 58, 66; economic interests 84, 145; energy 148–9; European Union 81–6, 90, 144, 147–8; executive, domination of 82–3; Free Trade Agreement with Russia, suspension of 91; geopolitical strategies 80, 84; Georgian Dream coalition 84, 92; judiciary as political tool 84–5; leverage 145; media 83; military 62, 68, 84; NATO 88, 91; Non-State Actors Local Authorities Program 82; Orthodox Church 91; Rose Revolution 80, 82–4, 87–8, 93; sanctions 88, 90–1, 143; South Ossetia, recognition of independence of 88; stability and security 145; statehood and territorial integrity, undermining 88, 90, 92–4, 143, 145; United National Movement 84; United States 81–6, 144, 148; Westernization 142
geostrategic interests 4, 6 *see also under* main entries
Germany: Bahrain 110; domestic politics 2; Hong Kong 31
globalization 4, 22
good governance 81–4, 130
governance model 2
Greenfield, Danya 104
Gulf Cooperation Council (GCC) 102, 106, 107–8, 109–10, 123, 141, 148

Hackenesch, Christine 27
hard power 2, 87
Hart, Clifford 30
Hawthorne, Amy 104
High Commission for the Realization of Revolutionary Goals 128
Hong Kong-China relations 21–3, 28–32: autonomy 21–2, 28; base for local and foreign forces, Hong Kong as 31; bilateral trade and investment relations 30–1; Chief Executive, election of 29; civil society 28; competition between pro-democracy and pro-Beijing groups 28–9; countervailing democracy promotion 28–9, 31, 32; democracy movement 2014 (Occupy Central) 22, 28–31, 142, 144; democracy promotion, activities aimed at 29, 30–1; diplomatic warnings from China 29–30; economic interests 28; EU 30–2; EU Office to Hong Kong and Macau 30; European External Action Service 30; human rights 21, 29–30; Human Rights and Democracy Act 2014 30; ICCPR, reports on 21; media 29; one country, two systems doctrine 21, 28–9, 33, 144; press freedom 28–9; regime survival 28, 32; repression 28–9; Sino-British Joint Declaration 30–1; tourists from mainland China, tension with 28;

INDEX

umbrella revolution 28, 144; United States 29–31; universal suffrage 29–32; white paper 29–30

human rights and EU/US 3–5, 23–7, 148: Africa 5, 45, 48–9, 128–9; aid 40, 149; Angola 45; Arab World 100–2, 104, 108, 110–11, 120–1, 128–9, 148–9; autocracy promotion 141; Bahrain 108, 110; China 5, 23–7, 29–30, 40, 45; countervailing democracy promotion 4, 7, 101, 143; Ethiopia 48–9; freedom of expression 29, 87; Hong Kong 21, 29–30; intention 7; Myanmar 24–6; opposition and protests 147; Saudi Arabia 100–2, 104, 108, 110–11, 120–1, 128–9; stability and security 2, 4, 7–8, 82, 148; Syria 148, 149; theoretical and policy implications 13, 148; Tunisia 128–9; Ukraine 62, 86, 91, 102; Vietnam 27; visa liberalization 82

Hungary 62, 70

illiberal regional powers, definition of 5
infrastructure projects 46, 49–50, 51, 130
institutions: Angola 43; Arab World 118; Democratic Institutions Programme (DIP) 48–9; Ethiopia 43, 47–9; European Neighbourhood Policy (ENP) 146; Russia 92; theoretical and policy implications 141; Tunisia 129
intention 8–9: autocracy promotion 9; human rights 7
International Monetary Fund (IMF) 126
investment *see* aids, loans and direct investment
Iran 100–1: Bahrain 107, 109–10, 143; Egypt 106; France 110; Germany 110; Saudi Arabia 101, 107, 109–10, 143
ISIS (Islamic State of Iraq and the Levant) 31
Islam: Arabellions/Arab Spring 2; Bahrain 107–10, 143–4; Egypt 103, 106, 142; elections 120, 128–9; ISIS 31; radical Islam 126, 129, 131–2; Salafists 126, 129, 131–2; Saudi Arabia 101–2, 106, 120, 142, 147; Shia Muslims 107–10, 143–4; Tunisia 126–9, 131–3, 147
Israel 100
Ivanishvili, Bidzina 84, 92

Jones, Lee 26
Jordan 121

judiciary as political tool 84–5

Kästner, Antje 27
Kazakhstan 66, 69, 142
Kerry, John 32
al-Khalifa regime 101, 107–8, 110, 143
Kuwait 106, 120
Kwasniewski, Aleksander 92
Kyrgyzstan, Tulip Revolution in 143

Lai, Jimmy 29
Lavrov, Sergey 65
League of Arab States 141
Lee Cheuk-yan 29
Lee, Martin 29, 31
legitimacy *see* credibility/legitimacy of West
Levada Center 64
leverage 2, 5, 10–11; Arab World 103, 105, 112, 118; China 21, 27, 33; Egypt 103, 105; linkage-leverage model 10; Moldova 145; Myanmar 27, 33; Russia 63, 86, 88, 90–1, 145; Saudi Arabia 112; theoretical and policy implications 144
Levitsky, Steven 10
liberalization: Arab World 104–7, 109, 118, 128, 132; Bahrain 109; competition 104–5; Egypt 107; Myanmar 21, 24–7; Russia 63, 91; Saudi Arabia 104–5, 107, 109, 128; Tunisia 128
Libya 2, 123, 126, 149
loans *see* aids, loans and direct investment
Lukashenko, Alexander 67

macro-financial assistance (MFA) (EU) 103–4
Malinowski, Tom 29
managed democracy 62
mass movements *see* opposition and protests
media: Angola 45, 47; Bahrain 109–10; Ethiopia 49; Georgia 83; Hong Kong 29; press freedom 28–9, 47; training 29, 109; Tunisia 129; Ukraine 83, 85; USAID 49, 83
Medvedev, Dmitry 67
MENA Trade and Investment Partnership (MENA-TIP) 103–4
Merkel, Angela 32
Middle East Free Trade Area (MEFTA) 104, 108–9

INDEX

Middle East Partnership Initiative (MEPI) 103–4, 109–10
Middle East Response Fund (MERF) 103
Millennium Challenge Corporation 41
Millennium Development Goals (MDGs) 47–8
military: Armenia 68; authoritarian regimes, pressures on 43; Egypt 105–7, 142; facilities provided by US 109; Georgia 62, 68, 84; Hong Kong as base for local and foreign forces 31; Peninsular Shield Force (Saudi Arabia) 108; Rapid Reaction Mechanism and Technical Assistance for CIS (TACIS) 82; Russia 62, 67–8; Tunisia 130
Minxin Pei 22
Mobility Partnerships 121, 128
modernization 104, 128
Moldova 67, 142, 145
money, markets and mobility (3Ms) 103, 105, 121
Morocco 121
Morsi, Mohammad 106
Mubarak, Hosni 102–4, 106, 126, 128, 149
Muslim Brotherhood 103–7, 123, 142
Myanmar-China relations 21, 23–7: aid 21; anti-China circle in SE Asia 24–5; arms embargo 24; autocracy promotion 27, 33; CASS 25; civil society 24–6; countervailing democracy promotion 25–7, 31; democratization 21, 23–7; diplomatic relations 21; economic interests 27; elites 26–7; ethnic and religious conflict 25; foreign direct investment, drop in China's 26; geostrategic interests 24–7, 33, 142; human rights 24–6; leverage 27, 33; liberalization 21, 24–7; projects 25–6; regime survival 33; regime-type-neutral approach 27; sanctions 21, 24–6; spillover or contagion, risk of 27; stability and security 26–7; Union Solidarity and Development Party 24

Nagorno Karabakh 69–70
Nathan, Andrew 22, 27
National Democratic Institute for International Affairs (NDI) 29
National Endowment for Democracy (NED) (United States) 29
NATO (North Atlantic Treaty Organization) 60, 63
natural resources 21, 45, 50, 145, *see also* energy
Neighbourhood Investment Facility (NIF) 103–4
New Citizen Movement (China) 23
non-government organizations (NGOs): China 23; foreign resources 23; restrictions 64, 80; Russia 64, 80, 83
nuclear energy 69

Obama, Barack 12, 24, 83–4, 103, 104, 109, 121
oil 25, 43–4, 46, 101–2
Oman 108
one-party rule, promotion of 61
opposition and protests: Arabellions/Arab Spring 2, 5, 7, 86, 9–12, 99–112, 118–24, 126, 140–8; authoritarian regimes, pressure on 43; Bahrain 6, 7, 107–11, 142, 146, 148; China 22, 28–31, 42–3, 48–50, 141–2, 144; Ethiopia 48–9, 50; Hong Kong 22, 28–31, 142, 144; Russia 64, 68–9, 80, 82, 86–7, 89, 91; Saudi Arabia 100–1, 126; Syria 123, 146; Tunisia 126; Ukraine 1–2, 80, 82–3, 86–7, 91, 93; Western agents, blamed on 31–2, 80
Overseas Private Investment Corporation (OPIC) (Saudi Arabia) 103

paradoxical outcomes 4, 9–11, 80–1, 84–6, 93, 144–8
Patten, Chris 30
PEW Global Attitudes survey 127
policy *see* theoretical and policy implications
political dialogue: Africa 51; Bahrain 109; China 41, 48–9, 50–1; Ethiopia 48–9, 50–1
Polity IV 8, 59
Poroshenko, Petro 67, 89
poverty 40
press freedom 28–9, 47
Privileged Partnerships 128–30
Putin, Vladimir 8, 60, 62–70, 142, 143–5, 147

Qualifying Industrial Zones (QIZs) (Saudi Arabia) 103
Qatar 106, 120, 123, 126, 130

INDEX

Rapid Reaction Mechanism and Technical Assistance for CIS (TACIS) 82
regime change 9, 83, 89, 116–17, 124
regime survival 5: Africa 40, 50–2, 103; China 28, 32–3, 40, 46, 50–2; democratization 145; Egypt 103; Ethiopia 50; Hong Kong 28, 32; Myanmar 33; Russia 59, 61, 64, 87, 142; theoretical and policy implications 142
religion 25, 89, 91–2, 146 *see also* Islam
rent-extraction 2, 61, 142–3
responsibility 2 protect (R2P) 2, 62
rhetoric 60, 62
Rice, Susan 31
Risse, Thomas 21, 59, 108, 111
rule of law 82–3, 86, 91, 120–1, 141
ruling parties 43, 61
Russia: aid 63, 70, 82–4, 144; Armenia 62, 68–70, 142, 145; association agreements with EU 59–60, 65, 67–9, 85–6, 89, 145, 147; autocracy promotion 6, 12, 59–62, 146; Azerbaijan 60, 65, 67–70; Belarus 60, 65, 66–7, 69, 142; civil society 61, 65, 81, 83, 87, 91–2; Collective Security Treaty Organization 69; competitive authoritarianism 80; conditionality 85, 88; consolidated authoritarianism 62; countervailing democracy promotion 59, 61, 65–9, 79–94, 118, 140–1, 147; Crimea, annexation of 64, 86, 89, 93; cross-conditionality 88; Deep and Comprehensive FTAs (DCFTA) 66–9, 82, 85, 142, 143–4; democracy promotion 5, 59–70, 79–94, 140–1; democratization 59–63, 65–7, 70, 79–94,142; Eastern Partnership (EaP) (EU) 5, 59–60, 64–9, 81–5, 87; economic interests 67, 70, 84, 89, 145; elections 61–2, 64, 83–5, 89–90, 142; elites 6, 62–3, 66, 69, 90–3; energy 64–9, 88–9, 91, 144, 149; enlargement of EU 60, 63, 88; Eurasian Customs Union 66, 68, 145; Eurasian Economic Union (EEU) 66–9, 87, 91, 92, 142; externally-driven or home-made, democratization as 81–4; geostrategic interests 12, 59, 65, 68–70, 87; great power status, restoration of 63–4, 70, 142; homosexual culture 62; human rights 62, 82, 91; Hungary 62, 70; institution-building 92; Kazakhstan 66, 69, 142; leverage 63, 86, 88, 90–1, 145; liberalization 63, 91; managed democracy 62; managed instability 143, 145; media 83; military 67, 84, 89; Moldova 142, 145; NATO 60, 63, 87–8, 91; near abroad, democracy promotion in Russia's 5, 58–70, 92–3; NGOs 64, 80, 83; opposition and protests 64, 68–9, 80, 82, 86–7, 89, 91; post-Soviet space 63, 66, 80, 83–4, 86–7, 93; regime survival 59, 61, 64, 87, 142; rent-extraction 61; rhetoric 59–60, 62, 66; sanctions 143; Soviet Union, collapse of 59, 63, 139; secessionists, support for 88–91, 145, 147; spillover or contagion, risk of 61, 64, 142; stability and security 61, 70, 82–3, 90, 92–3, 143, 145, 148; statehood and territorial integrity, undermining 2, 88–90, 92–4, 143–5, 147; Syria, blocking of action in 2; theoretical and policy implications 140; US-Russia relations 2009, reset of 64; veto powers in Security Council 8 *see also* Georgia-Russia relations; Ukraine-Russia relations

Saakashvili, Mikheil 84–5, 86, 88
Salafists 126, 129, 131–2
sanctions: Crimea, annexation of 64; Georgia 88, 90–1; Myanmar 21, 24–6; Russia 64–5, 67, 88, 90–1, 142–4, 147; Ukraine 65, 67, 142, 143–4, 147
Sargsyan, Serzh 68–9
Sarkisian, Tigran 69
Saudi Arabia 3, 12, 100–12: aid 106, 123–4, 144; Arab Spring 5, 12, 99–112, 140–4, 146, 148; autocracy promotion 146; competitive liberalization strategy 104–5; conflicts of interest 100–1; countervailing democracy promotion 5, 12, 99–112, 140–4, 146, 148; democracy promotion 99–112, 140–3, 146; democratization 70, 104–7, 109, 111, 123, 129–30, 143; elites 102; energy 100–2, 106; Euro-Mediterranean FTA 105; foreign policy 101–2, 111–12; Freedom Agenda (US) 104; geostrategic interests 70, 102, 104, 111–12, 130; human rights 100–2, 104, 108, 110–11, 120–1, 128–9; infrastructure 130; Iran 101; Islam 101–2, 106, 120, 142, 147;

164

INDEX

leverage 112; liberalization 104–5; oil 101–2; regime competition 13, 117–18, 120–4, 131–2; regime survival/strengthening 12, 64, 70; soft loans 123; stability and security 100–2, 148; Turkey 106 *see also* Bahrain-Saudi relations; Egypt-Saudi relations; Tunisia-Saudi relations
Schimmelfennig, Frank 119
Schumacher, Tobias 110
secessionists/separatists, support for 2, 64, 86, 88–93, 145, 147
security *see* stability and security
Security Council (UN): China 2, 8; Libya 2; Russia 2, 8; Syria, blocking of action in 2; veto powers 8
Sedelmeier, Hanno 119
semi-authoritarianism 141
Sharaf, Essam 106
Shevardnadze, Eduard 88
Serbia, NATO bombing of 63
Shanghai Cooperation Organization 141
Shia Muslims 107–10, 143–4
single market 128
al-Sisi, Abd-al-Fattah 106–7
small and medium-sized enterprises (SMEs) 103–4, 126–7
Soares de Oliveira, Ricardo 45
socio-political conditions in target States 3
soft power 2, 145
Solana, Javier 66
South Ossetia, recognition of independence of 88
sovereign debt crisis 23
Soviet Union, collapse of 63, 139
spillover or contagion, risk of: autocracy promotion 2; Bahrain 142; China 22, 27, 32; democratization 2, 61, 87; Myanmar 27; Russia 61, 64, 87, 142; Ukraine 87, 142
SPRING (Support for Partnership, Reforms and Inclusive Growth) programme 127–9
stability and security 4, 10; Africa 41; Arab World 2, 7, 107–9, 120, 143; Bahrain 107–8, 143; China 22–3, 26–7, 41; consolidation 139; democratization 143, 146, 148–9; Eastern Partnership (EaP) 81; Egypt 103–4, 107, 142–3; energy 100, 102; EU 10, 81; human rights 2, 4, 7–8, 82, 148; managed instability 143, 145; Myanmar 26–7; Russia 61, 67, 70, 82–3, 90, 92–3, 143, 145, 148; Saudi Arabia 100–4, 107–8, 126–8, 142–3, 148–9; soft security interests 128; theoretical and policy implications 139–40, 142, 143–4, 146–9; Ukraine 83, 92, 143–5, 148; United States 2, 4, 7, 10, 40, 70, 101–2, 120, 123, 142–3, 148–9
statehood and territorial integrity, undermining: borders, contesting 146; credibility of democracy promoters 146; Georgia 88, 90, 92–4, 143, 145; Moldova 145; political authority, contesting 146; Russia 2, 88–90, 92–4, 143–5, 147; secessionists, support for 2, 64, 86, 89, 92–3, 145, 147; theoretical and policy implications 146; Ukraine 2, 8, 64, 86, 89–90, 92–4, 143–5
subprime mortgage crisis 23
Suez Canal 100, 105
Suu Kyi, Aung San 26
Syria: human rights 148, 149; opposition and protests 123, 146; Security Council action, blocking by Russia and China of 2

TACIS (Rapid Reaction Mechanism and Technical Assistance for CIS) 82
Tai, Benny 32
Thant Myint-U 24
Thein Sein 25
theoretical and policy implications 139–49: agency-centred perspective 148; Arab World 120, 141, 143, 146, 148; autocracy promotion 140–2, 145, 148; democratization 140; enlargement of EU 140; hybrid regimes 140; conflicts of interest 143; countervailing democracy promotion 139–40, 143, 145; credibility 141–2, 146; democracy promotion 139–49; democratization 140, 146–8; economic interests 142, 144; elections 145, 147; geostrategic interests 142–3, 148–9; human rights 13, 148; institutions 141; leverage 144; paradoxical outcomes 4, 9–13, 80–1, 84–6, 93, 140, 144–8 ; regime change 124; regime survival 142; rent-seeking 142–3; stability and security 139–40, 142, 143–4, 146–9; statehood and territorial integrity, undermining 146

165

INDEX

Tiananmen crisis 1989 22
Tolstrup, Jakob 90
transparency 44–5
Tunisia-Saudi relations 124–31: Action Plan 128–30; aid 126–7, 147; Association Council 129–30; authoritarian powers, influence of regional 130–1; civil society 127, 128; conditionality 128; conflicts of interest 128; constitution 129; cooperation on democracy promotion 128–30; credibility 127–8; Deep and Comprehensive FTAs (DCFTA) 128; democracy promotion 126–7, 132, 141, 149; democratization 129–30; economic conditions 126; elections 126–7, 128–9; elites 129–30, 146; Erasmus Mundus/Tempus programmes 128; EU, role of 127–30; Euromed Justice 130; European Neighbourhood Policy (ENP) 128; human rights 128–9; infrastructure projects 130; institutions, building 129; Instrument for Stability 127; Islam 126–9, 131–3, 147; liberalization 128; media 129; military 130; Mobility Partnership 128; modernization 128; opposition and protests 126; Privileged Partnership 128–30; radical Islam 126, 129, 131–2; regime competition 12–13, 117–18, 124–31, 132; Salafists 126, 129, 131–2; SPRING programme 127–9; stability and security 126–8, 149; soft security interests 128; Tunisian-American Enterprise fund for SMEs 126–7; United States 126, 130–1; veto players 130–1
Turkey 69, 106
Tymoshenko, Yulia 85, 144

Uganda 39–40
Ugulava, Gigi 84
Ukraine-Russia relations 12, 62, 64–8, 92–3, 117, 142–4; aid 89; association agreements 1–2, 67–8, 85–6, 89, 91, 143–4, 147; autocracy promotion 61; Belarus 142; civil society 83, 92; conditionality 85, 88, 144, 147; contagion 87, 142; countervailing democracy promotion 86–9, 147; credibility 86; Crimea by Russia, annexation of 2, 8, 64, 86, 89, 93; Deep and Comprehensive FTAs (DCFTA) 67, 142, 143–4; democracy promotion 6, 67, 79–89, 117; democratization 9, 79–93; Donbass, support of separatism in 89, 92; eastern Ukraine, conflict in 2, 8, 92–3; Eastern Partnership (EaP) 5, 59, 66, 68, 83; elections 89; elites 91–2; energy 88–9, 144, 149; EU 1–2, 12, 61–2, 81–6, 92, 143, 147, 149; Eurasian Economic Union 142; geopolitical strategies 80; grey area between democratization and authoritarianism 80; human rights 62, 86, 91, 102; institution-building 92; Kazakhstan 142; Maidan protests 1–2, 80, 83, 86, 91, 93; media 83, 85; Novorossiya, support of separatism in 89; opposition and protests 80, 82, 86–7, 93; Orange Revolution 80, 82, 86–7, 93; Party of Regions (Ukraine) 85; sanctions 65, 67, 142, 143–4, 147; separatism, Russia's support of 2, 64, 86, 89, 92–3; south-eastern Ukraine 89, 92; spillover or contagion, risk of 142; stability and security 83, 92, 143–5, 148; statehood and territorial integrity, undermining 2, 8, 64, 86, 89–90, 92–4, 143–5; United States 11, 31, 61–2, 81–6, 143; Vilnius Summit 85; Westernization 142
United Arab Emirates (UAE) 106
United Kingdom: Africa 40; Hong Kong 30–1; Sino-British Joint Declaration 30–1
United National Movement (Georgia) 84
United Nations see Security Council (UN)
United States, 29–31, 110: aid 49, 64, 70, 82–3, 103, 126–7; allies 7; Bahrain 7, 109; civil society, promotion of 10; Congressional Commission on China roundtable discussion 29; Defence Cooperation Agreement (DCA) with Bahrain 109; Egypt, Enterprise Fund for 103; embassy, attacks on 131; EU, convergence with 2, 10–11, 81, 104; Georgia 81–6, 144, 148; hard power 2; Hong Kong 29–31; military facilities, provision of 109; Millennium Challenge Corporation 41; Myanmar 24–5; normative power, as 7–8; Russia, 2009 re-set of relations with 64; Saudi Arabia 126–7, 130–1; stability and security 2, 4, 7, 10, 40, 70, 101–2, 120, 123, 142–3, 148–9; subprime mortgage crisis 23;

INDEX

Tunisia 126–7, 130–1; Ukraine 2, 11, 31, 61–2, 81–6, 143; USAID 49, 64, 70, 82–3
use of force, condoning 111

Vietnam 27
visa procedures 63, 81–2, 91, 121–2, 127–8

Wang Yi 32
Way, Lucan A 10
Westernization 63, 70, 142
Westminster Foundation for Democracy (UK) 30
Whitehead, Laurence 61, 86

Wolczuk, Kataryna 59, 67–8
Wong, Joshua 32
World Bank's Governance Indicator 126
World Trade Organization (WTO) 67
Wu Hailong 23

Xi Jinping 21, 25
Xie Yue 22–3
Xu Zhiyong 23

Yanukovych, Viktor 1–2, 85–6, 88–9, 91, 144, 147
Yemen 123, 126
Young, Stephen 29
Yunnan Center for Myanmar Studies 26